exit wounds rutu modan

Israel Lottery Council
for the Arts

Entire contents © copyright 2007 by Rutu Modan. All rights reserved. (Except "I've Got You Under my Skin"; Words and Music by Cole Porter; © 1936 (Renewed) by Chappell & Co.; Copyright assigned to Robert H. Montgomery, Trustee of the Cole Porter Musical & Literary Property Trusts; Publications and Allied Rights Assigned to Chappell & Co.; All rights reserved. Used by permission.) Published by Jonathan Cape 2007. Copyright © Rutu Modan 2007. Rutu Modan has asserted her right under the Copyright, Designs and Patents Act 1988 to be identified as the author of this work. This book is sold subject to the condition that it shall not, by way of trade or otherwise, be lent, resold, hired out, or otherwise circulated without the publisher's prior consent in any form of binding or cover other than that in which it is published and without a similar condition including this condition being imposed on the subsequent purchaser. First published in Great Britain in 2007 by Jonathan Cape Random House, 20 Vauxhall Bridge Road, London SW1V 2SA. www.randomhouse.co.uk Addresses for companies within The Random House Group Limited can be found at: www.randomhouse.co.uk The Random House Group Limited Reg. No. 954009. A CIP catalogue record for this book is available from the British Library. ISBN 9780224081665. Printed and bound in Singapore. Story advisor: Yirmi Pinkus. Acknowledgements: I would like to thank Yirmi Pinkus, for his eye-opening comments, ingenious solutions and advice; and Batia Kolton, who, in her nonchalant way, helped me more than I can say. There would be no book without either of you. Thanks to Chris Oliveros for convincing me that I was capable of creating this book. Thanks to my younger sister, Dana Modan, for guiding me through the writing process and to Noah Stollman for translating, editing, and giving me a title. Thanks to Rachel Marani of the Israel Cultural Excellence Foundation for her attentive support and to Thomas Gabison for his good words and intentions. For support and friendship: thanks to Itzik Renert, Mira Friedmann, Moran Palmoni and Lilian Bareto, Alona Palmoni, Orit Bergman, Orit Mazor and Yotam Burnstein, Meirav and Amnon Salomon-Dekel, Ephrat Beloosesky, Tamar and Zeev Bergman, and Zvia Cagan. Thanks to Tom Devlin for the design and for being so nice; to Shachar Kober—such a faithful assistant; to the real Koby Franco for his name; and to David Ofek—whose documentary No 17. inspired this story. Most of all, thank you to my patient husband Ofer Bergman.

exit wounds rutu modan

Jonathan Cape
London

To Yirmi and Ofer.

chapter one
father figure

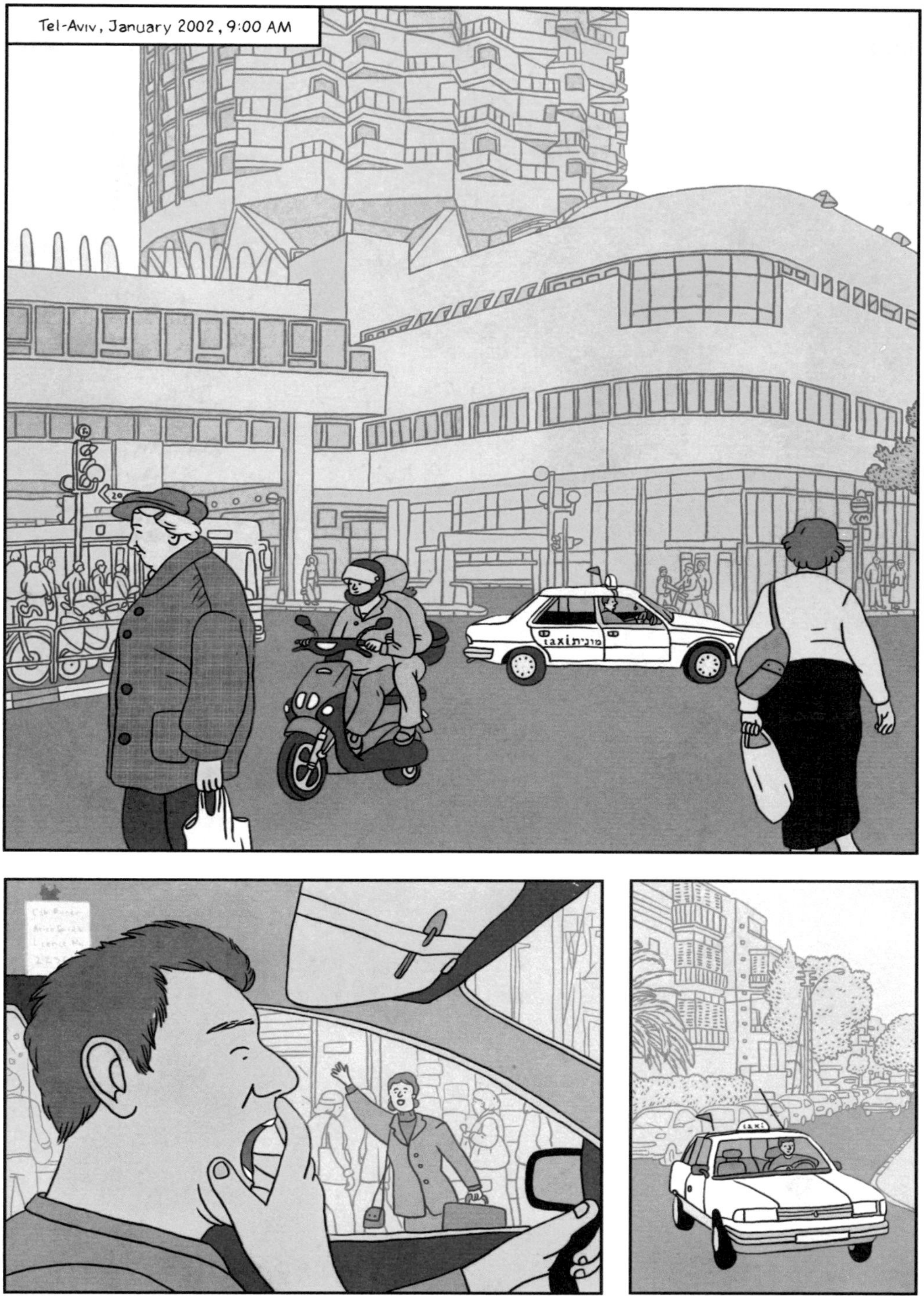
Tel-Aviv, January 2002, 9:00 AM

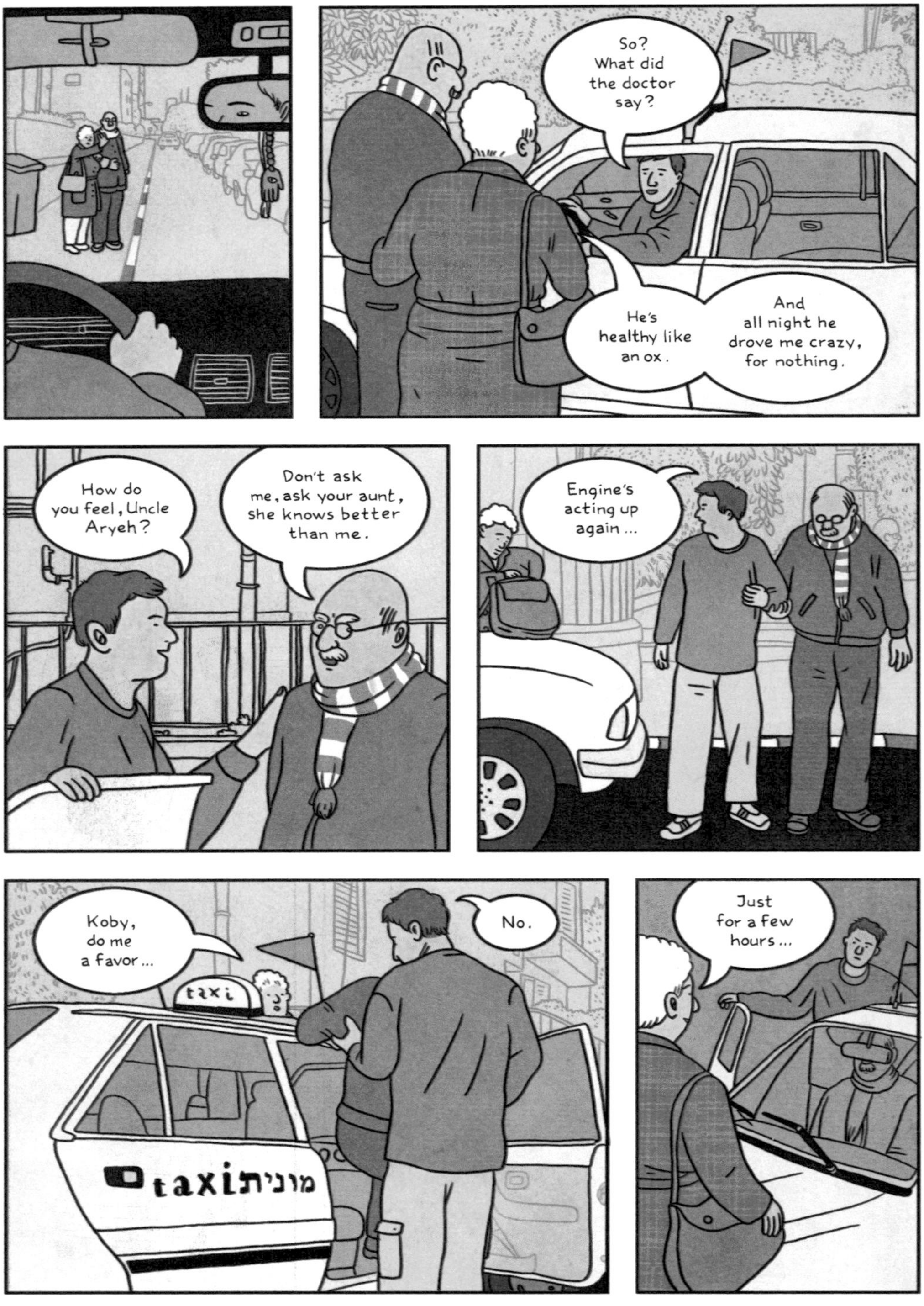
So? What did the doctor say?
He's healthy like an ox.
And all night he drove me crazy, for nothing.
How do you feel, Uncle Aryeh?
Don't ask me, ask your aunt, she knows better than me.
Engine's acting up again...
Koby, do me a favor...
No.
taxi
taxi מונית
Just for a few hours...

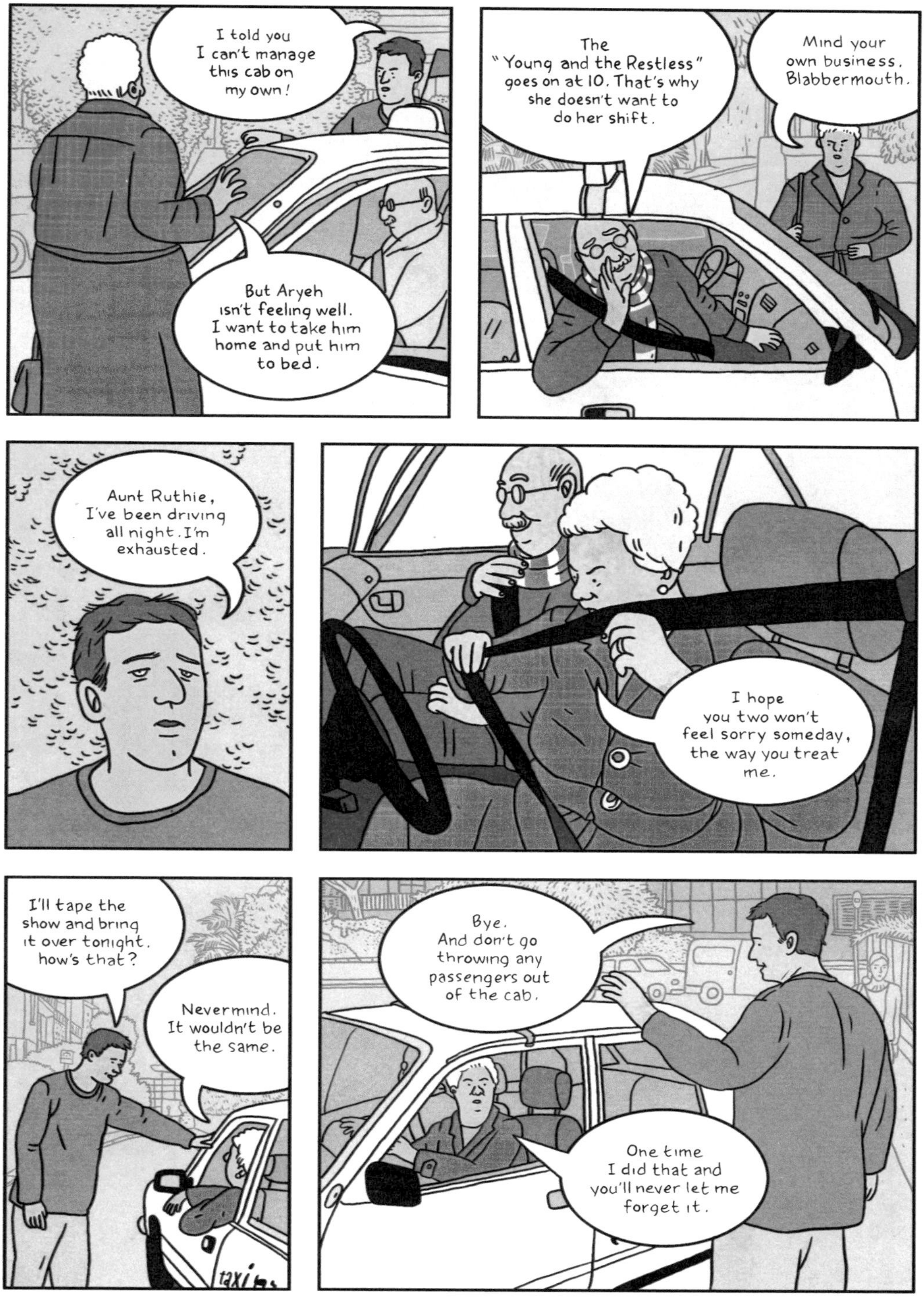
I told you I can't manage this cab on my own!
But Aryeh isn't feeling well. I want to take him home and put him to bed.
The "Young and the Restless" goes on at 10. That's why she doesn't want to do her shift.
Mind your own business, Blabbermouth.
Aunt Ruthie, I've been driving all night. I'm exhausted.
I hope you two won't feel sorry someday, the way you treat me.
I'll tape the show and bring it over tonight, how's that?
Nevermind. It wouldn't be the same.
Bye. And don't go throwing any passengers out of the cab.
One time I did that and you'll never let me forget it.

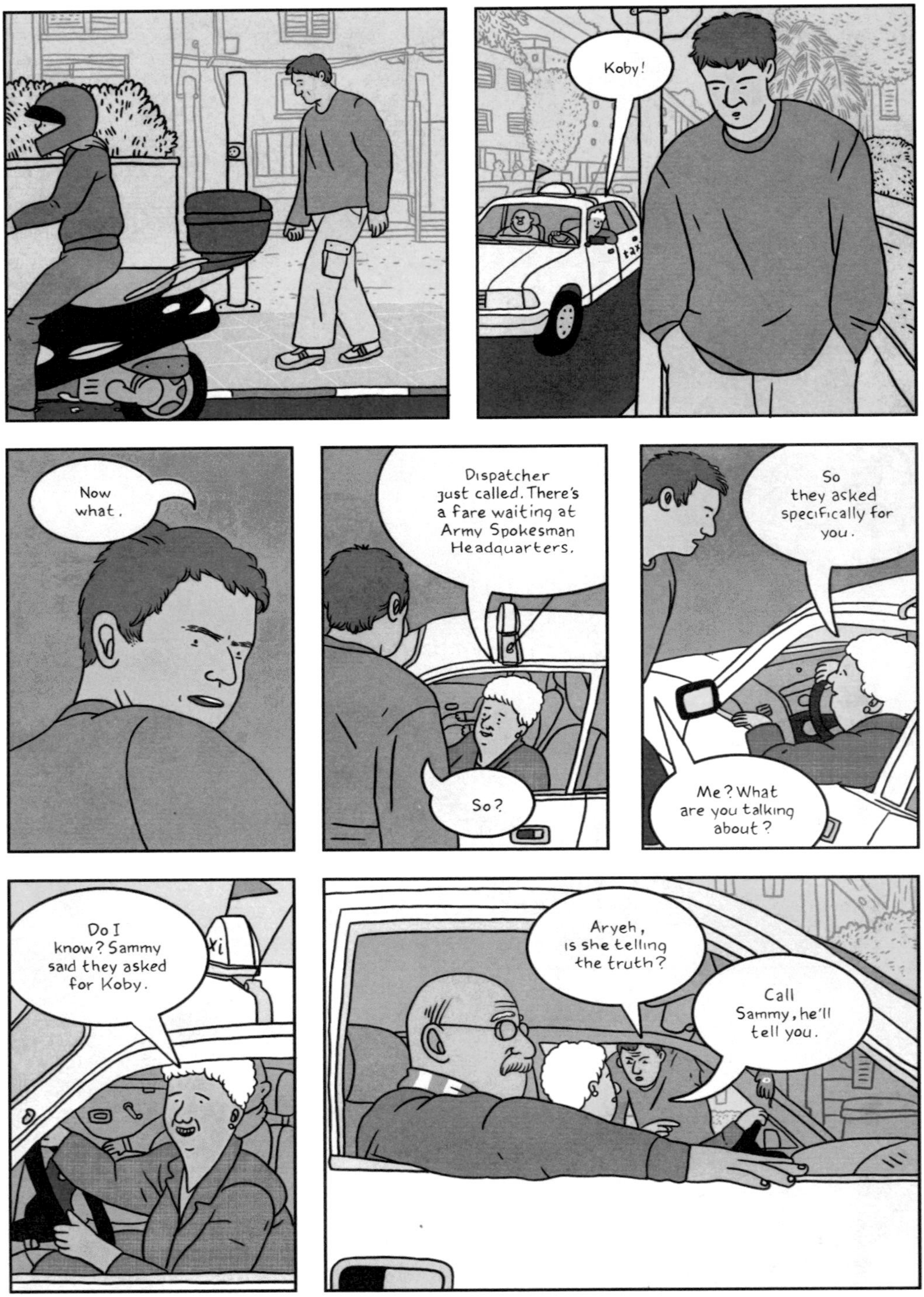

Koby!
Now what.
Dispatcher just called. There's a fare waiting at Army Spokesman Headquarters.
So?
So they asked specifically for you.
Me? What are you talking about?
Do I know? Sammy said they asked for Koby.
Aryeh, is she telling the truth?
Call Sammy, he'll tell you.

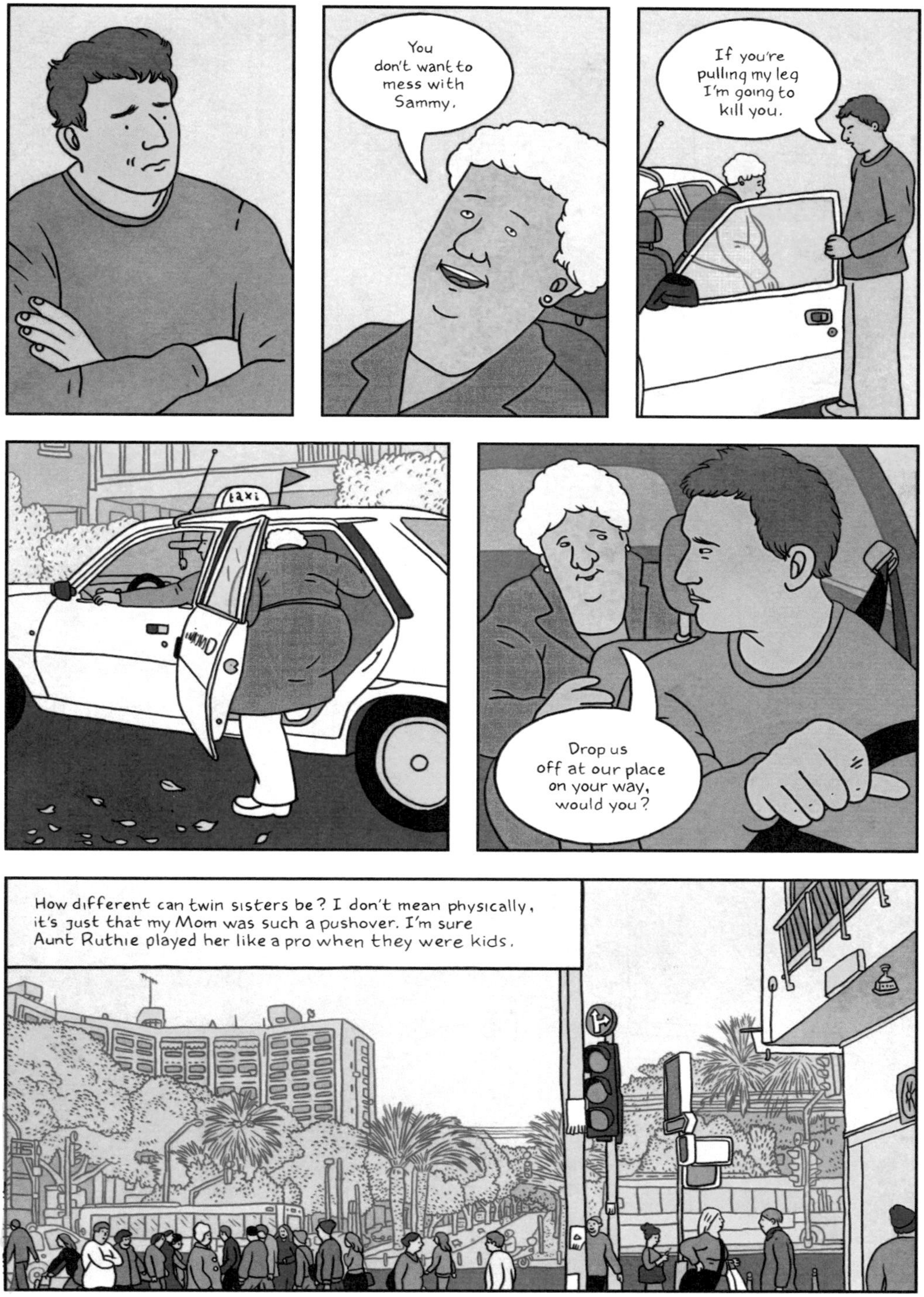

You don't want to mess with Sammy.
If you're pulling my leg I'm going to kill you.
taxi
Drop us off at our place on your way, would you?
How different can twin sisters be? I don't mean physically, it's just that my Mom was such a pushover. I'm sure Aunt Ruthie played her like a pro when they were kids.

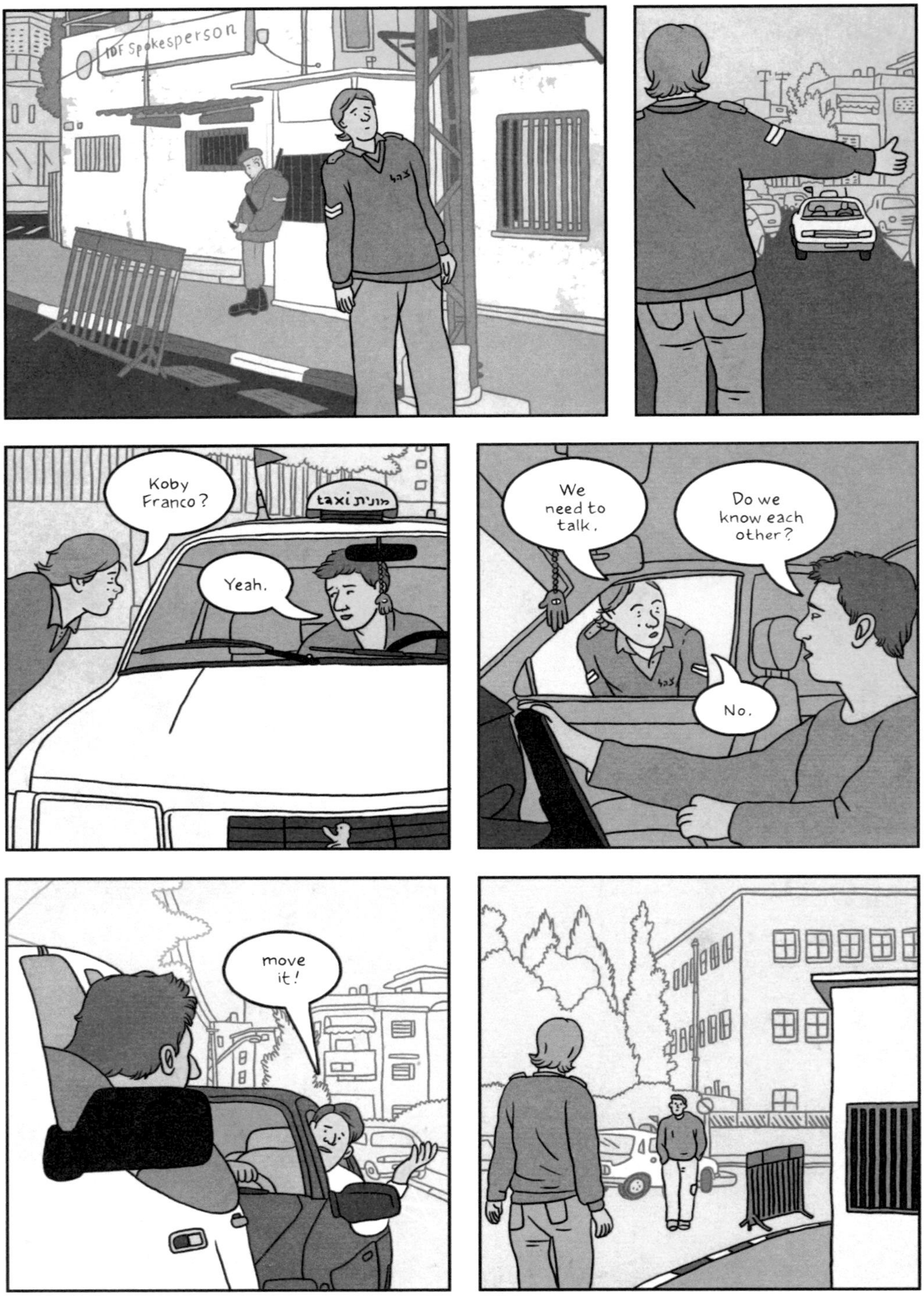
IDF Spokesperson
Koby Franco?
Yeah.
taxi
We need to talk.
Do we know each other?
No.
move it!

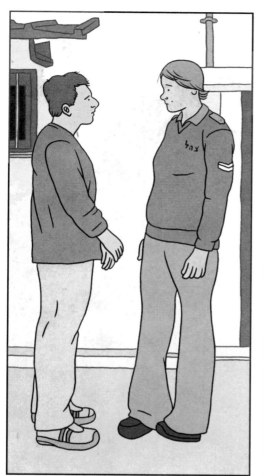

Well?

We should speak in private.

I guess we could sit in the park.

Let's make it quick, I'm parked on the sidewalk.

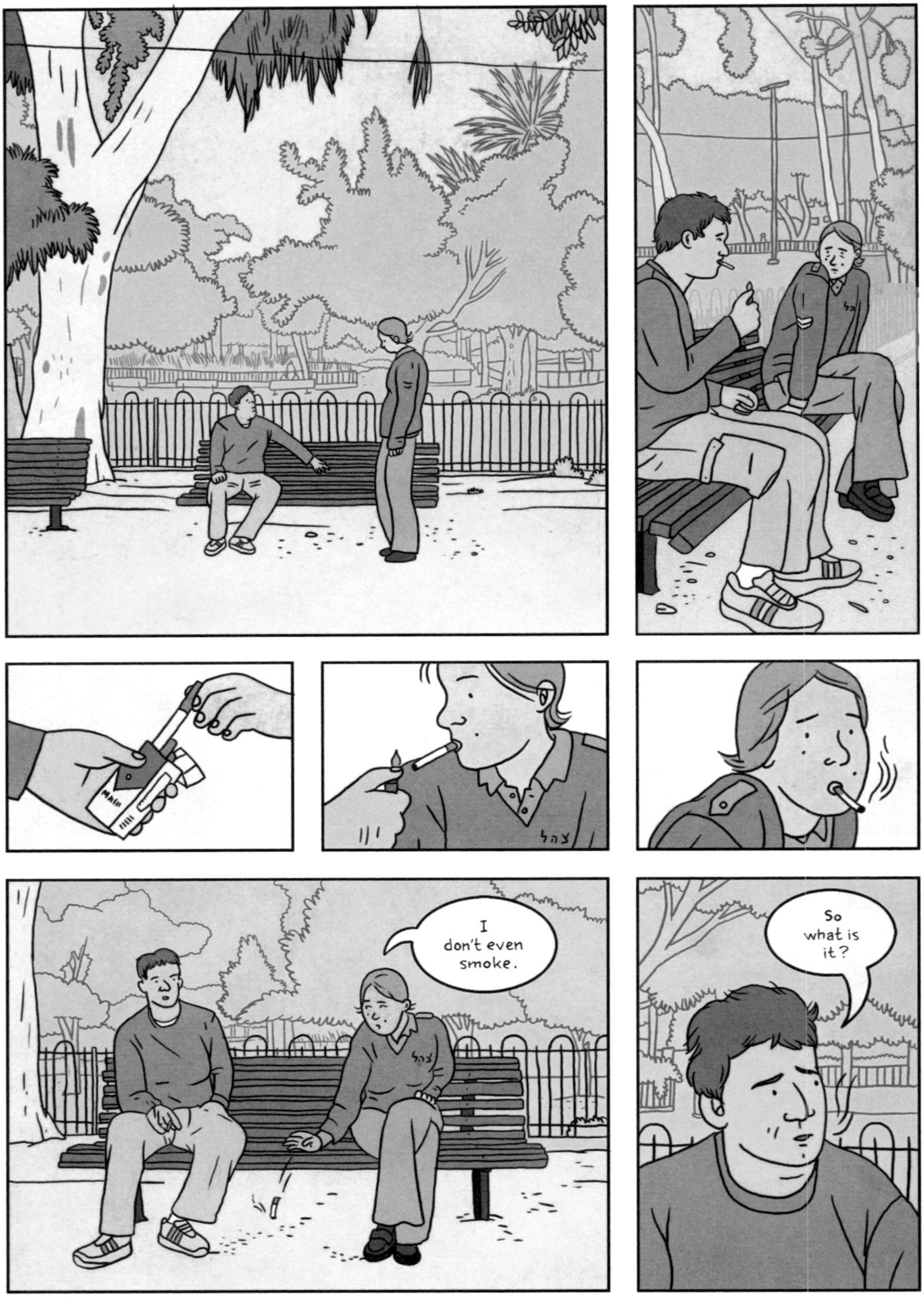
I don't even smoke.
So what is it?

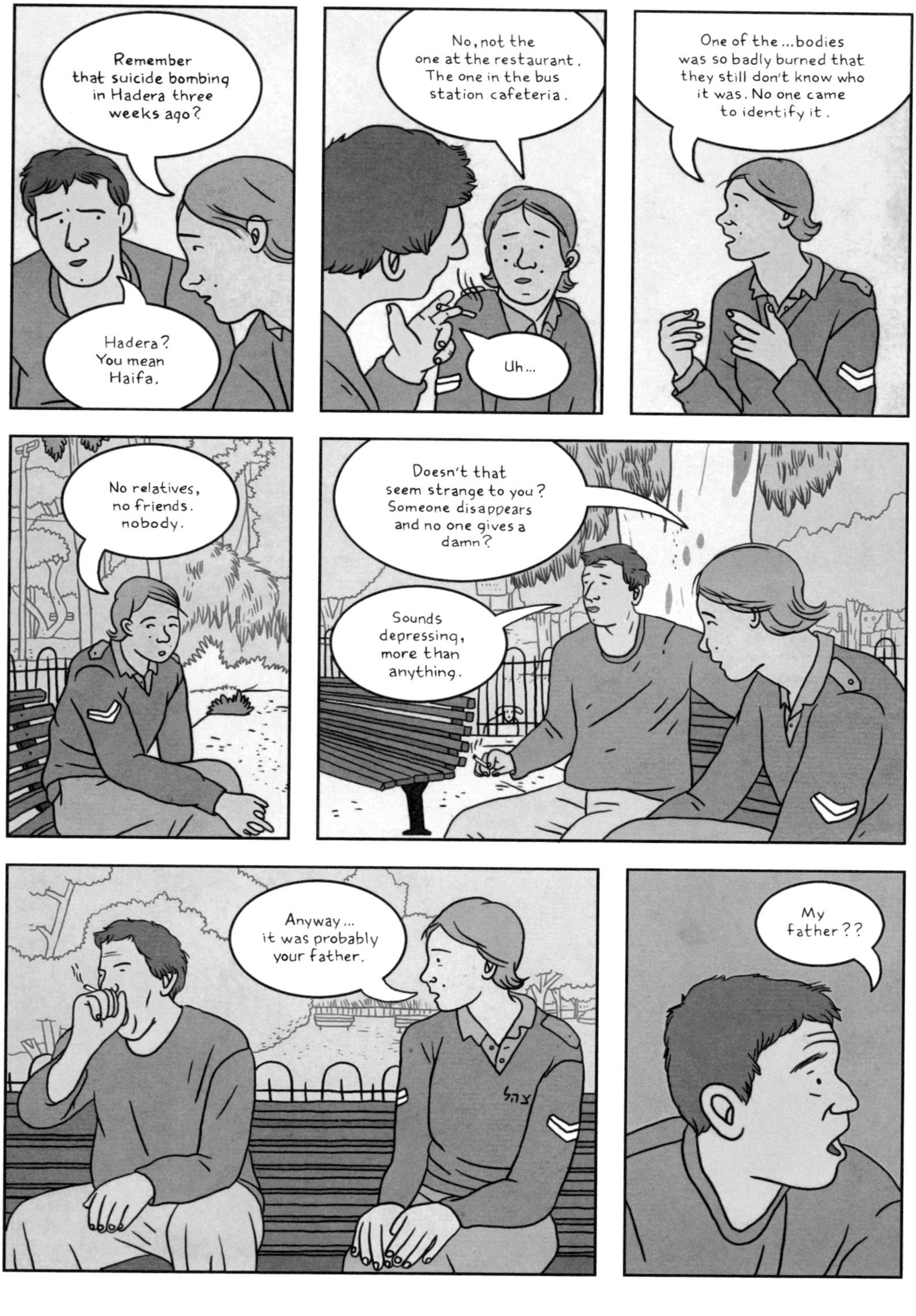
Remember that suicide bombing in Hadera three weeks ago?
Hadera? You mean Haifa.
No, not the one at the restaurant. The one in the bus station cafeteria.
Uh...
One of the ...bodies was so badly burned that they still don't know who it was. No one came to identify it.
No relatives, no friends. nobody.
Doesn't that seem strange to you? Someone disappears and no one gives a damn?
Sounds depressing, more than anything.
Anyway... it was probably your father.
צהל
My father??

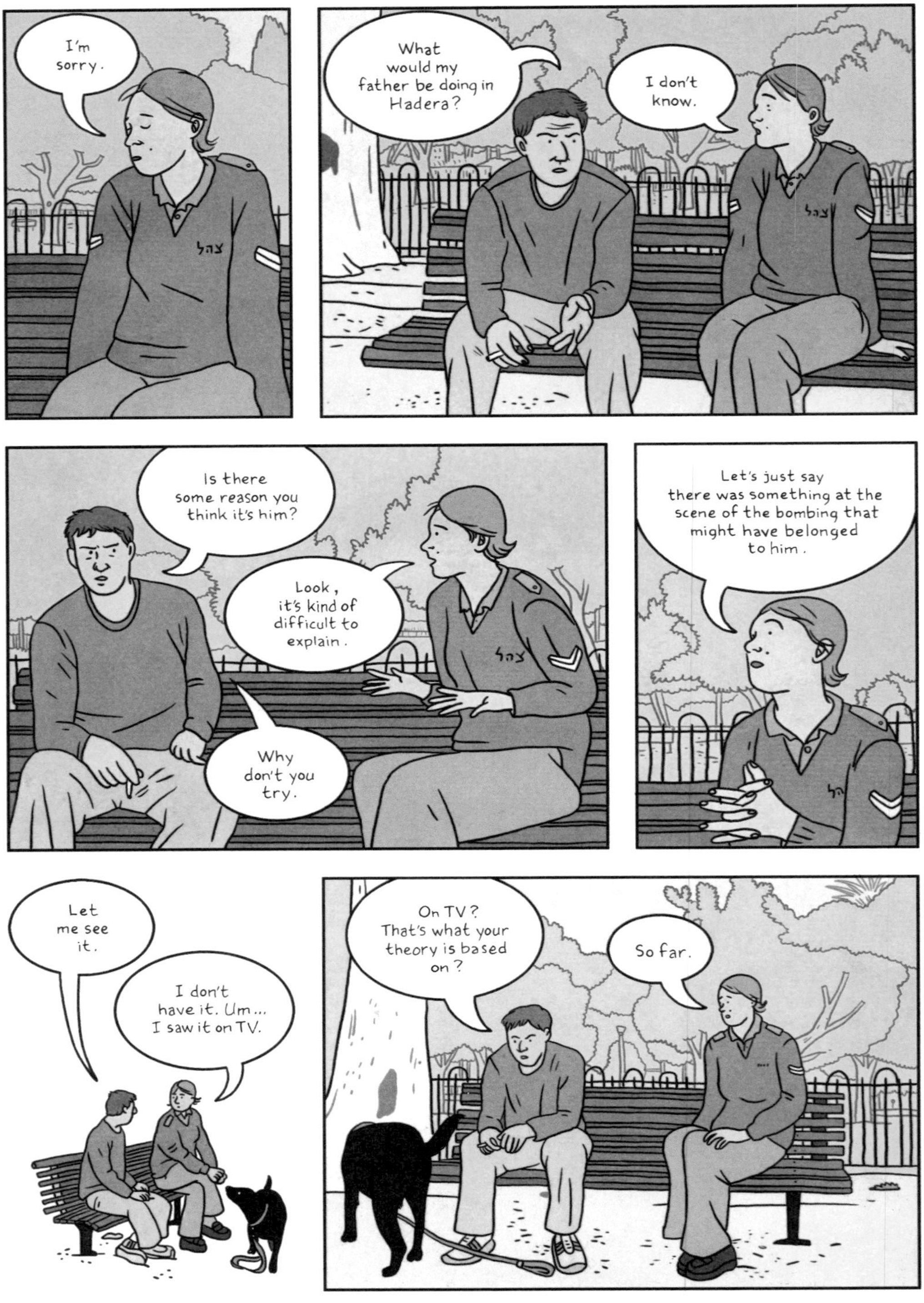
I'm sorry.
What would my father be doing in Hadera?
I don't know.
Is there some reason you think it's him?
Look, it's kind of difficult to explain.
Why don't you try.
Let's just say there was something at the scene of the bombing that might have belonged to him.
Let me see it.
I don't have it. Um... I saw it on TV.
On TV? That's what your theory is based on?
So far.

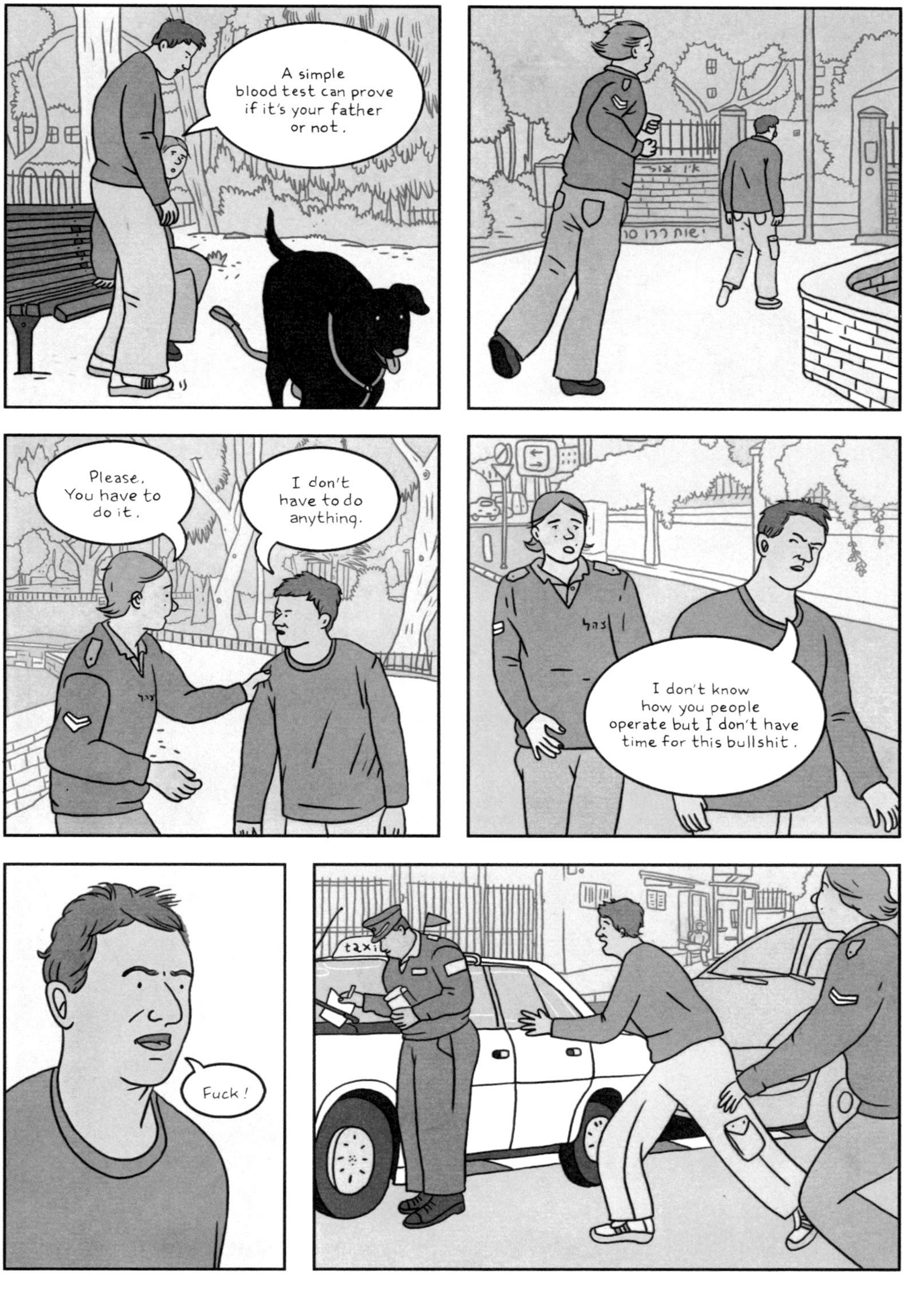
A simple blood test can prove if it's your father or not.
Please. You have to do it.
I don't have to do anything.
I don't know how you people operate but I don't have time for this bullshit.
Fuck!

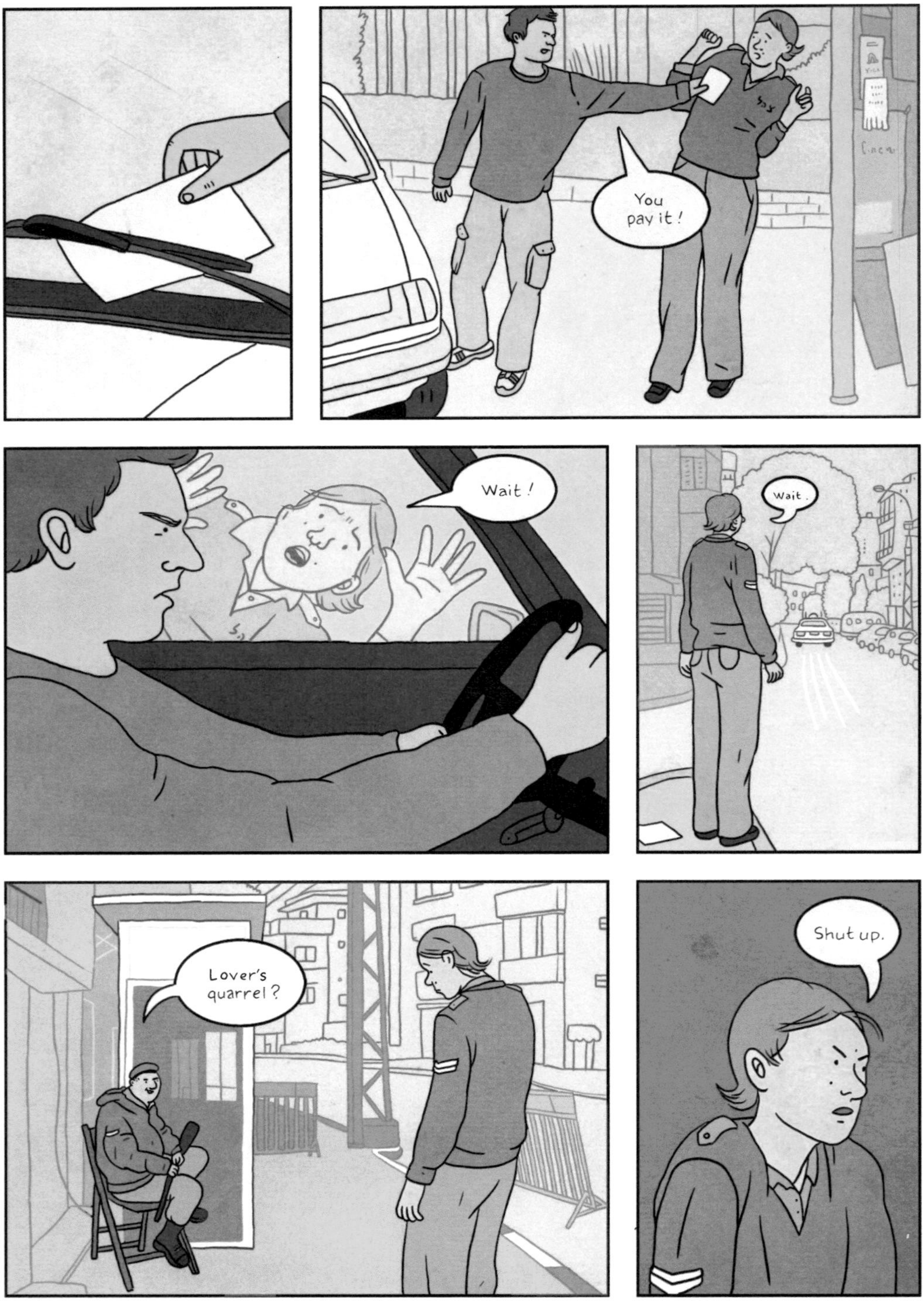
You pay it!
Wait!
Wait.
Lover's quarrel?
Shut up.

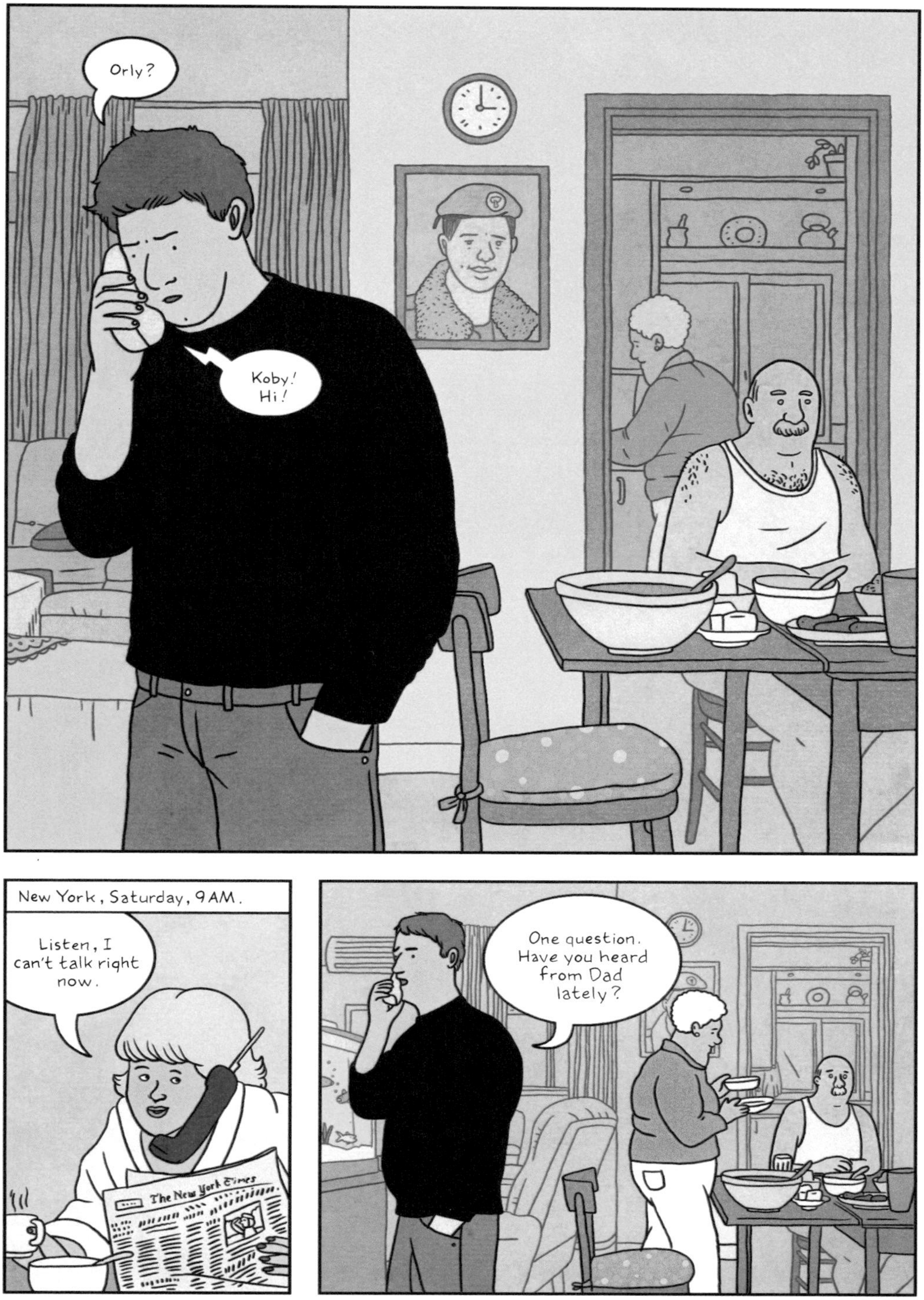
Orly?
Koby! Hi!
New York, Saturday, 9AM.
Listen, I can't talk right now.
The New York Times
One question. Have you heard from Dad lately?

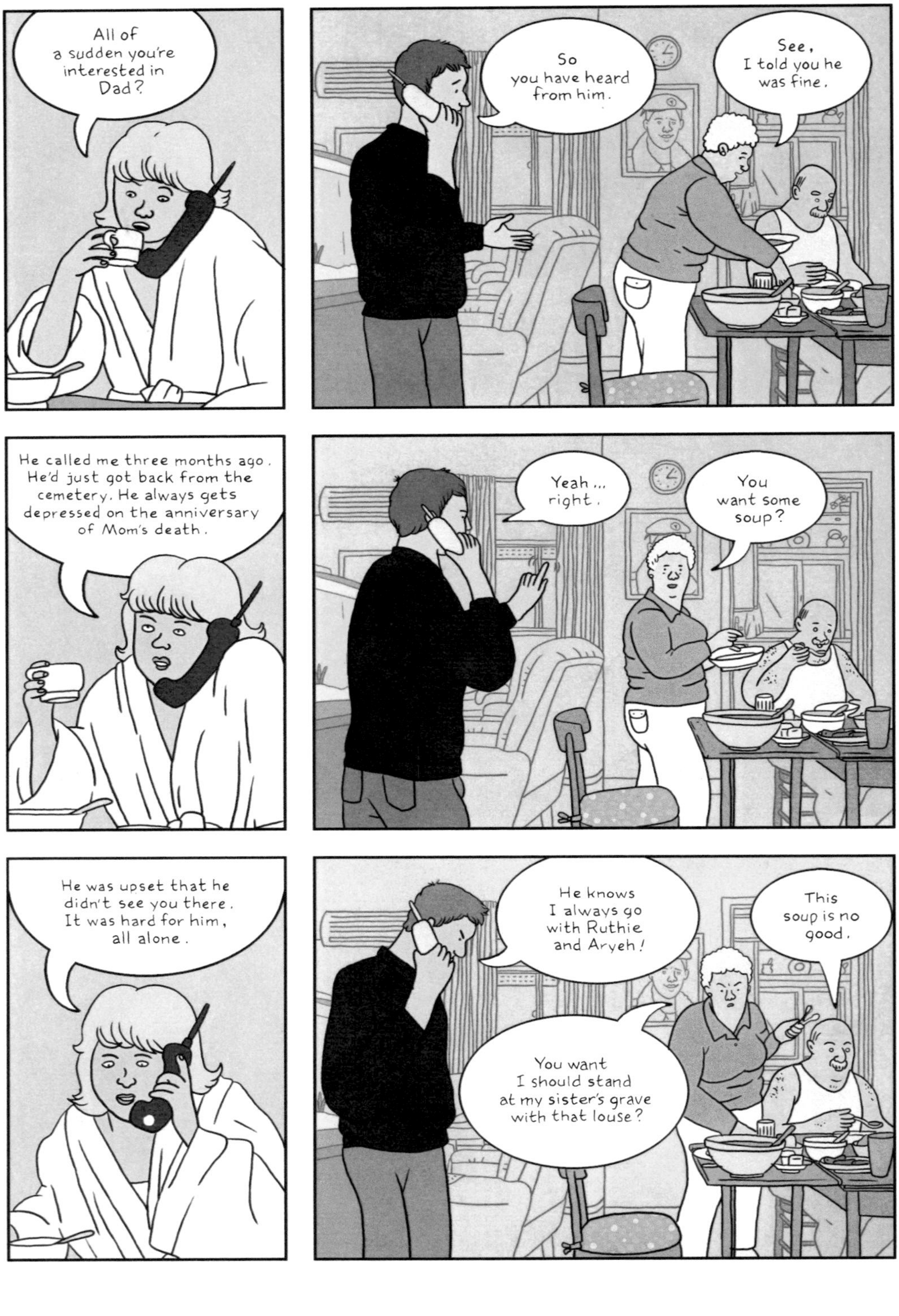
All of a sudden you're interested in Dad?
So you have heard from him.
See, I told you he was fine.
He called me three months ago. He'd just got back from the cemetery. He always gets depressed on the anniversary of Mom's death.
Yeah... right.
You want some soup?
He was upset that he didn't see you there. It was hard for him, all alone.
He knows I always go with Ruthie and Aryeh!
This soup is no good.
You want I should stand at my sister's grave with that louse?

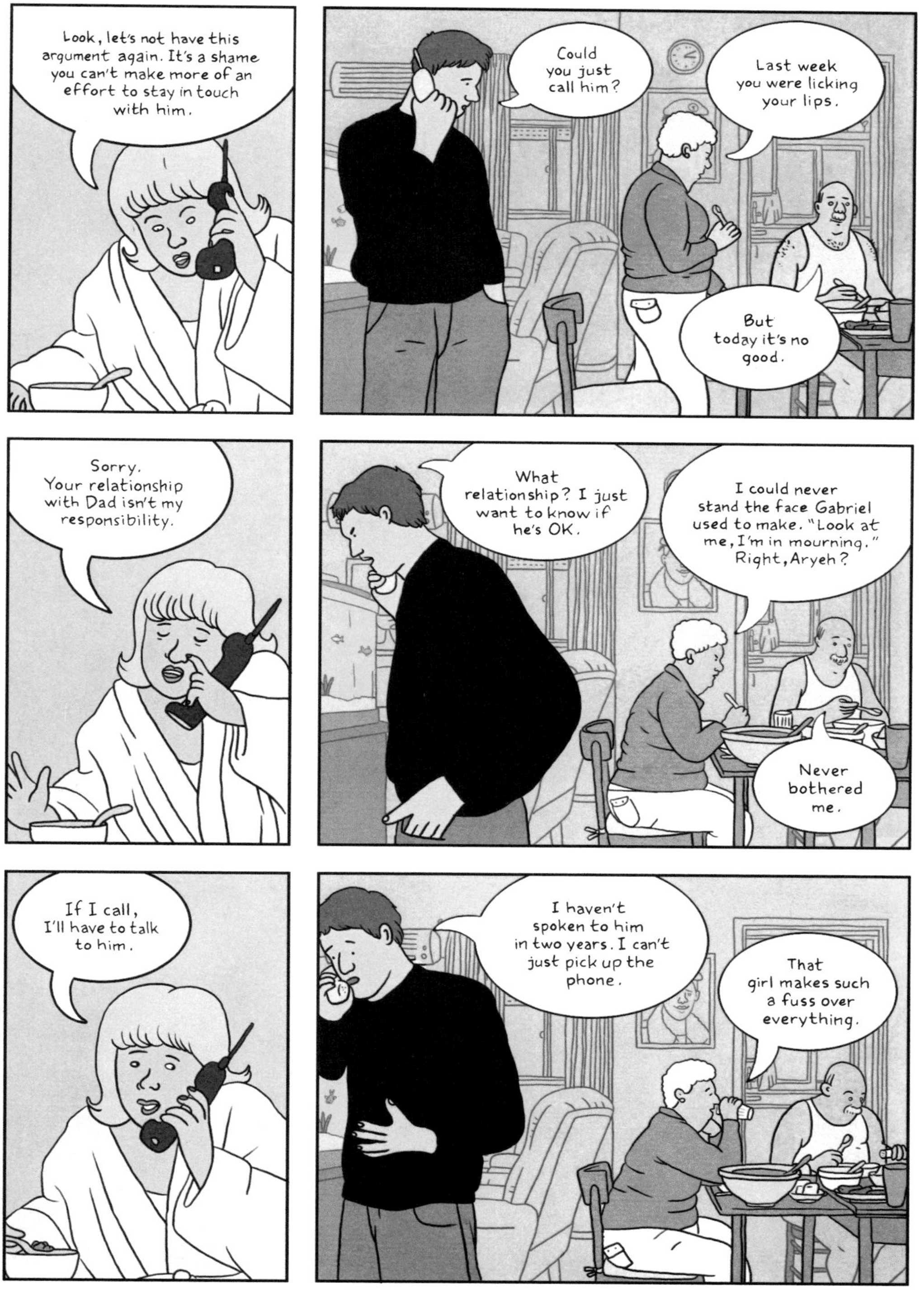
Look, let's not have this argument again. It's a shame you can't make more of an effort to stay in touch with him.
Could you just call him?
Last week you were licking your lips.
But today it's no good.
Sorry. Your relationship with Dad isn't my responsibility.
What relationship? I just want to know if he's OK.
I could never stand the face Gabriel used to make. "Look at me, I'm in mourning." Right, Aryeh?
Never bothered me.
If I call, I'll have to talk to him.
I haven't spoken to him in two years. I can't just pick up the phone.
That girl makes such a fuss over everything.

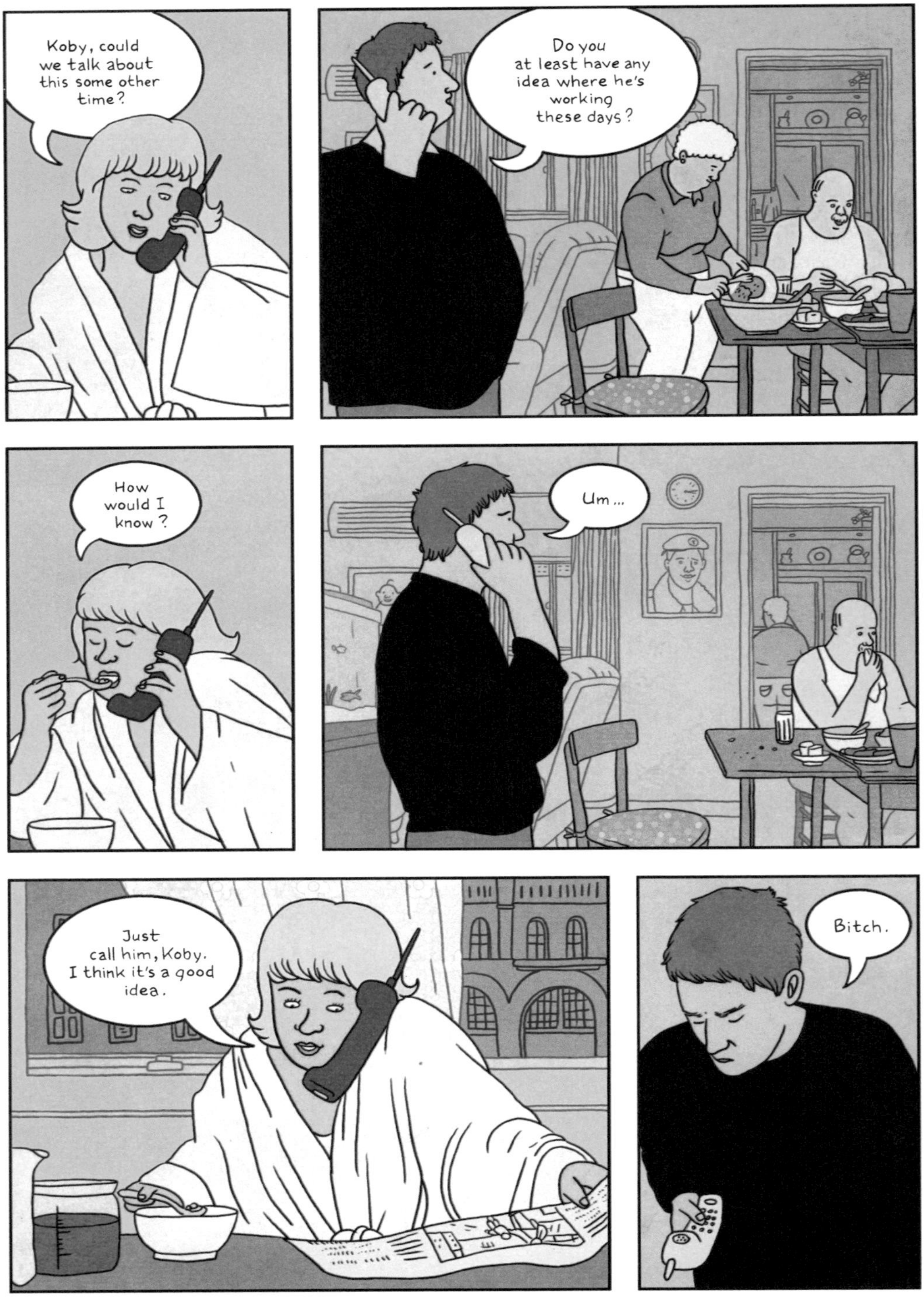
Koby, could we talk about this some other time?
Do you at least have any idea where he's working these days?
How would I know?
Um...
Just call him, Koby. I think it's a good idea.
Bitch.

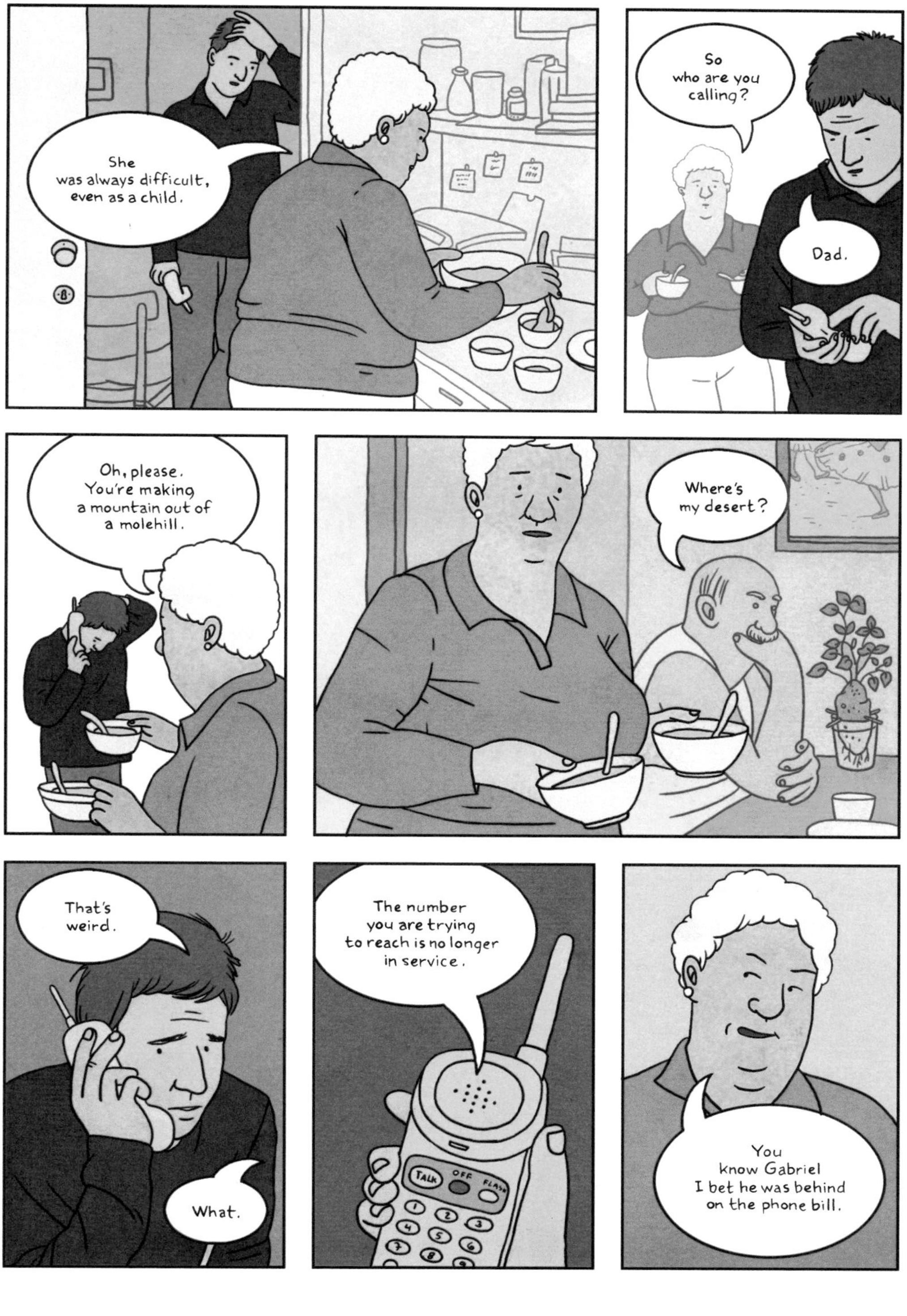
She was always difficult, even as a child.
So who are you calling?
Dad.
Oh, please. You're making a mountain out of a molehill.
Where's my desert?
That's weird.
What.
The number you are trying to reach is no longer in service.
TALK
OFF
FLASH
You know Gabriel I bet he was behind on the phone bill.

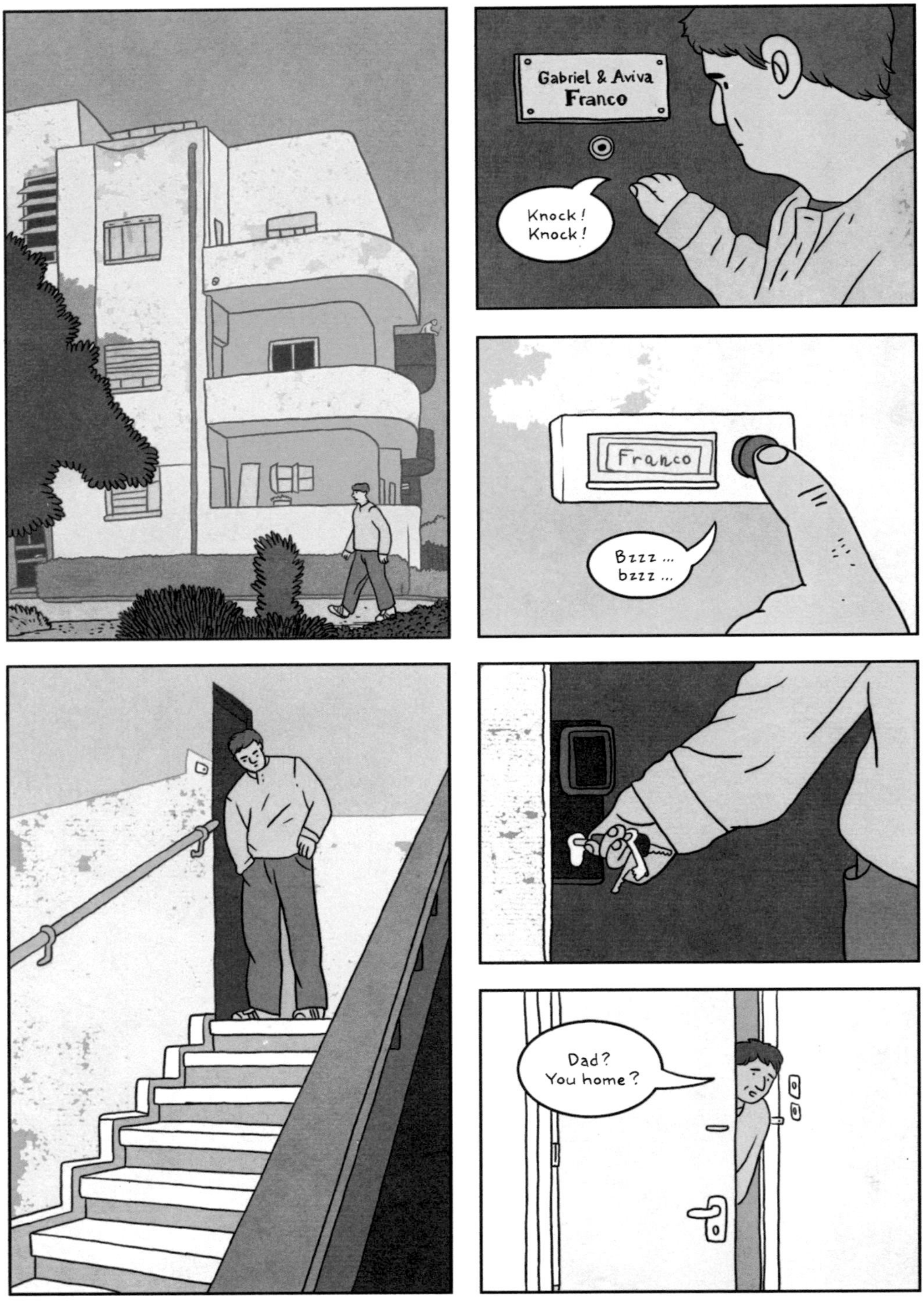
Gabriel & Aviva
Franco
Knock!
Knock!
Franco
Bzzz ...
bzzz ...
Dad?
You home?

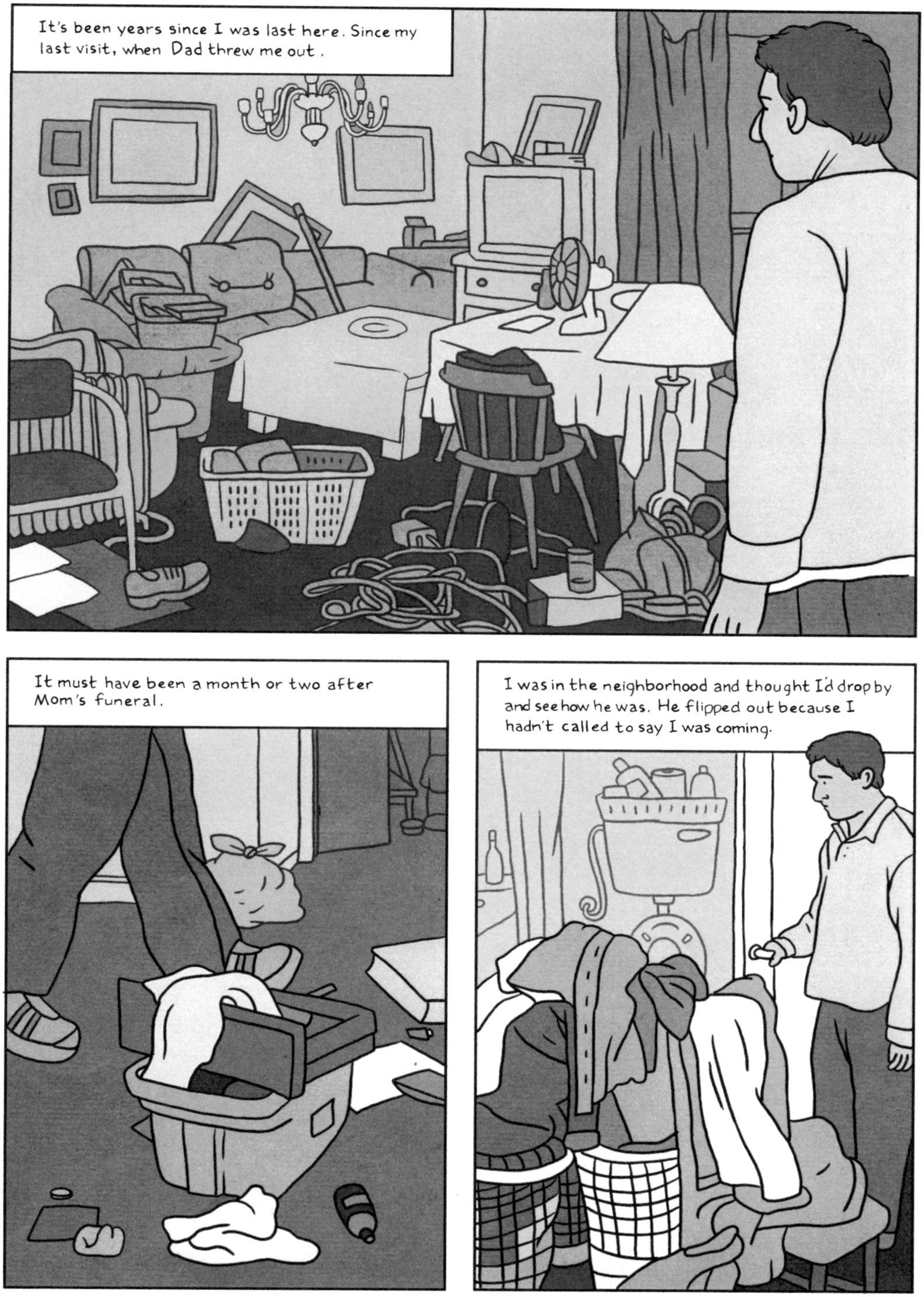
It's been years since I was last here. Since my last visit, when Dad threw me out.
It must have been a month or two after Mom's funeral.
I was in the neighborhood and thought I'd drop by and see how he was. He flipped out because I hadn't called to say I was coming.

Aunt Ruthie was here, she tried to calm him down but he went on and on. I need my privacy, he said. I need my goddamn privacy.

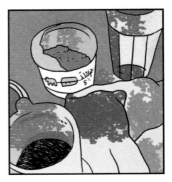

Later he kind of apologized, but from then on I wouldn't see him at home. Only in cafes, or in the park.

Five times in three years.

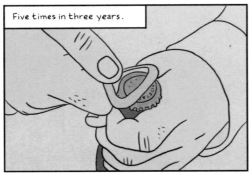

And then not even that.

Wonder how much this apartment is worth. Not very well maintained. Still, we could probably get about 180,000 for it. Half for Orly, which leaves me with 90 grand. Not bad.

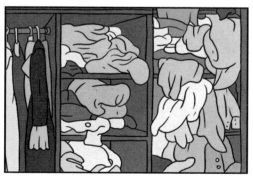

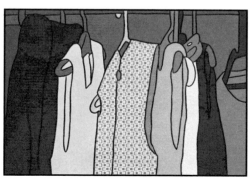

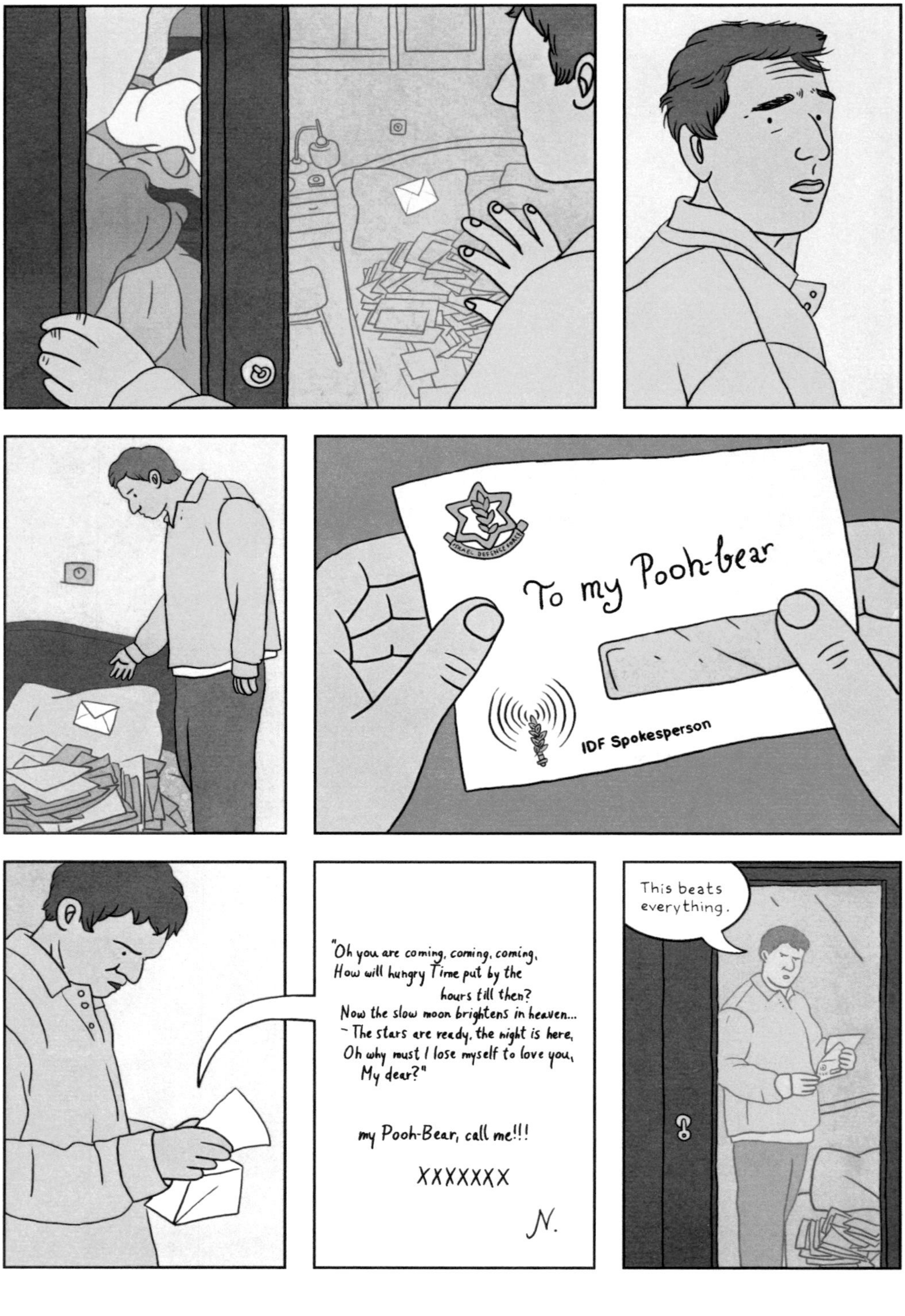
To my Pooh-bear
IDF Spokesperson
"Oh you are coming, coming, coming,
How will hungry Time put by the
hours till then?
Now the slow moon brightens in heaven...
- The stars are ready, the night is here,
Oh why must I lose myself to love you,
My dear?"
my Pooh-Bear, call me!!!
XXXXXXX
N.
This beats everything.

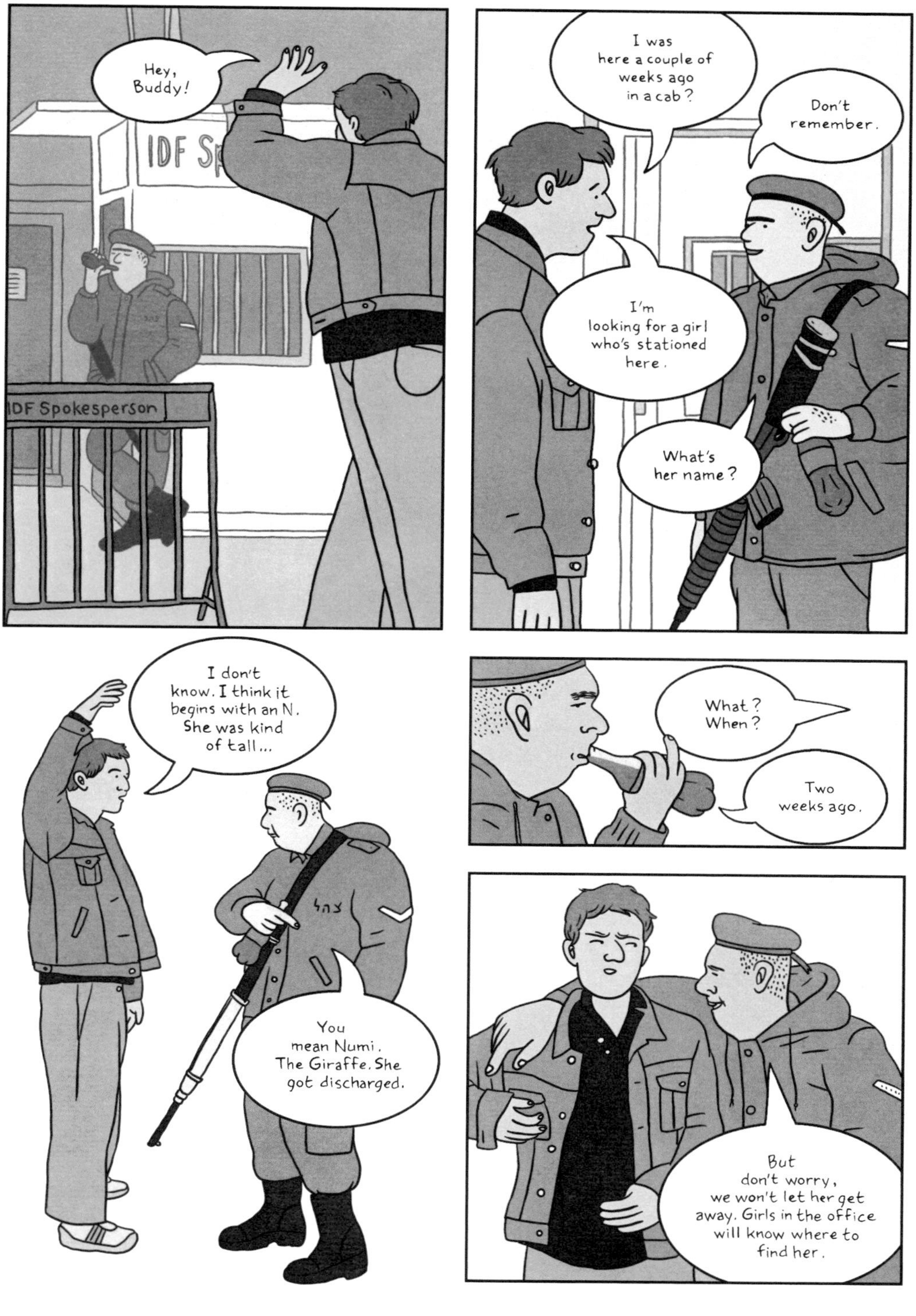
Hey, Buddy!
IDF Sp
IDF Spokesperson
I was here a couple of weeks ago in a cab?
Don't remember.
I'm looking for a girl who's stationed here.
What's her name?
I don't know. I think it begins with an N. She was kind of tall...
You mean Numi. The Giraffe. She got discharged.
What? When?
Two weeks ago.
But don't worry, we won't let her get away. Girls in the office will know where to find her.

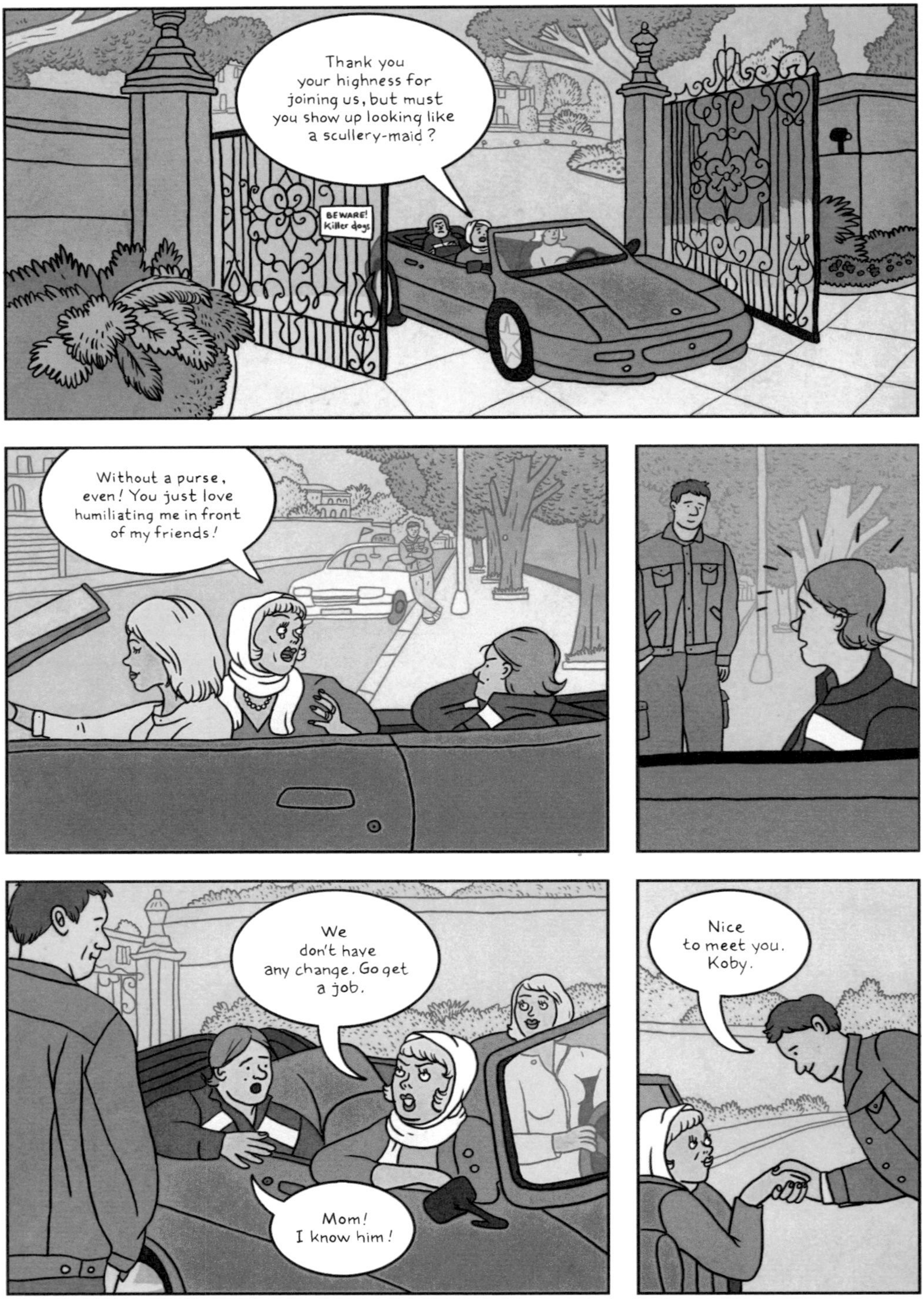
Thank you your highness for joining us, but must you show up looking like a scullery-maid?
BEWARE! Killer dogs
Without a purse, even! You just love humiliating me in front of my friends!
We don't have any change. Go get a job.
Mom! I know him!
Nice to meet you. Koby.

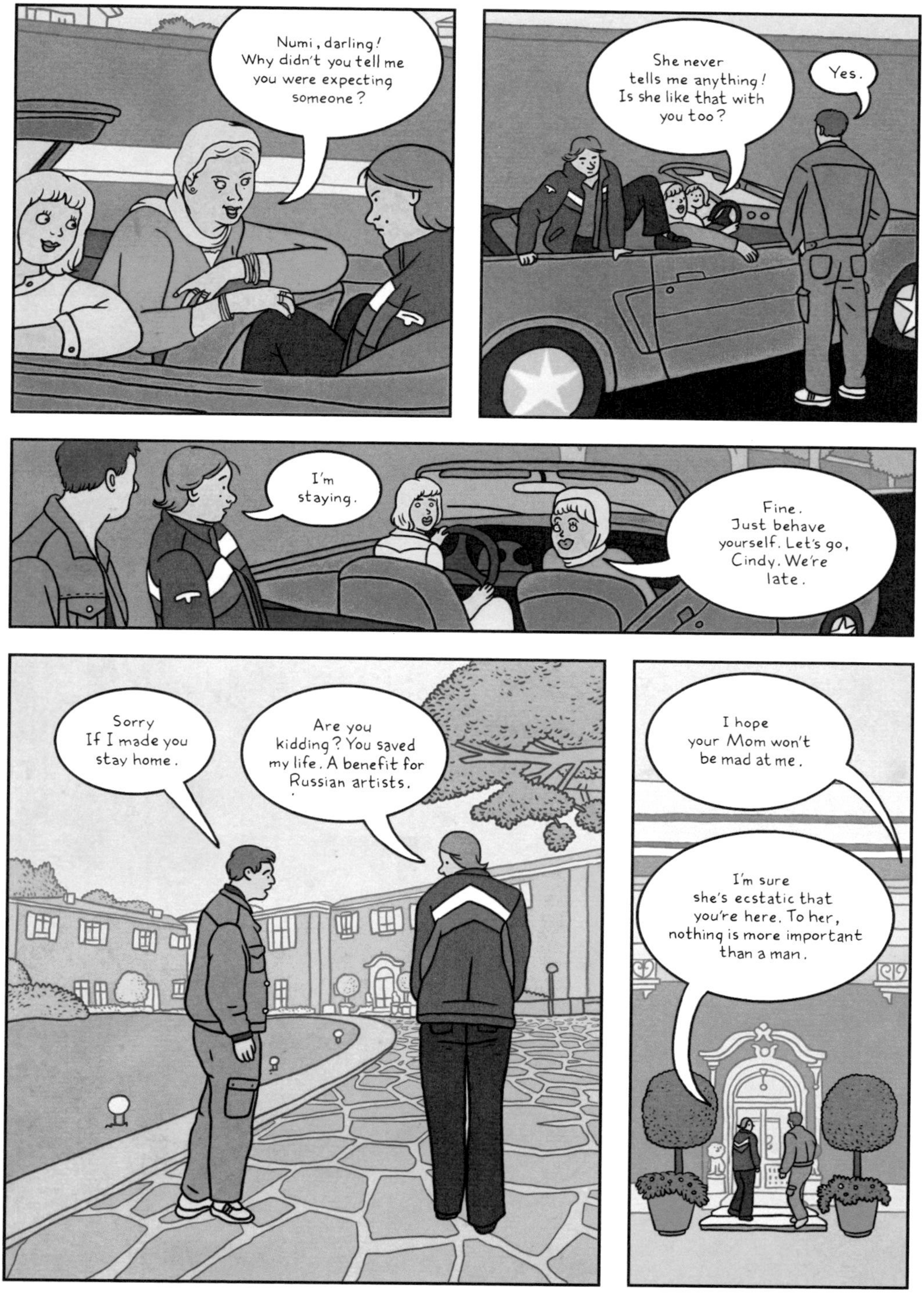
Numi, darling! Why didn't you tell me you were expecting someone?
She never tells me anything! Is she like that with you too?
Yes.
I'm staying.
Fine. Just behave yourself. Let's go, Cindy. We're late.
Sorry If I made you stay home.
Are you kidding? You saved my life. A benefit for Russian artists.
I hope your Mom won't be mad at me.
I'm sure she's ecstatic that you're here. To her, nothing is more important than a man.

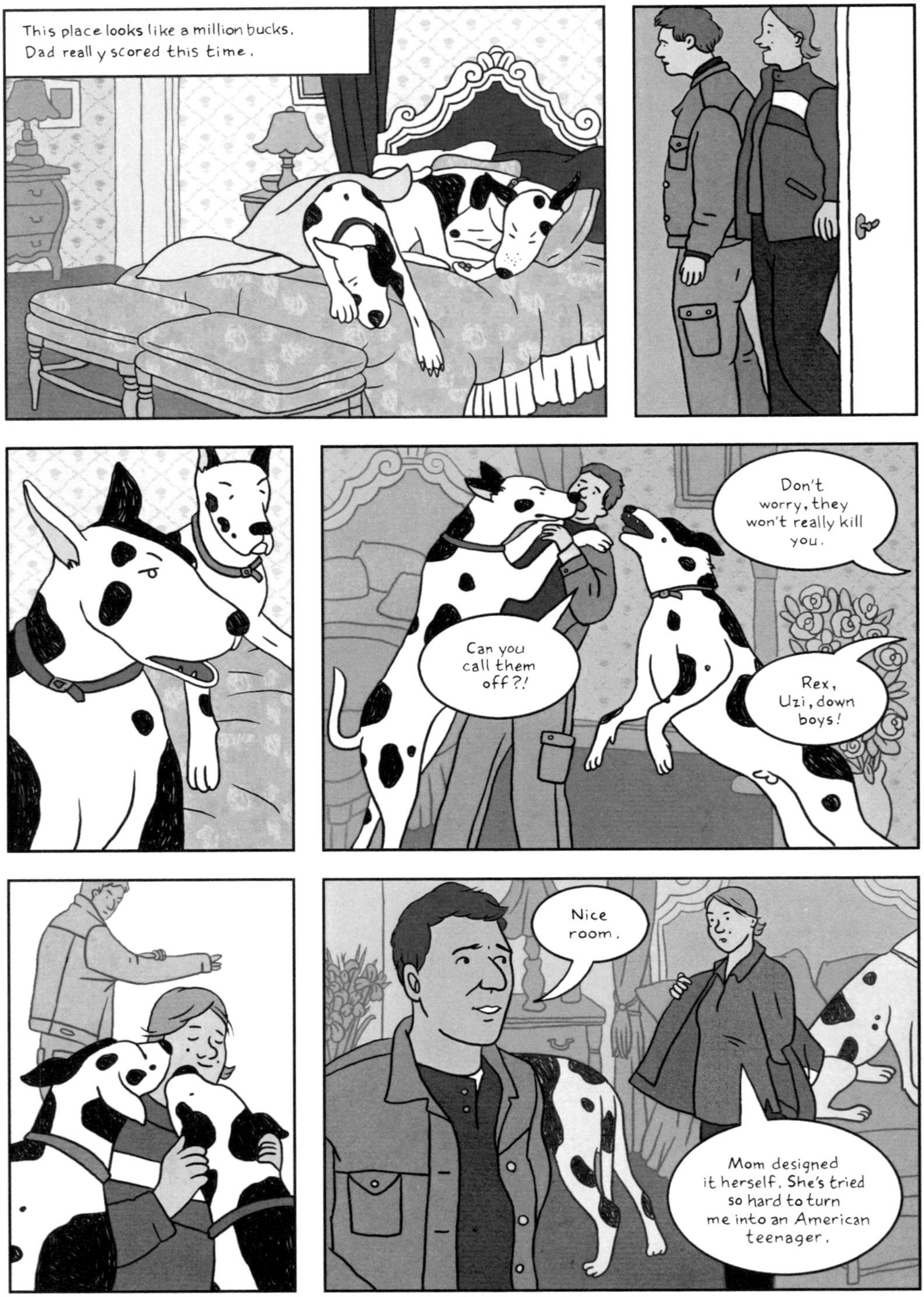
This place looks like a million bucks. Dad reall y scored this time.
Don't worry, they won't really kill you.
Can you call them off?!
Rex, Uzi, down boys!
Nice room.
Mom designed it herself. She's tried so hard to turn me into an American teenager.

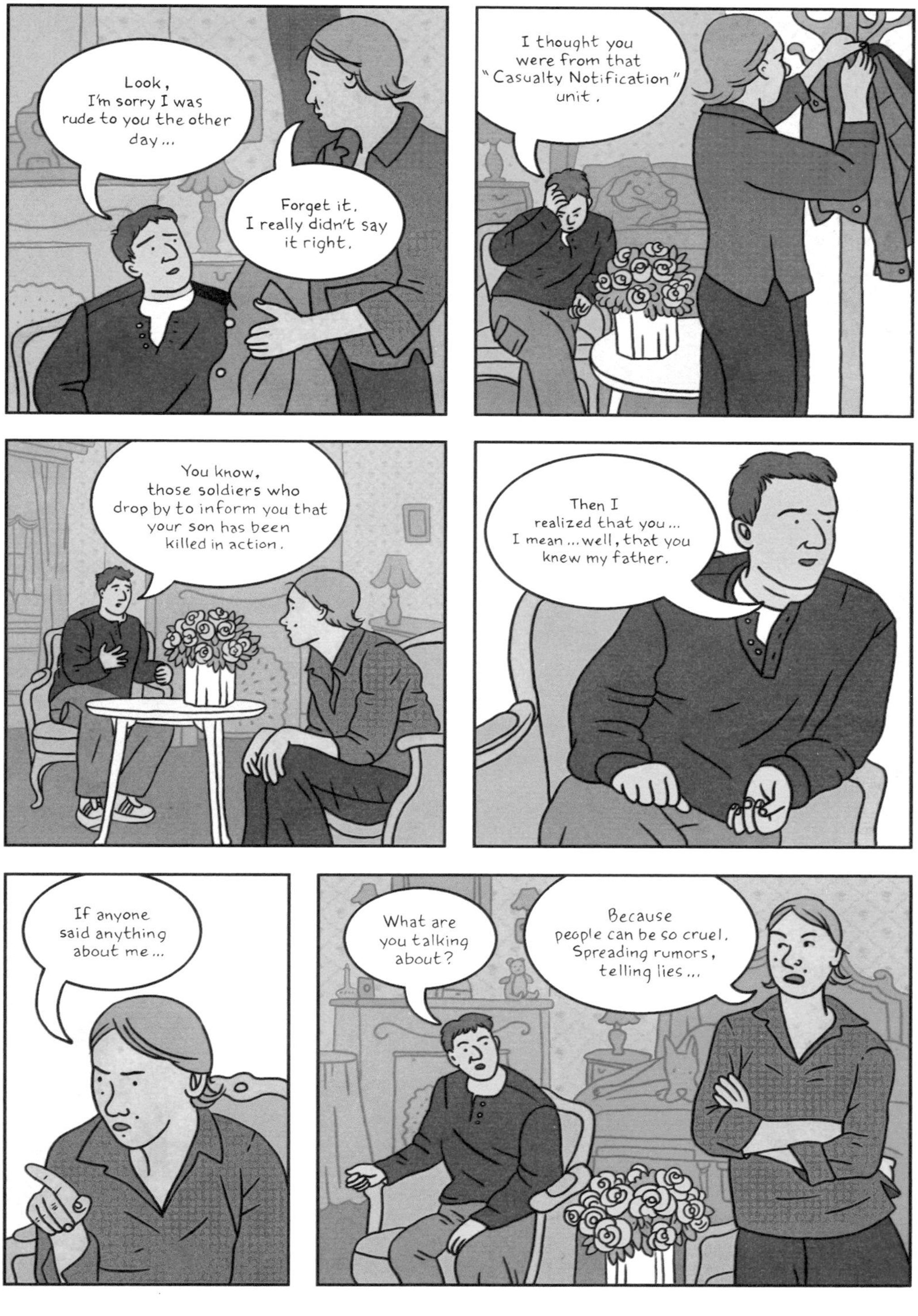
Look, I'm sorry I was rude to you the other day...
Forget it. I really didn't say it right.
I thought you were from that "Casualty Notification" unit.
You know, those soldiers who drop by to inform you that your son has been killed in action.
Then I realized that you... I mean... well, that you knew my father.
If anyone said anything about me...
What are you talking about?
Because people can be so cruel. Spreading rumors, telling lies...

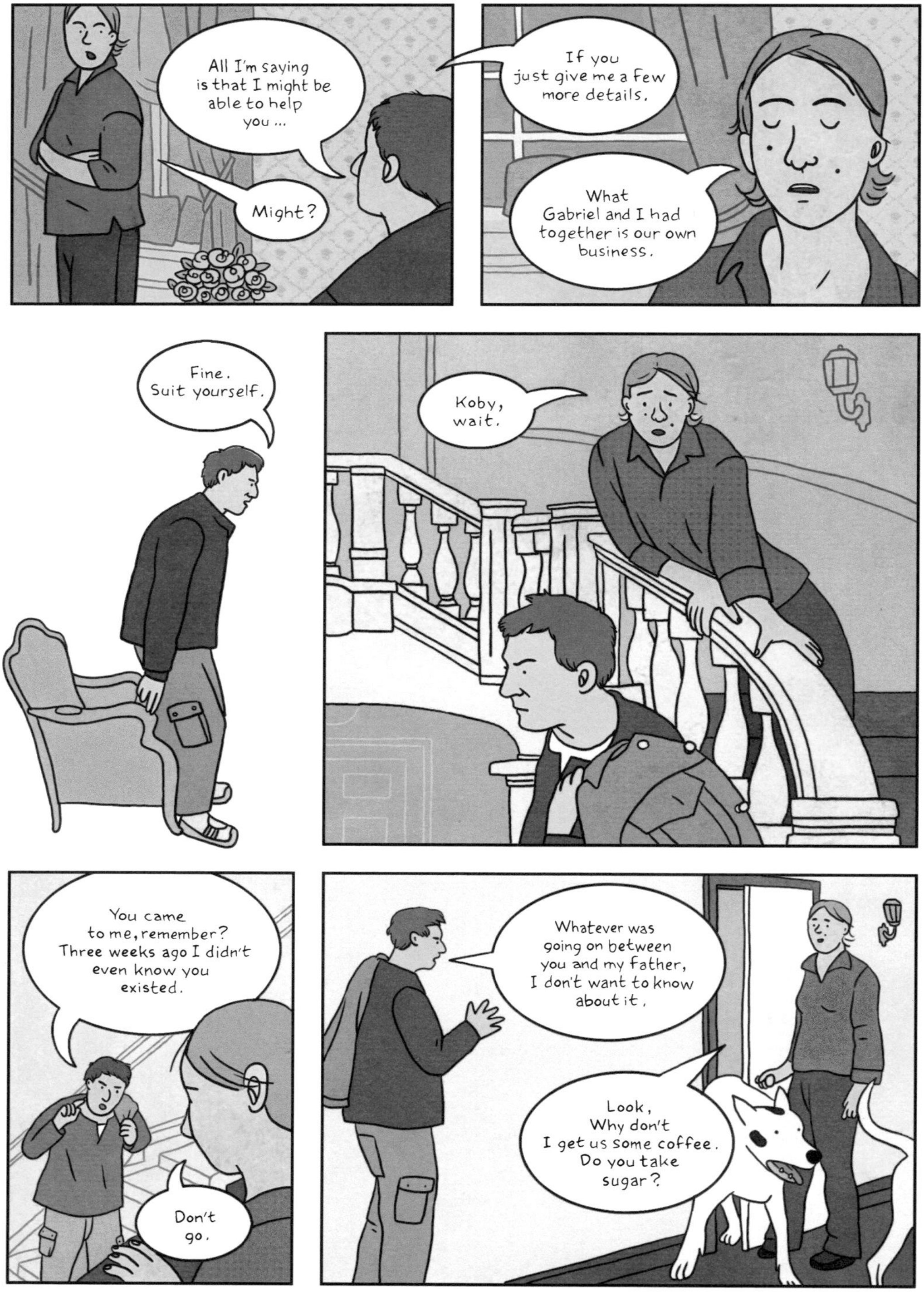
All I'm saying is that I might be able to help you ...
Might?
If you just give me a few more details.
What Gabriel and I had together is our own business.
Fine. Suit yourself.
Koby, wait.
You came to me, remember? Three weeks ago I didn't even know you existed.
Don't go.
Whatever was going on between you and my father, I don't want to know about it.
Look, Why don't I get us some coffee. Do you take sugar?

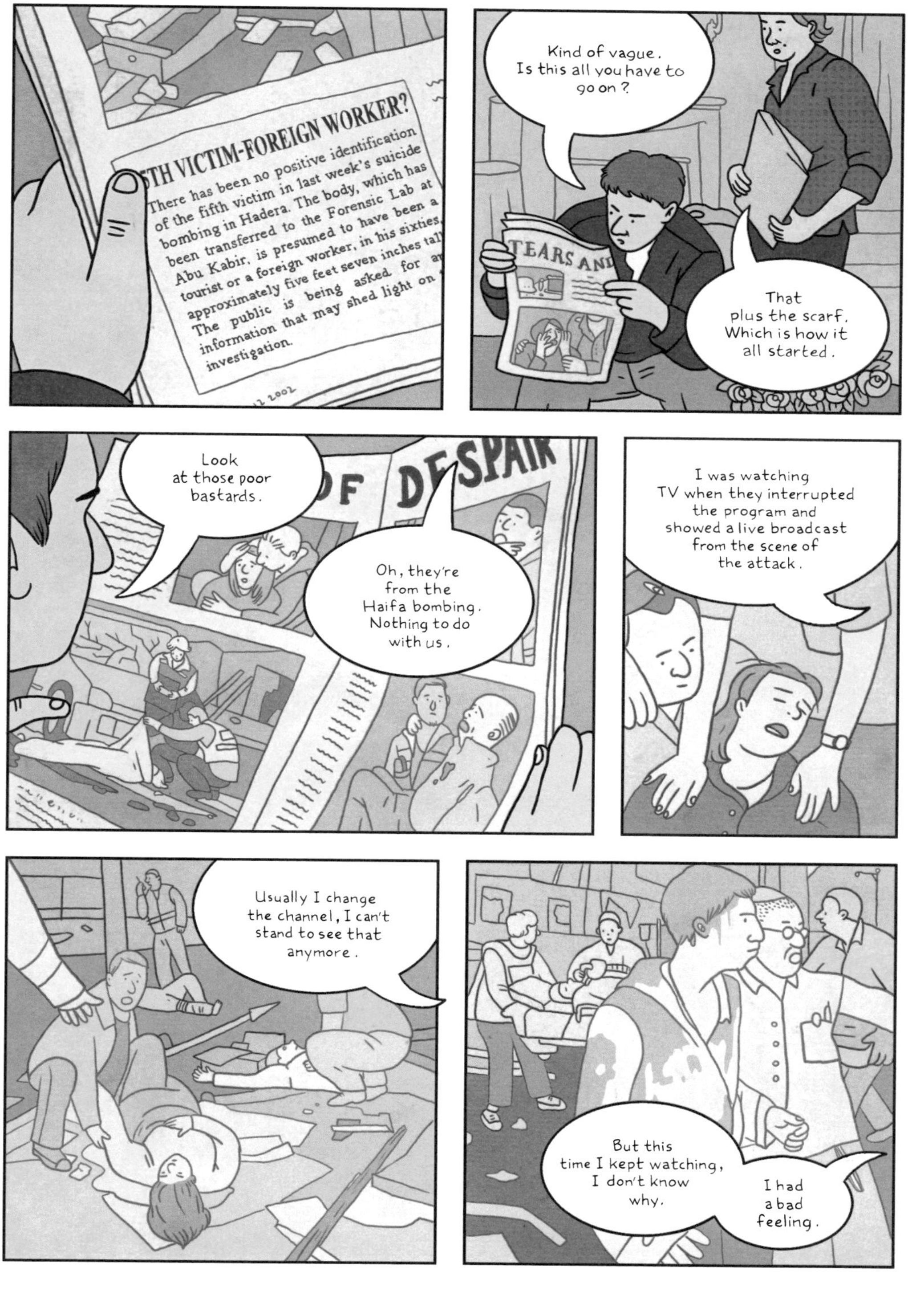
5TH VICTIM-FOREIGN WORKER?
There has been no positive identification of the fifth victim in last week's suicide bombing in Hadera. The body, which has been transferred to the Forensic Lab at Abu Kabir, is presumed to have been a tourist or a foreign worker, in his sixties, approximately five feet seven inches tall. The public is being asked for any information that may shed light on the investigation.
Kind of vague. Is this all you have to go on?
TEARS AND
That plus the scarf. Which is how it all started.
OF DESPAIR
Look at those poor bastards.
Oh, they're from the Haifa bombing. Nothing to do with us.
I was watching TV when they interrupted the program and showed a live broadcast from the scene of the attack.
Usually I change the channel, I can't stand to see that anymore.
But this time I kept watching, I don't know why.
I had a bad feeling.

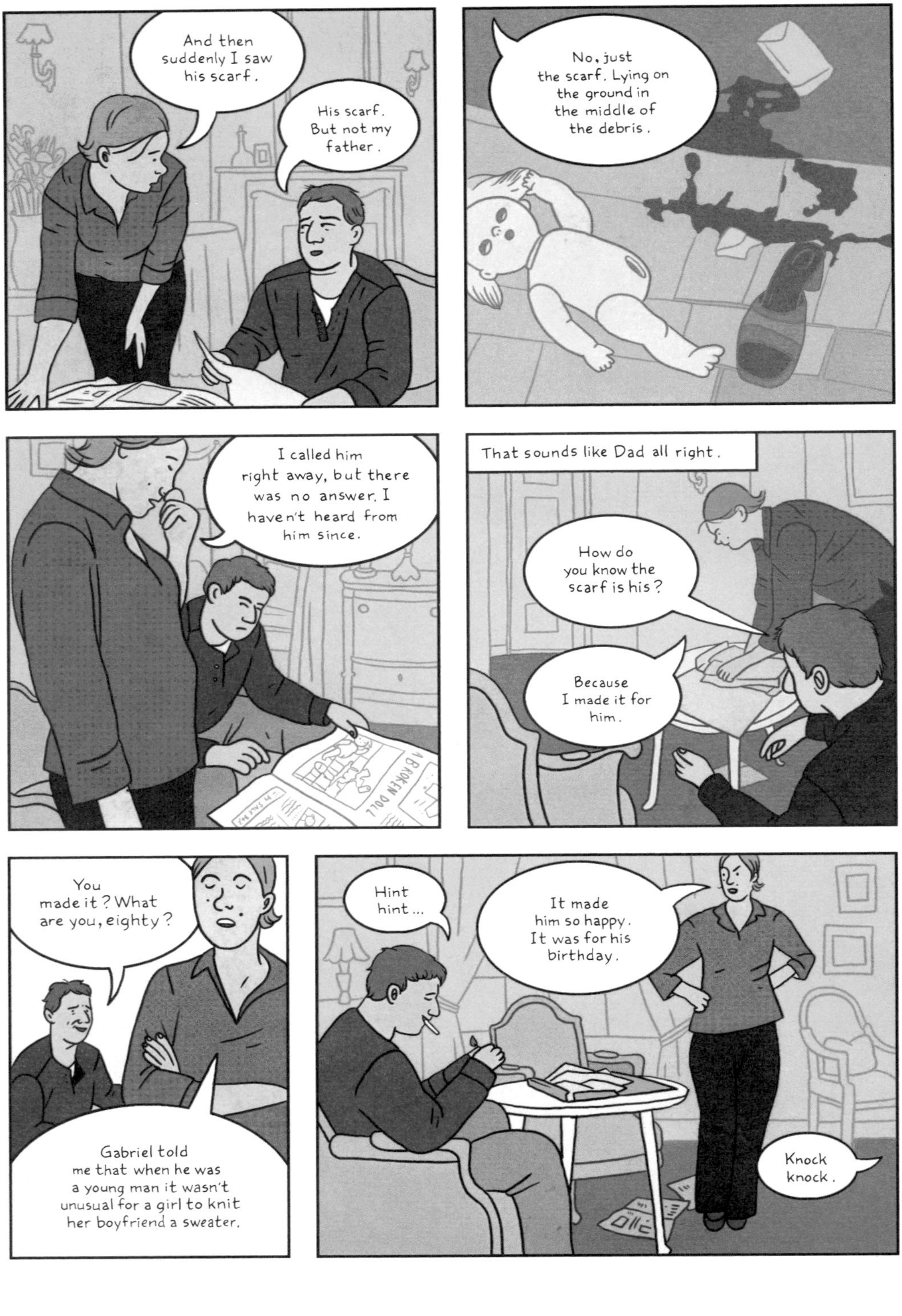
And then suddenly I saw his scarf.
His scarf. But not my father.
No, just the scarf. Lying on the ground in the middle of the debris.
I called him right away, but there was no answer. I haven't heard from him since.
A BROKEN DOLL
That sounds like Dad all right.
How do you know the scarf is his?
Because I made it for him.
You made it? What are you, eighty?
Gabriel told me that when he was a young man it wasn't unusual for a girl to knit her boyfriend a sweater.
Hint hint...
It made him so happy. It was for his birthday.
Knock knock.

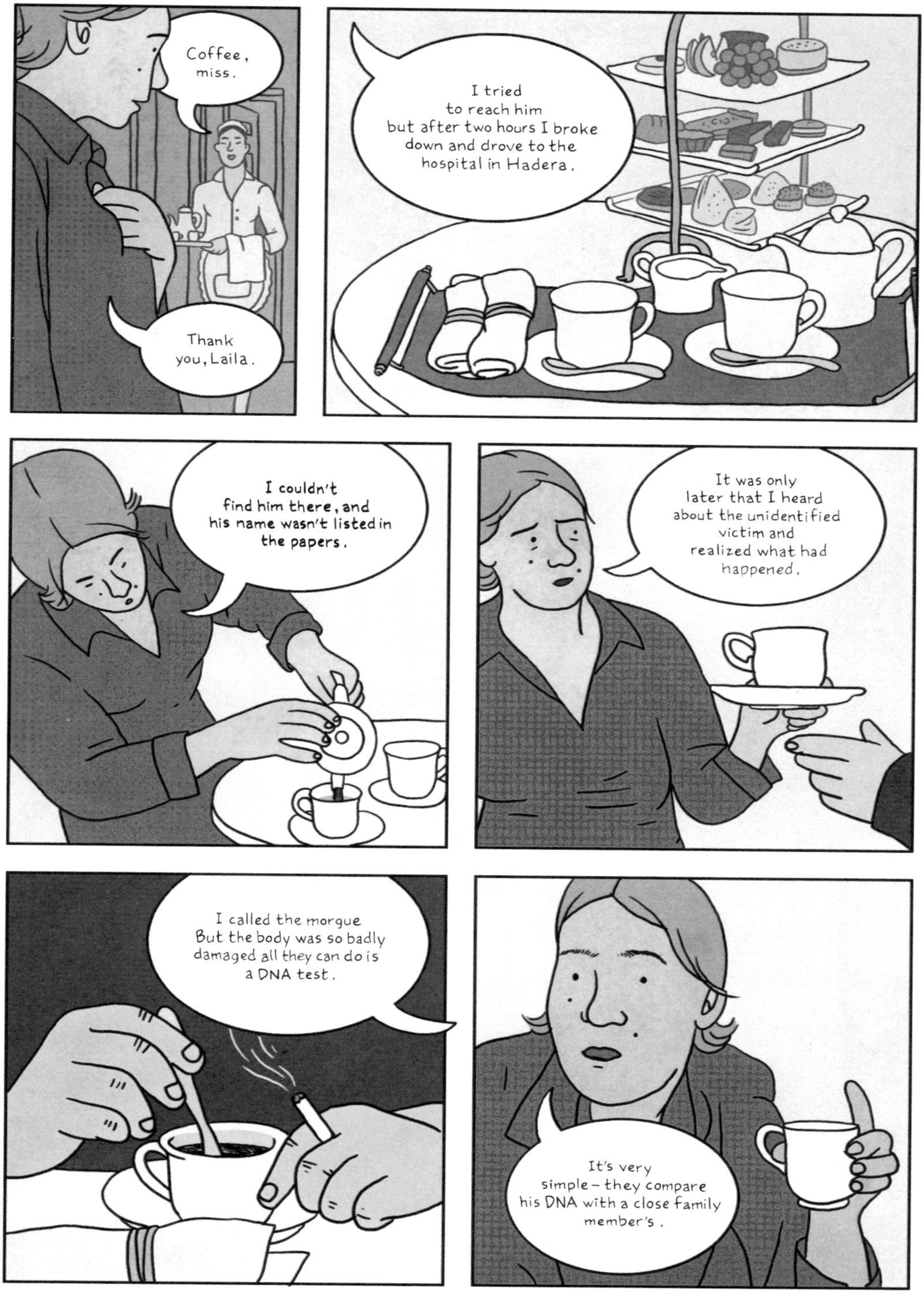
Coffee, miss.
Thank you, Laila.
I tried to reach him but after two hours I broke down and drove to the hospital in Hadera.
I couldn't find him there, and his name wasn't listed in the papers.
It was only later that I heard about the unidentified victim and realized what had happened.
I called the morgue But the body was so badly damaged all they can do is a DNA test.
It's very simple – they compare his DNA with a close family member's.

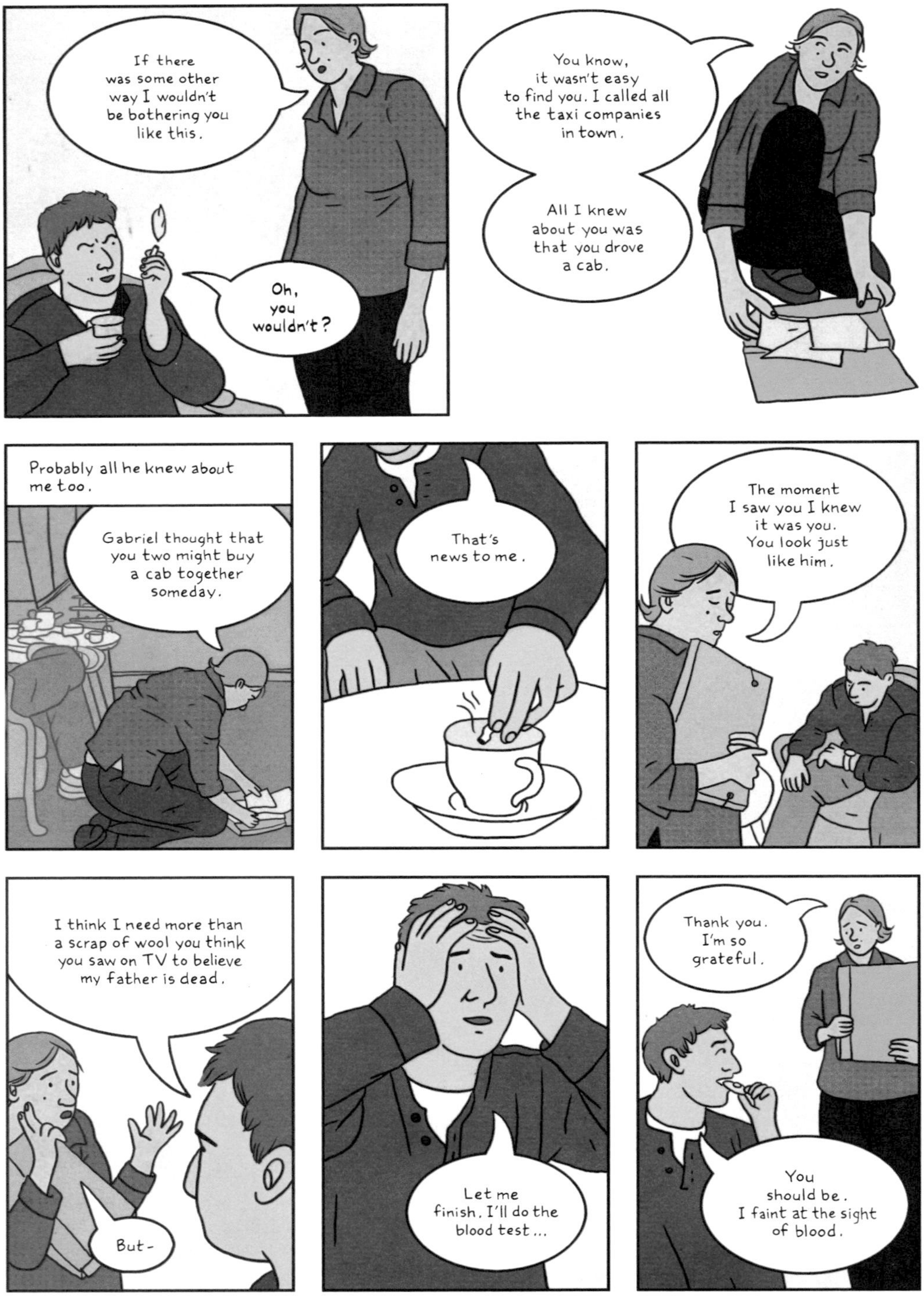
If there was some other way I wouldn't be bothering you like this.
Oh, you wouldn't?
You know, it wasn't easy to find you. I called all the taxi companies in town.
All I knew about you was that you drove a cab.
Probably all he knew about me too.
Gabriel thought that you two might buy a cab together someday.
That's news to me.
The moment I saw you I knew it was you. You look just like him.
I think I need more than a scrap of wool you think you saw on TV to believe my father is dead.
But-
Let me finish. I'll do the blood test...
Thank you. I'm so grateful.
You should be. I faint at the sight of blood.

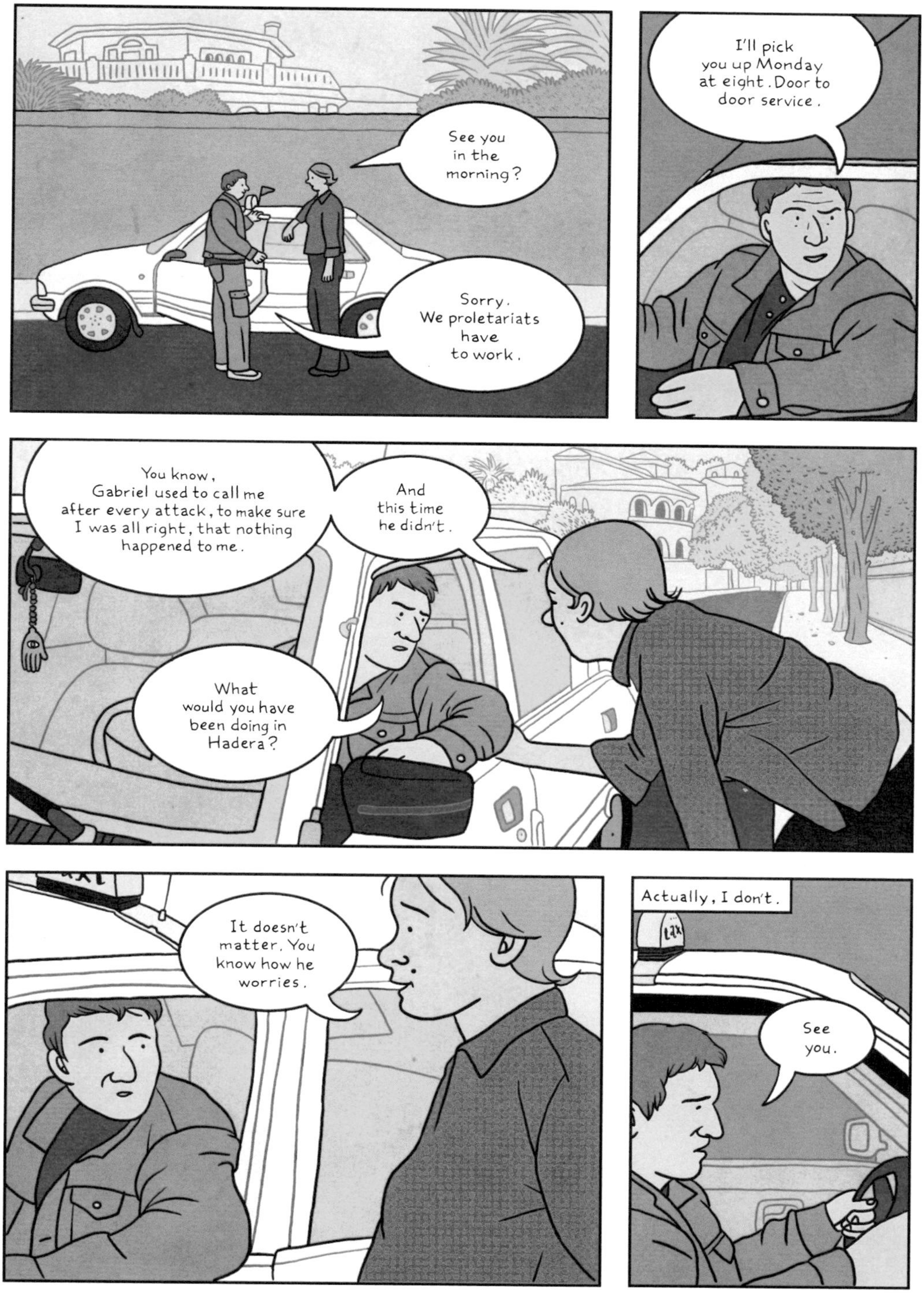
See you in the morning?
Sorry. We proletariats have to work.
I'll pick you up Monday at eight. Door to door service.
You know, Gabriel used to call me after every attack, to make sure I was all right, that nothing happened to me.
And this time he didn't.
What would you have been doing in Hadera?
It doesn't matter. You know how he worries.
Actually, I don't.
See you.

chapter two
my travels with the giraffe

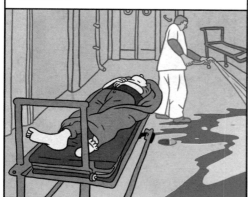

Pathological Institute for Forensic Medicine, Abu Kabir.

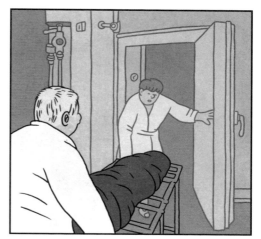

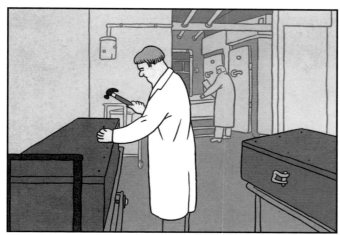

Any thoughts on lunch?

How about Chinese?

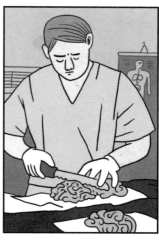

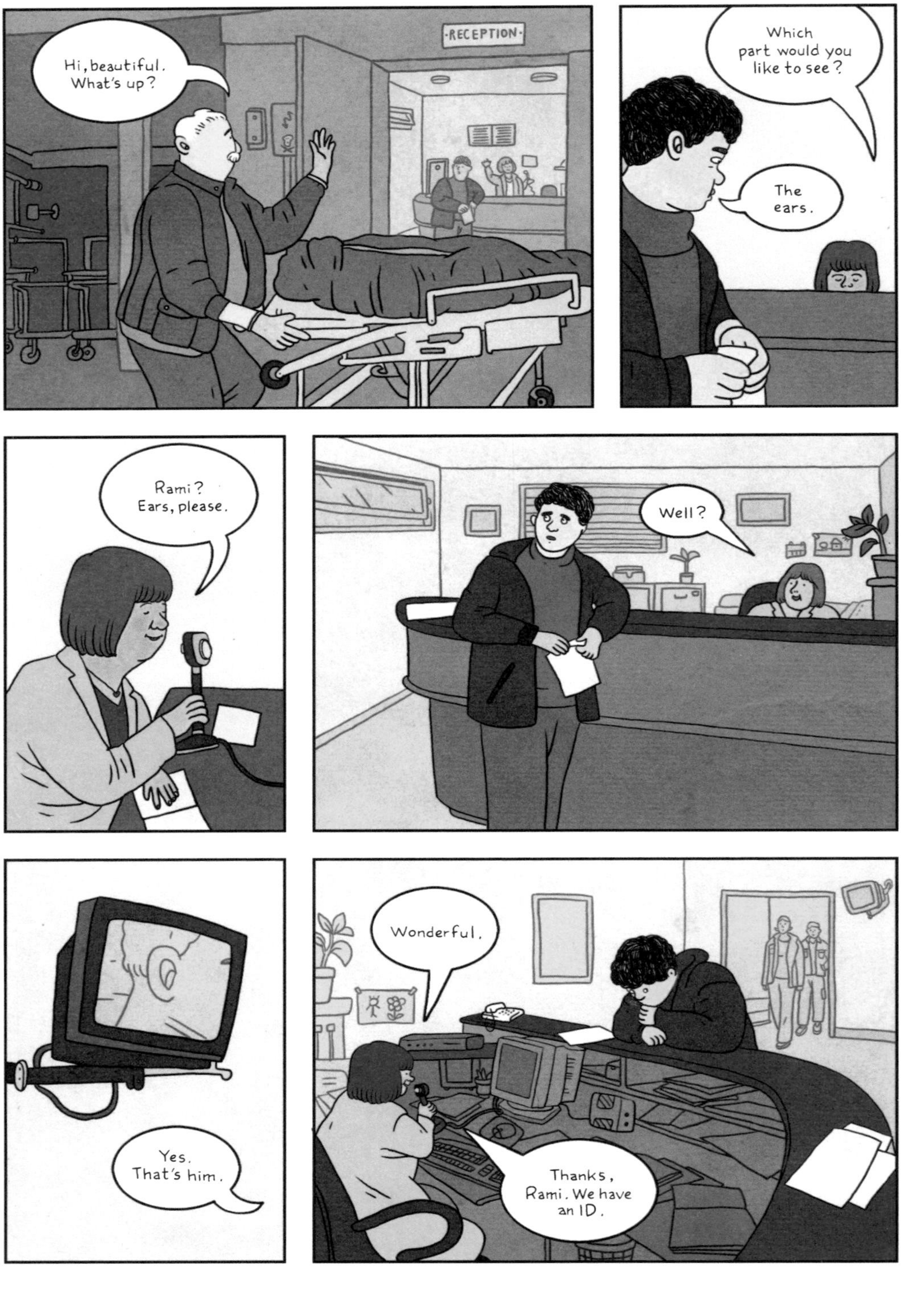
RECEPTION
Hi, beautiful. What's up?
Which part would you like to see?
The ears.
Rami? Ears, please.
Well?
Yes. That's him.
Wonderful.
Thanks, Rami. We have an ID.

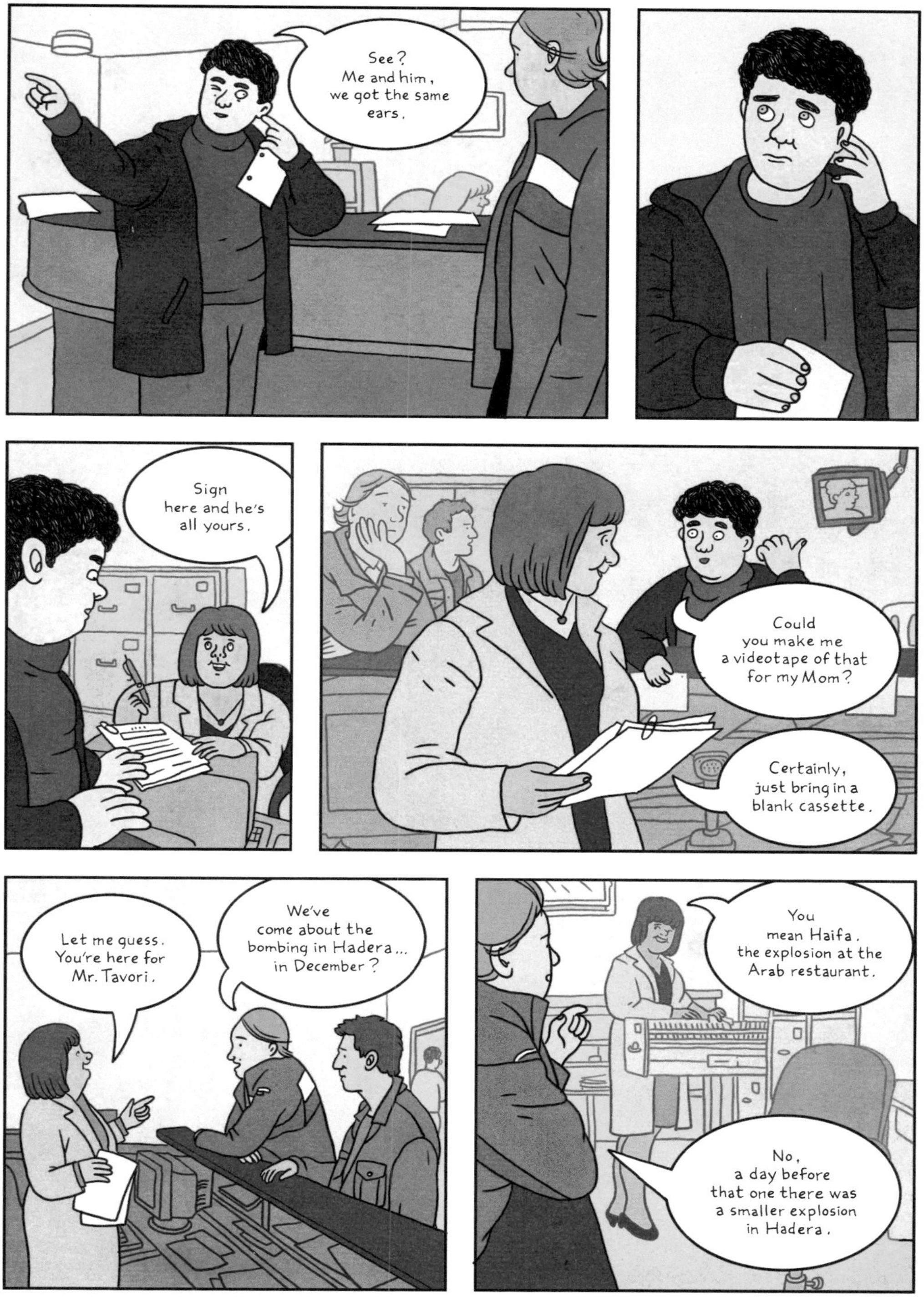
See? Me and him, we got the same ears.
Sign here and he's all yours.
Could you make me a videotape of that for my Mom?
Certainly, just bring in a blank cassette.
Let me guess. You're here for Mr. Tavori.
We've come about the bombing in Hadera... in December?
You mean Haifa, the explosion at the Arab restaurant.
No, a day before that one there was a smaller explosion in Hadera.

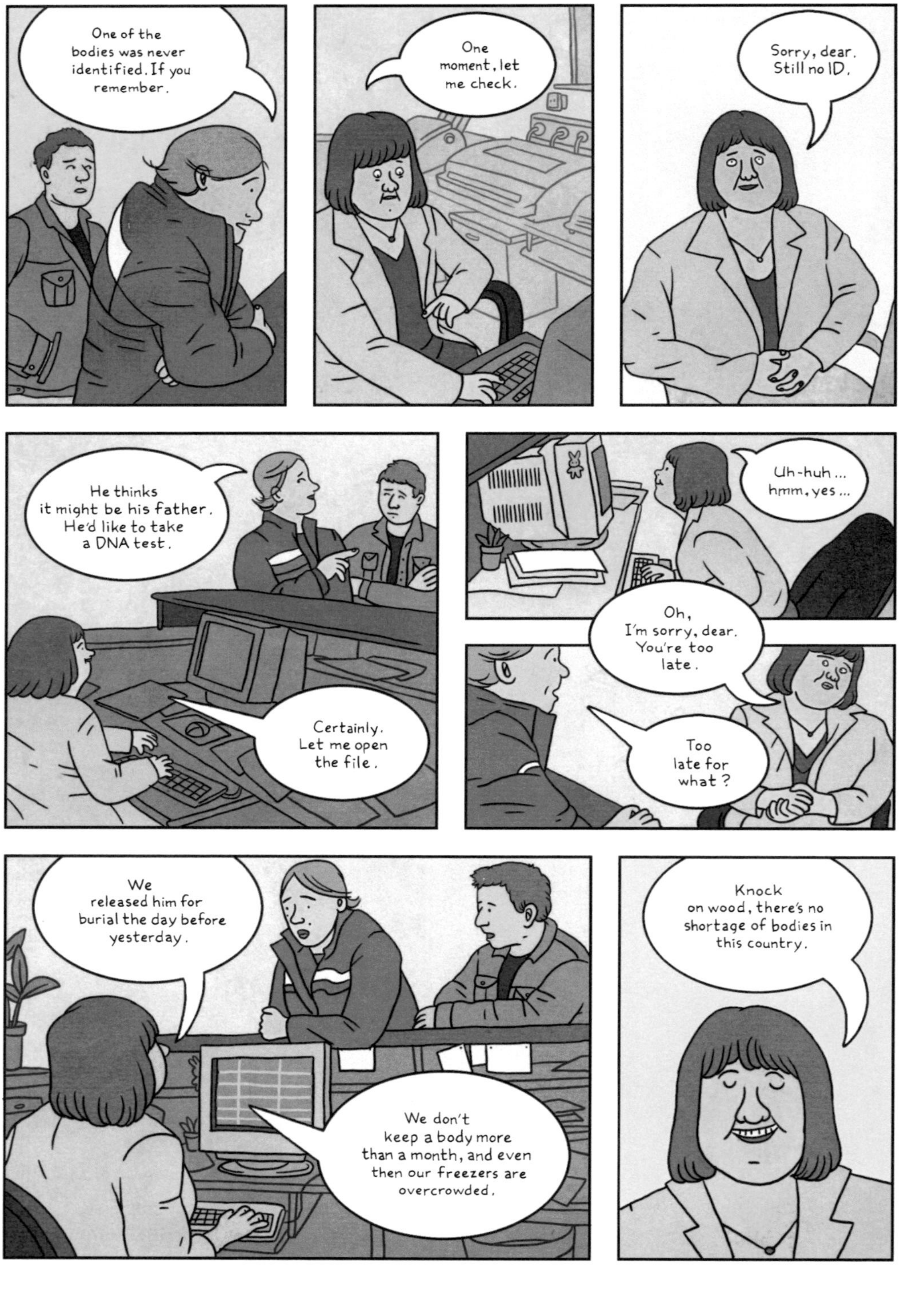

One of the bodies was never identified. If you remember.
One moment, let me check.
Sorry, dear. Still no ID.
He thinks it might be his father. He'd like to take a DNA test.
Certainly. Let me open the file.
Uh-huh... hmm, yes...
Oh, I'm sorry, dear. You're too late.
Too late for what?
We released him for burial the day before yesterday.
We don't keep a body more than a month, and even then our freezers are overcrowded.
Knock on wood, there's no shortage of bodies in this country.

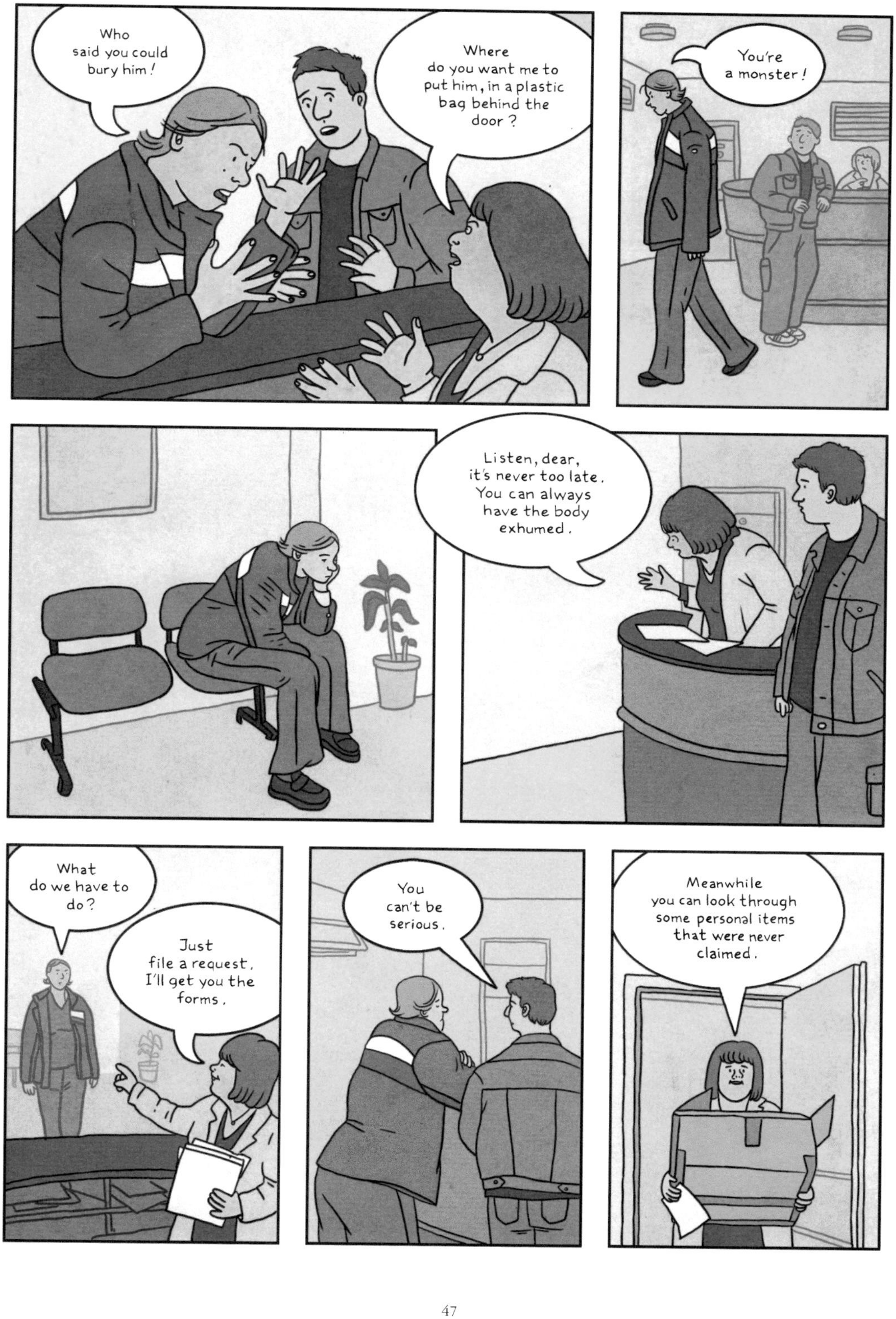
Who said you could bury him!
Where do you want me to put him, in a plastic bag behind the door?
You're a monster!
Listen, dear, it's never too late. You can always have the body exhumed.
What do we have to do?
Just file a request, I'll get you the forms.
You can't be serious.
Meanwhile you can look through some personal items that were never claimed.

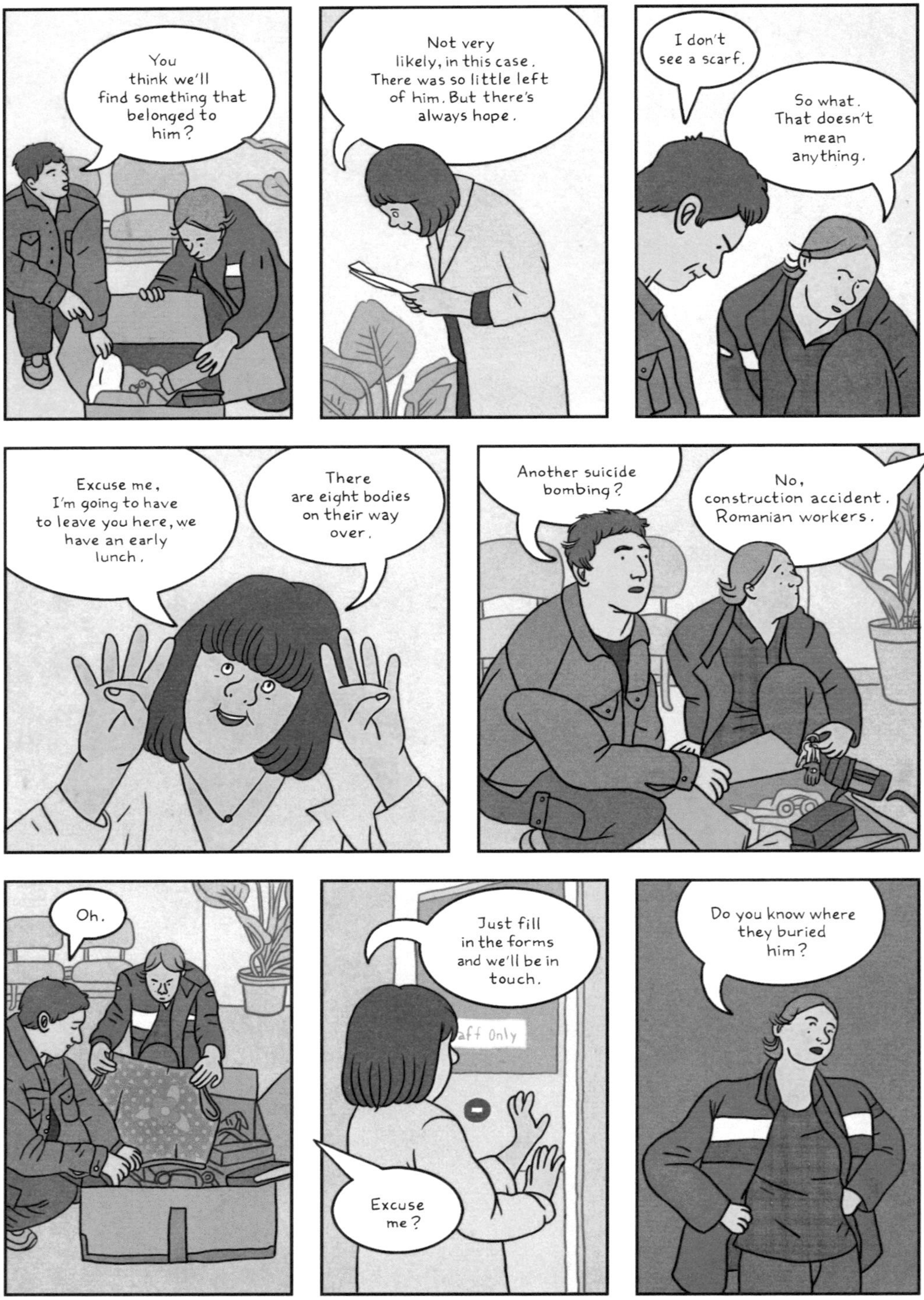
You think we'll find something that belonged to him?
Not very likely, in this case. There was so little left of him. But there's always hope.
I don't see a scarf.
So what. That doesn't mean anything.
Excuse me, I'm going to have to leave you here, we have an early lunch.
There are eight bodies on their way over.
Another suicide bombing?
No, construction accident. Romanian workers.
Oh.
Just fill in the forms and we'll be in touch.
aff Only
Excuse me?
Do you know where they buried him?

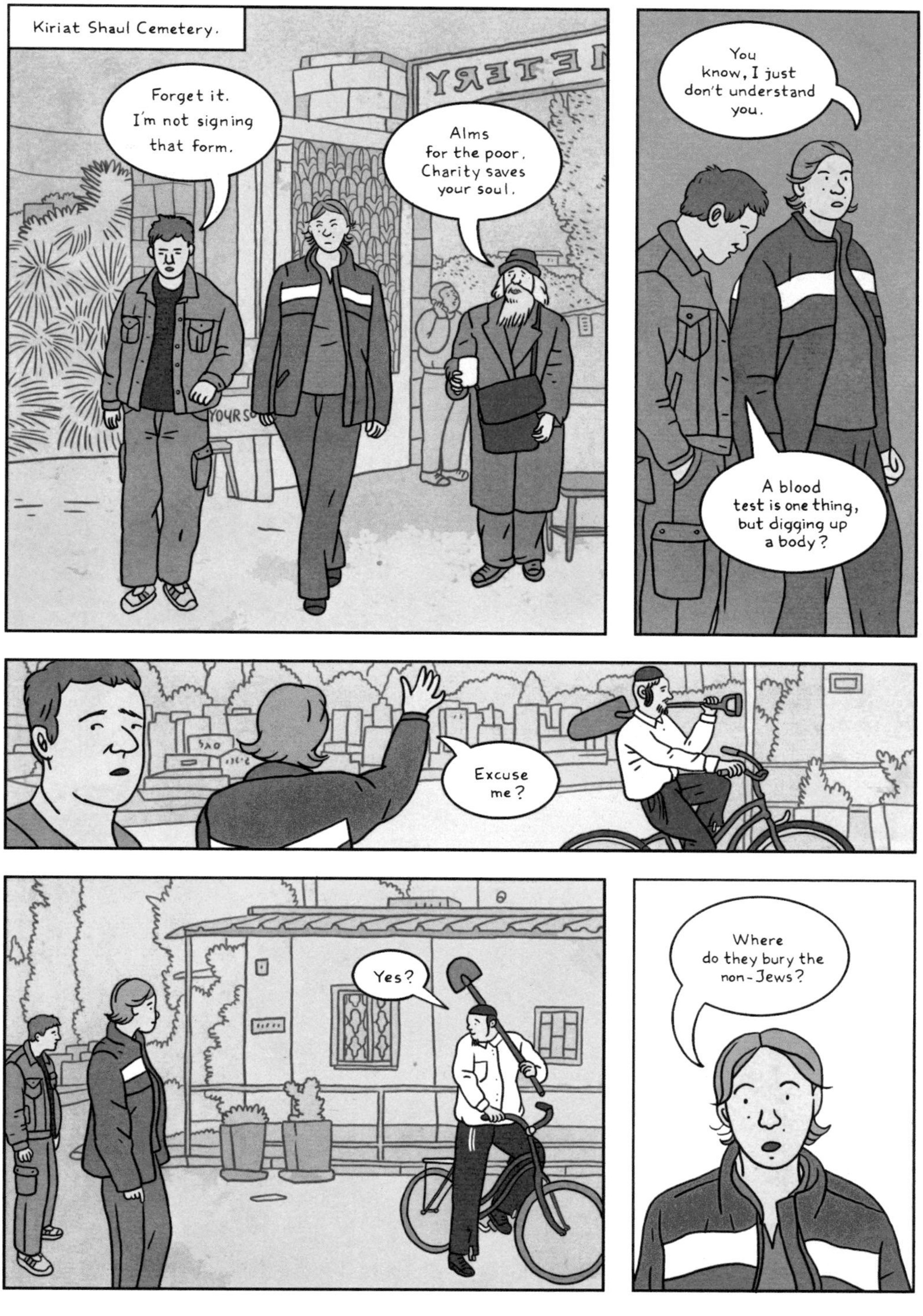
Kiriat Shaul Cemetery.
Forget it. I'm not signing that form.
Alms for the poor. Charity saves your soul.
You know, I just don't understand you.
A blood test is one thing, but digging up a body?
Excuse me?
Yes?
Where do they bury the non-Jews?

She your girlfriend?
What? No!
Here it is.
22/12/02
John Doe
A relative?
How would I know?
Yeah, I see your point.

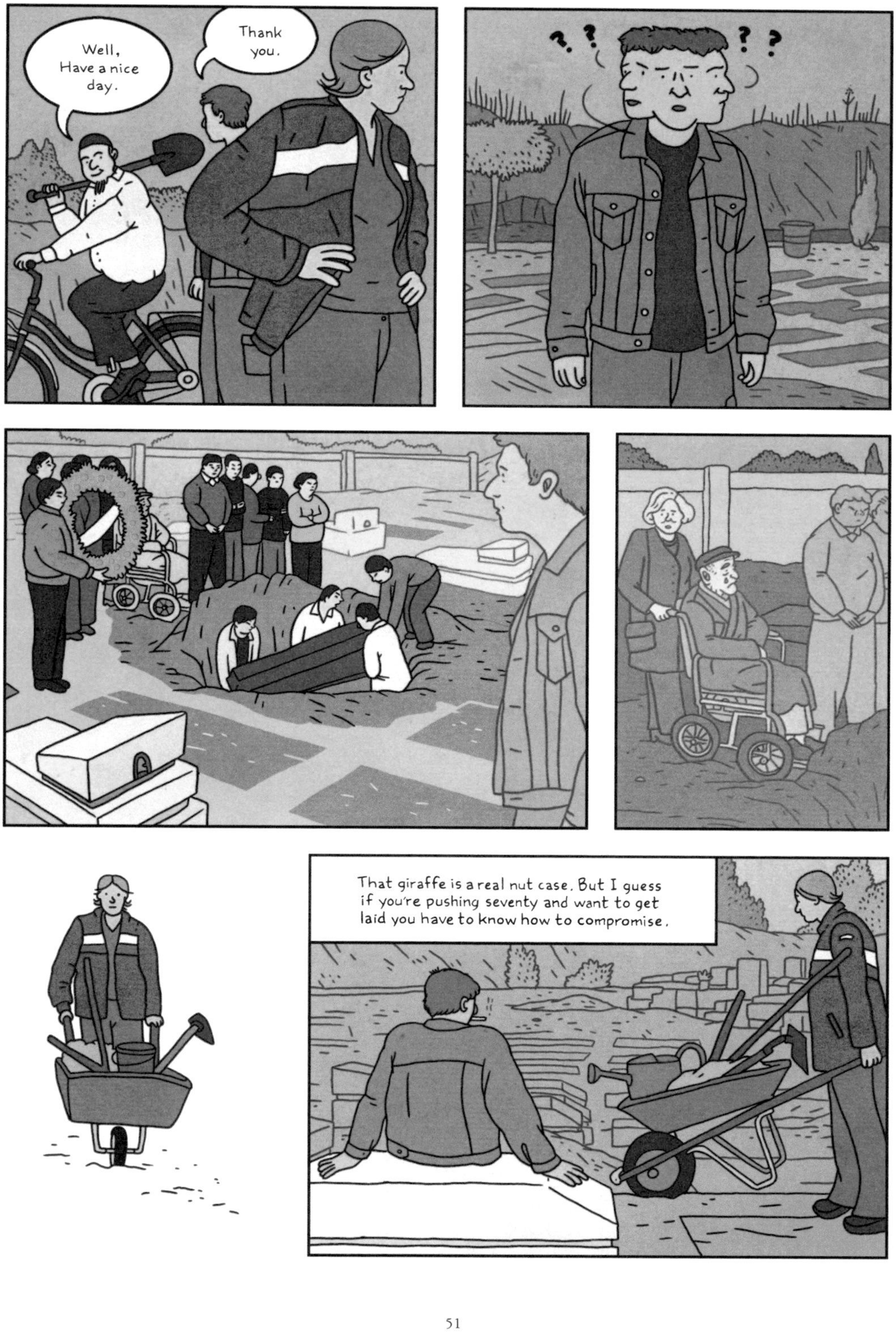
Well, Have a nice day.
Thank you.
? ? ? ?
That giraffe is a real nut case. But I guess if you're pushing seventy and want to get laid you have to know how to compromise.

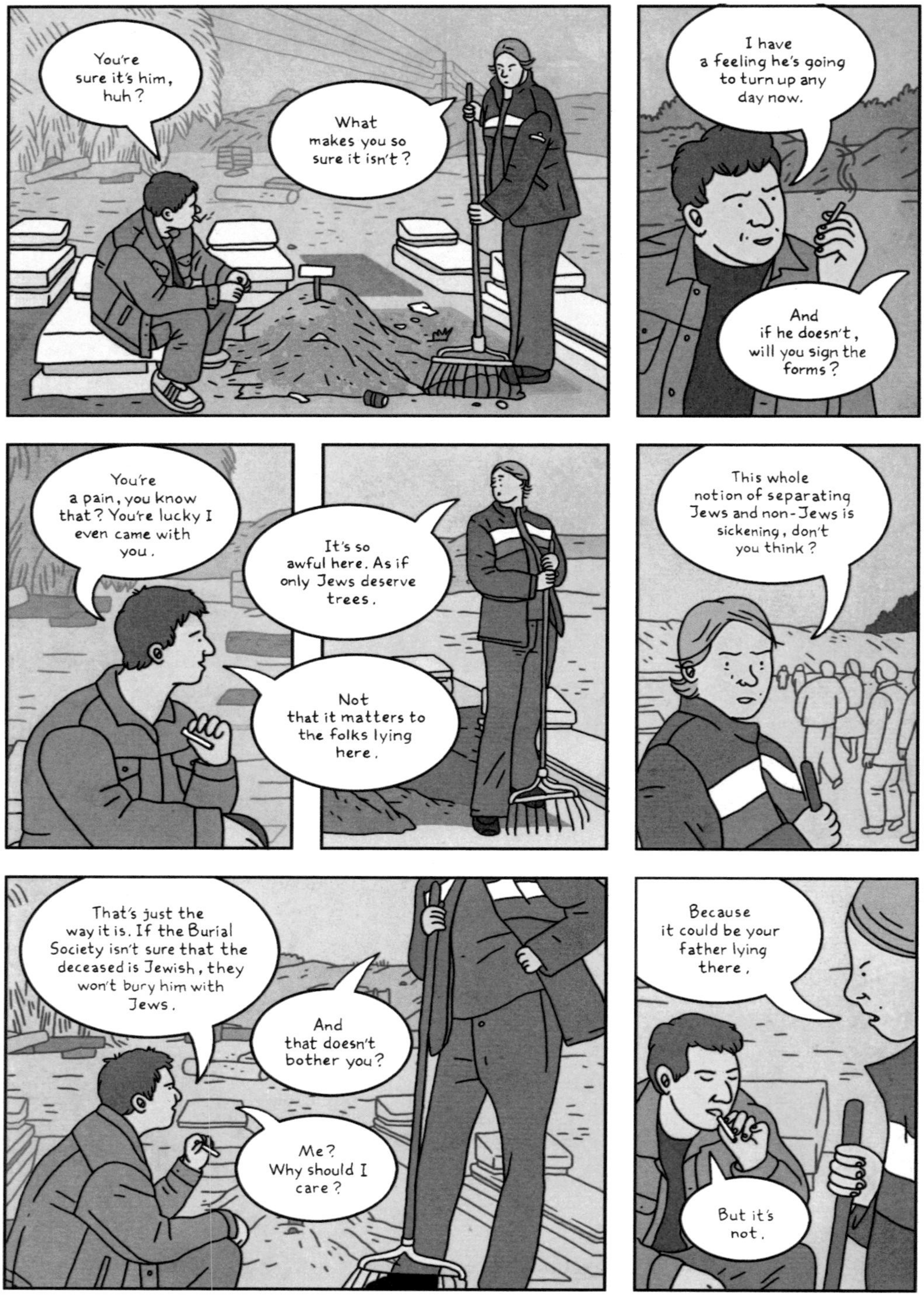
You're sure it's him, huh?
What makes you so sure it isn't?
I have a feeling he's going to turn up any day now.
And if he doesn't, will you sign the forms?
You're a pain, you know that? You're lucky I even came with you.
It's so awful here. As if only Jews deserve trees.
Not that it matters to the folks lying here.
This whole notion of separating Jews and non-Jews is sickening, don't you think?
That's just the way it is. If the Burial Society isn't sure that the deceased is Jewish, they won't bury him with Jews.
And that doesn't bother you?
Me? Why should I care?
Because it could be your father lying there.
But it's not.

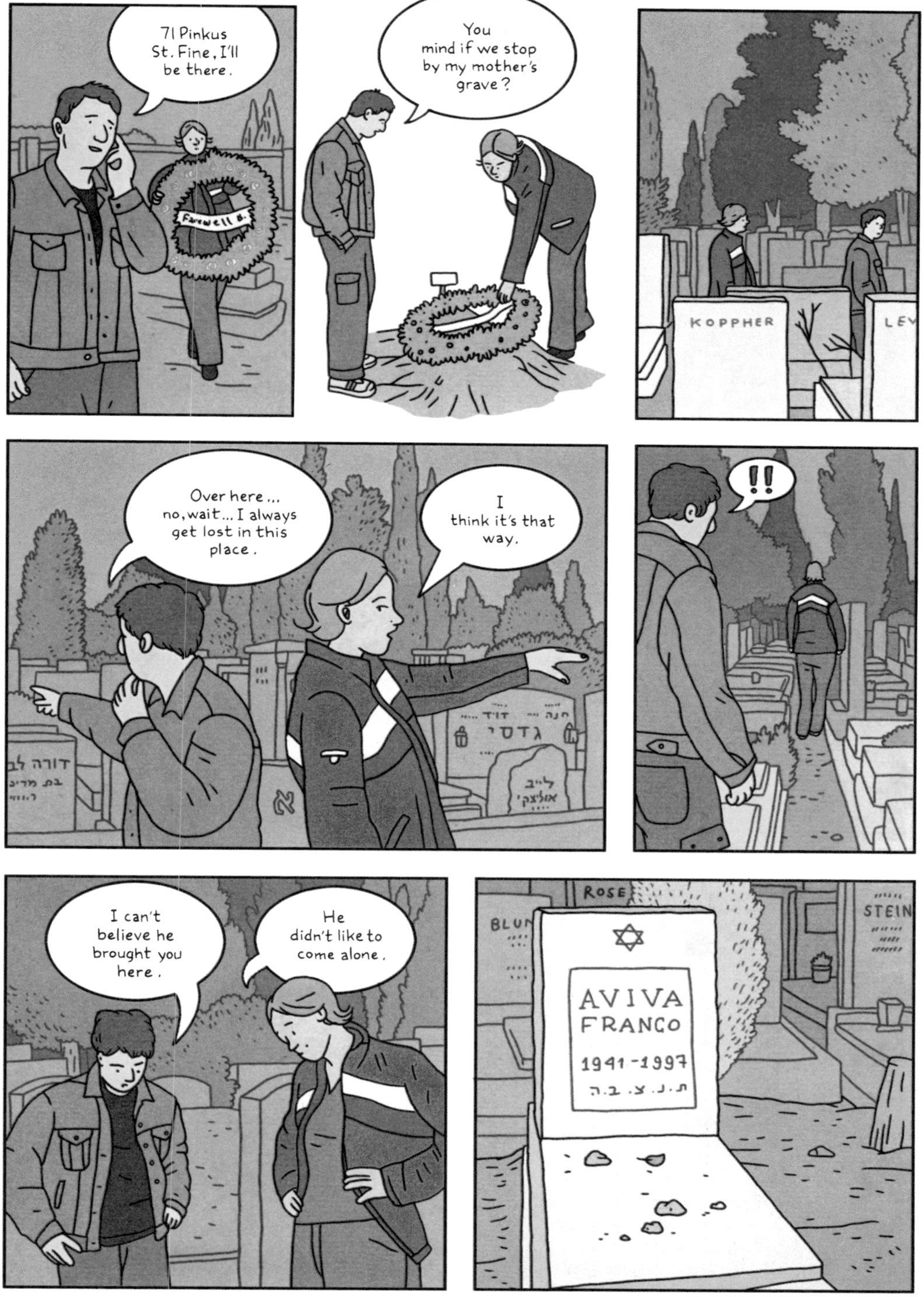
71 Pinkus St. Fine, I'll be there.
Farewell B.
You mind if we stop by my mother's grave?
KOPPHER
LEV
Over here... no, wait... I always get lost in this place.
I think it's that way.
!!
I can't believe he brought you here.
He didn't like to come alone.
ROSE
BLUN
STEIN
AVIVA FRANCO
1941-1997
ת.נ.צ.ב.ה

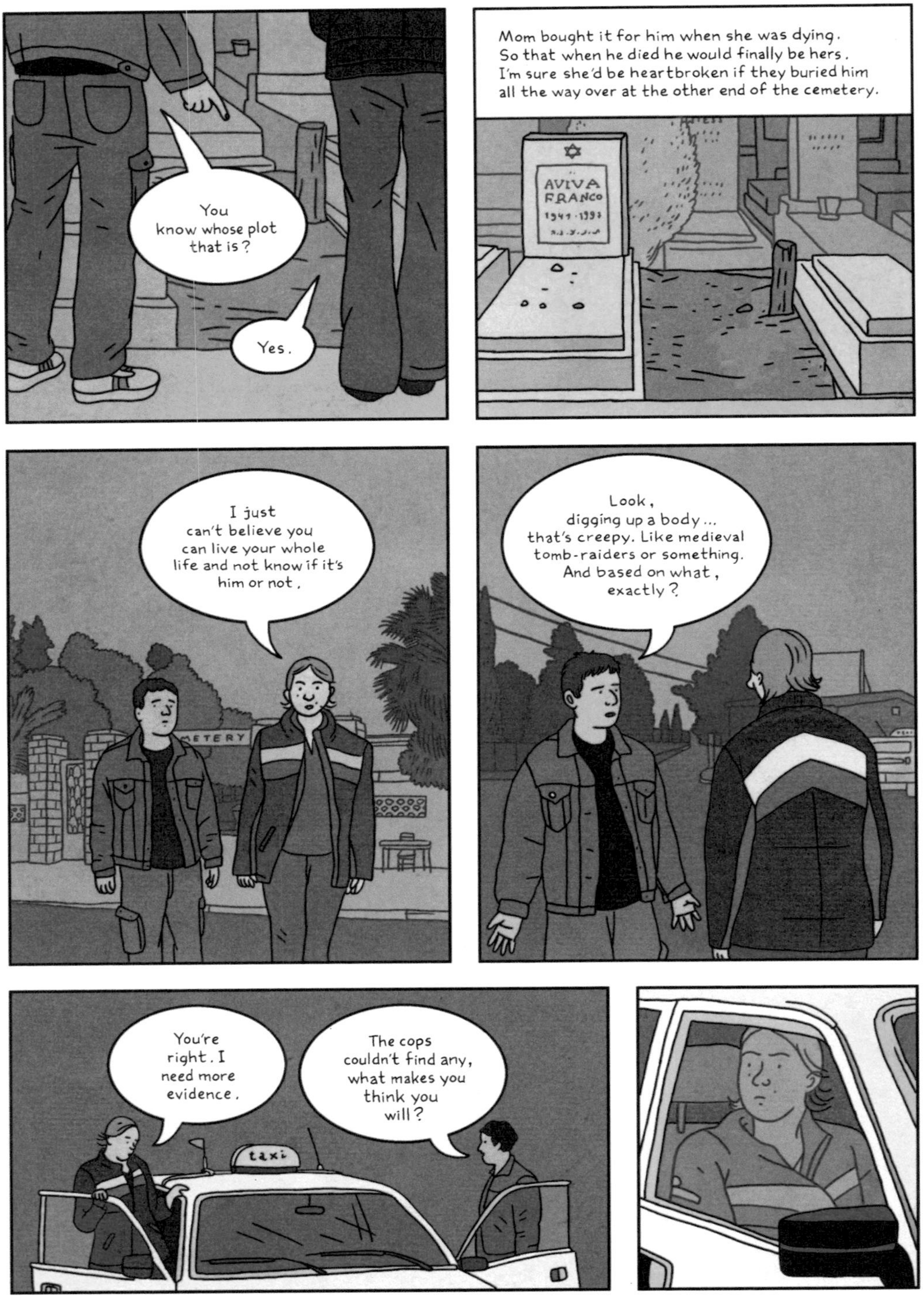
You know whose plot that is?
Yes.
Mom bought it for him when she was dying. So that when he died he would finally be hers. I'm sure she'd be heartbroken if they buried him all the way over at the other end of the cemetery.
AVIVA FRANCO
I just can't believe you can live your whole life and not know if it's him or not.
Look, digging up a body... that's creepy. Like medieval tomb-raiders or something. And based on what, exactly?
You're right. I need more evidence.
The cops couldn't find any, what makes you think you will?
taxi

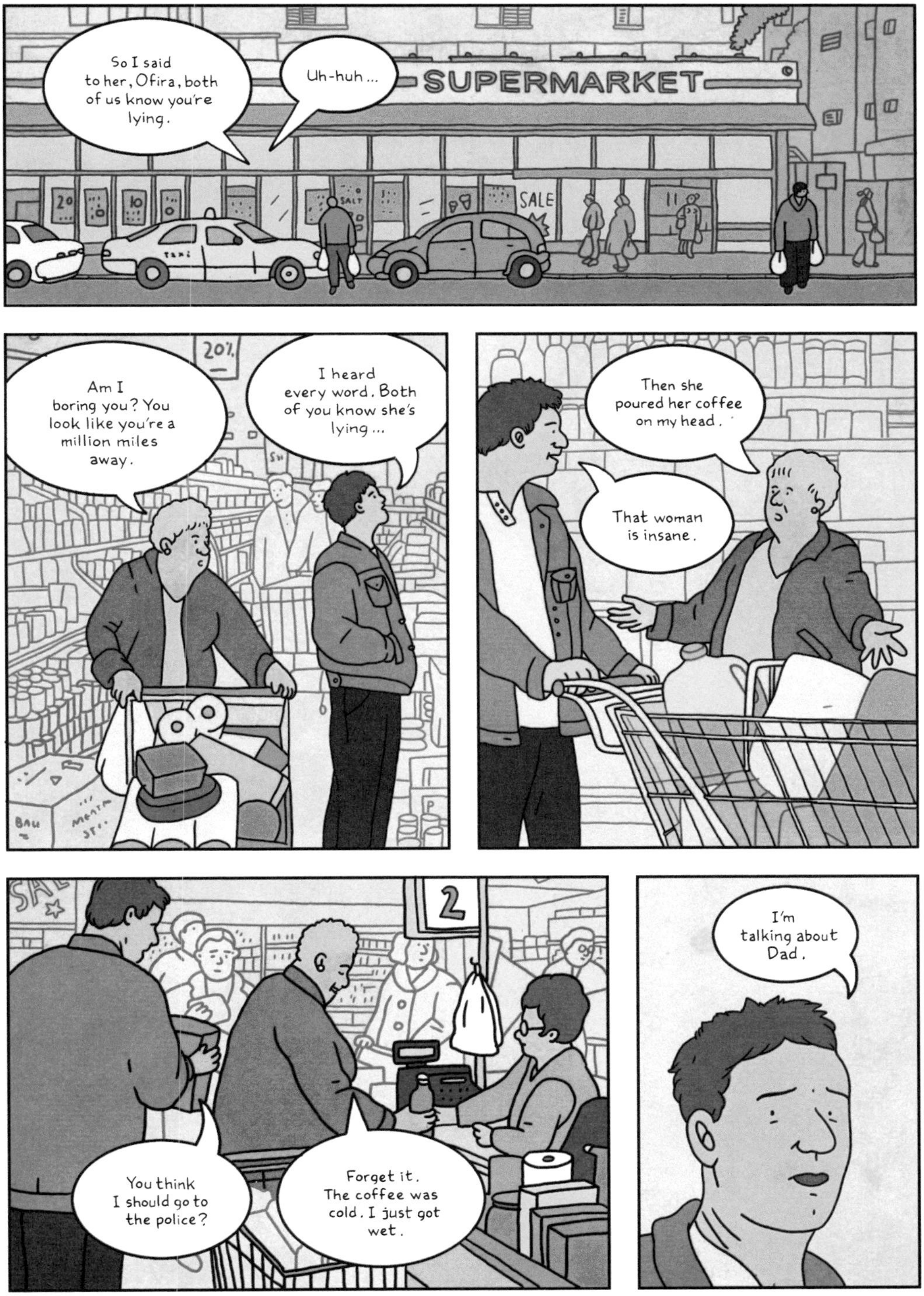
SUPERMARKET
SALE
So I said to her, Ofira, both of us know you're lying.
Uh-huh ...
20%
Am I boring you? You look like you're a million miles away.
I heard every word. Both of you know she's lying ...
Then she poured her coffee on my head.
That woman is insane.
2
You think I should go to the police?
Forget it. The coffee was cold. I just got wet.
I'm talking about Dad.

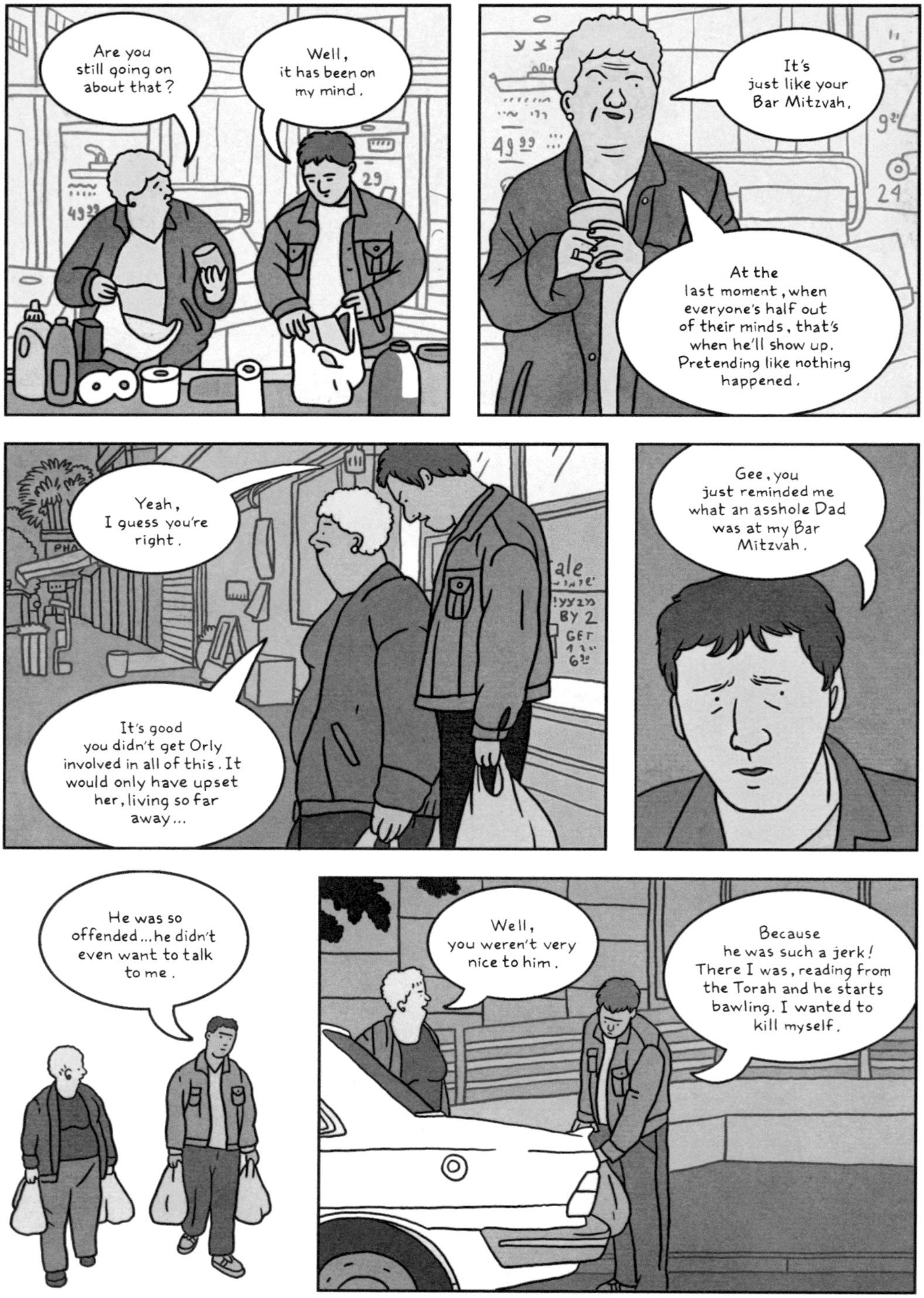

Are you still going on about that?
Well, it has been on my mind.
It's just like your Bar Mitzvah.
At the last moment, when everyone's half out of their minds, that's when he'll show up. Pretending like nothing happened.
Yeah, I guess you're right.
It's good you didn't get Orly involved in all of this. It would only have upset her, living so far away...
Gee, you just reminded me what an asshole Dad was at my Bar Mitzvah.
He was so offended... he didn't even want to talk to me.
Well, you weren't very nice to him.
Because he was such a jerk! There I was, reading from the Torah and he starts bawling. I wanted to kill myself.

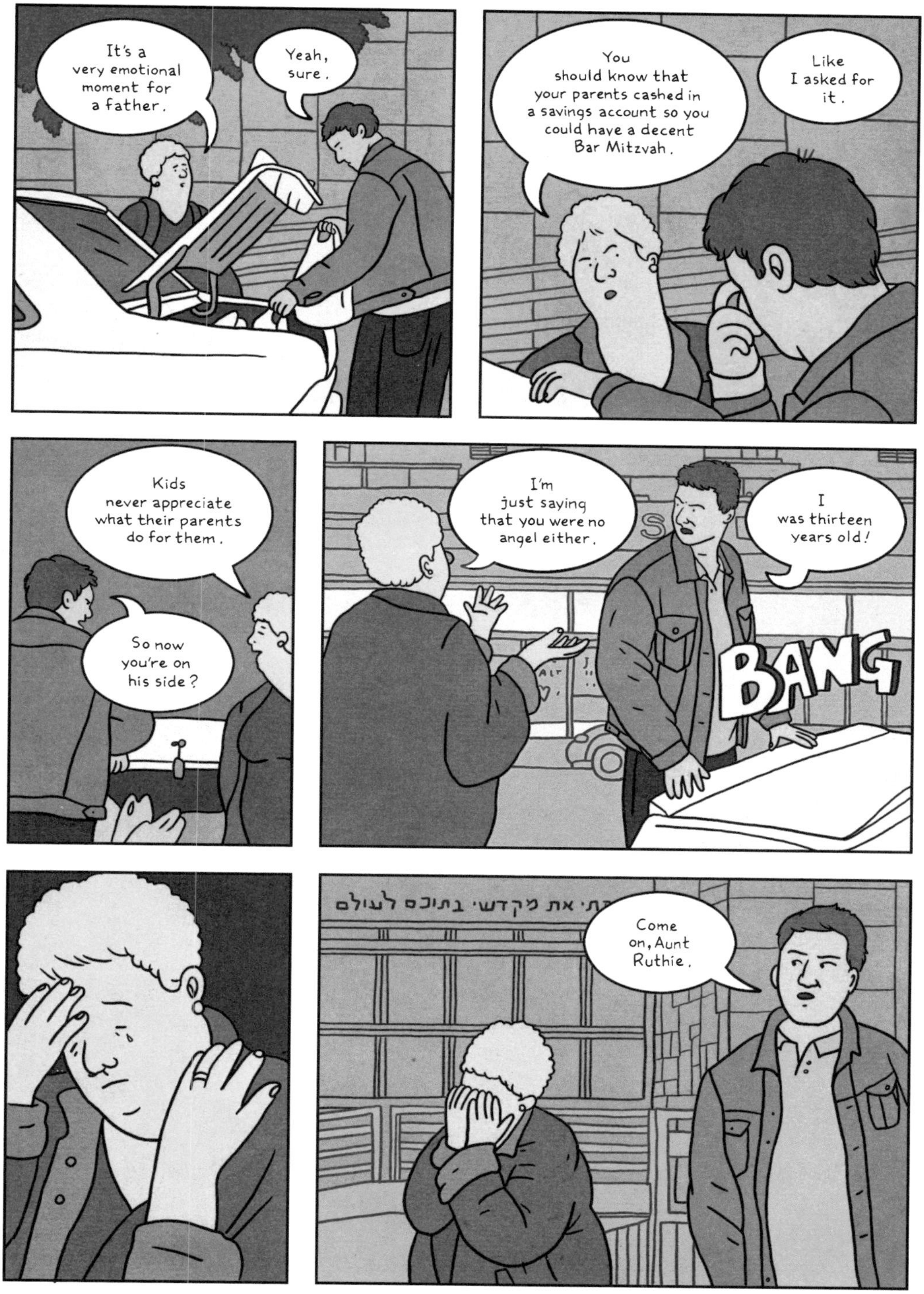

It's a very emotional moment for a father.
Yeah, sure.
You should know that your parents cashed in a savings account so you could have a decent Bar Mitzvah.
Like I asked for it.
Kids never appreciate what their parents do for them.
So now you're on his side?
I'm just saying that you were no angel either.
I was thirteen years old!
BANG
תי את מקדשי בתוכם לעולם
Come on, Aunt Ruthie.

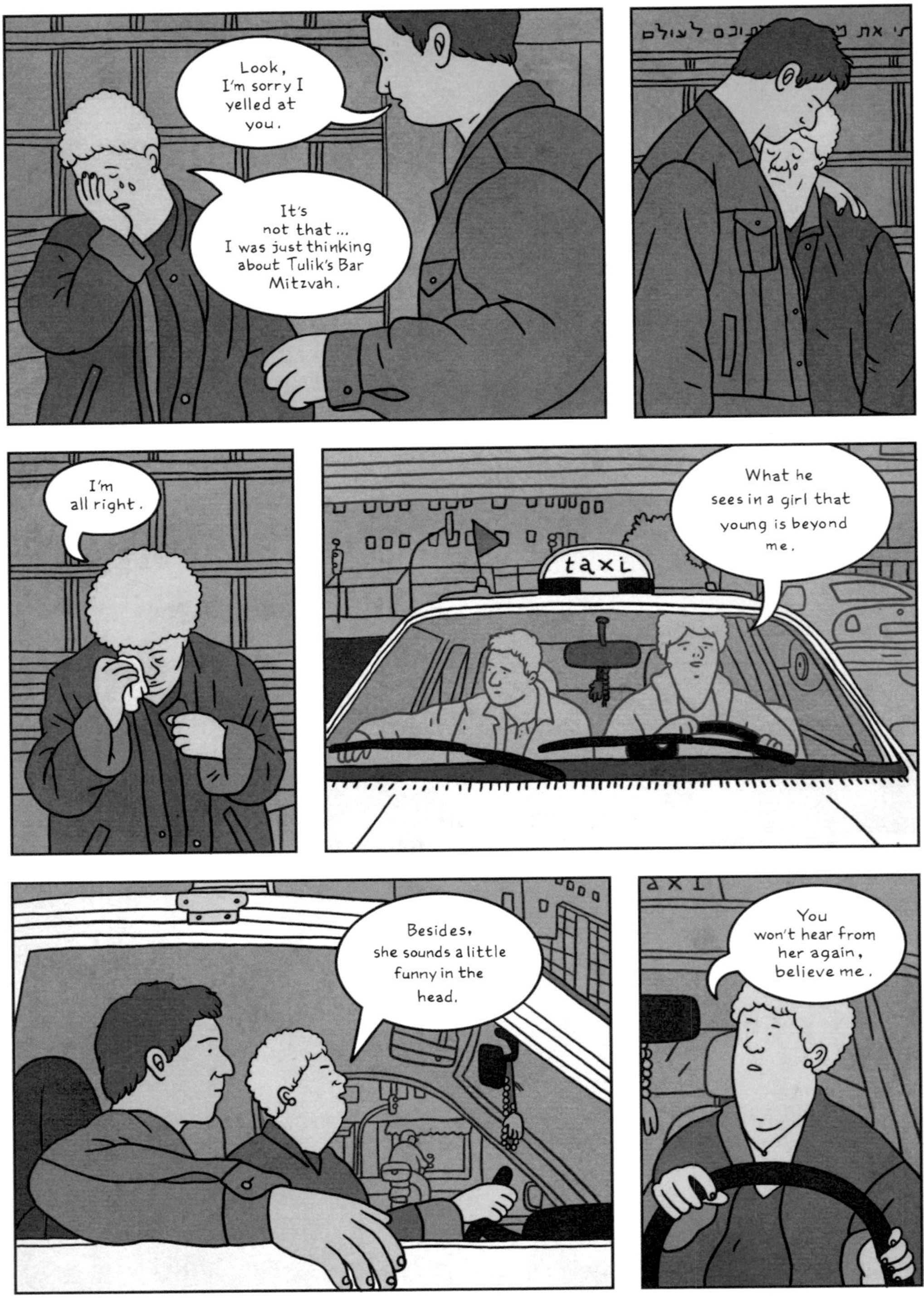
Look, I'm sorry I yelled at you.
It's not that... I was just thinking about Tulik's Bar Mitzvah.
I'm all right.
taxi
What he sees in a girl that young is beyond me.
Besides, she sounds a little funny in the head.
You won't hear from her again, believe me.

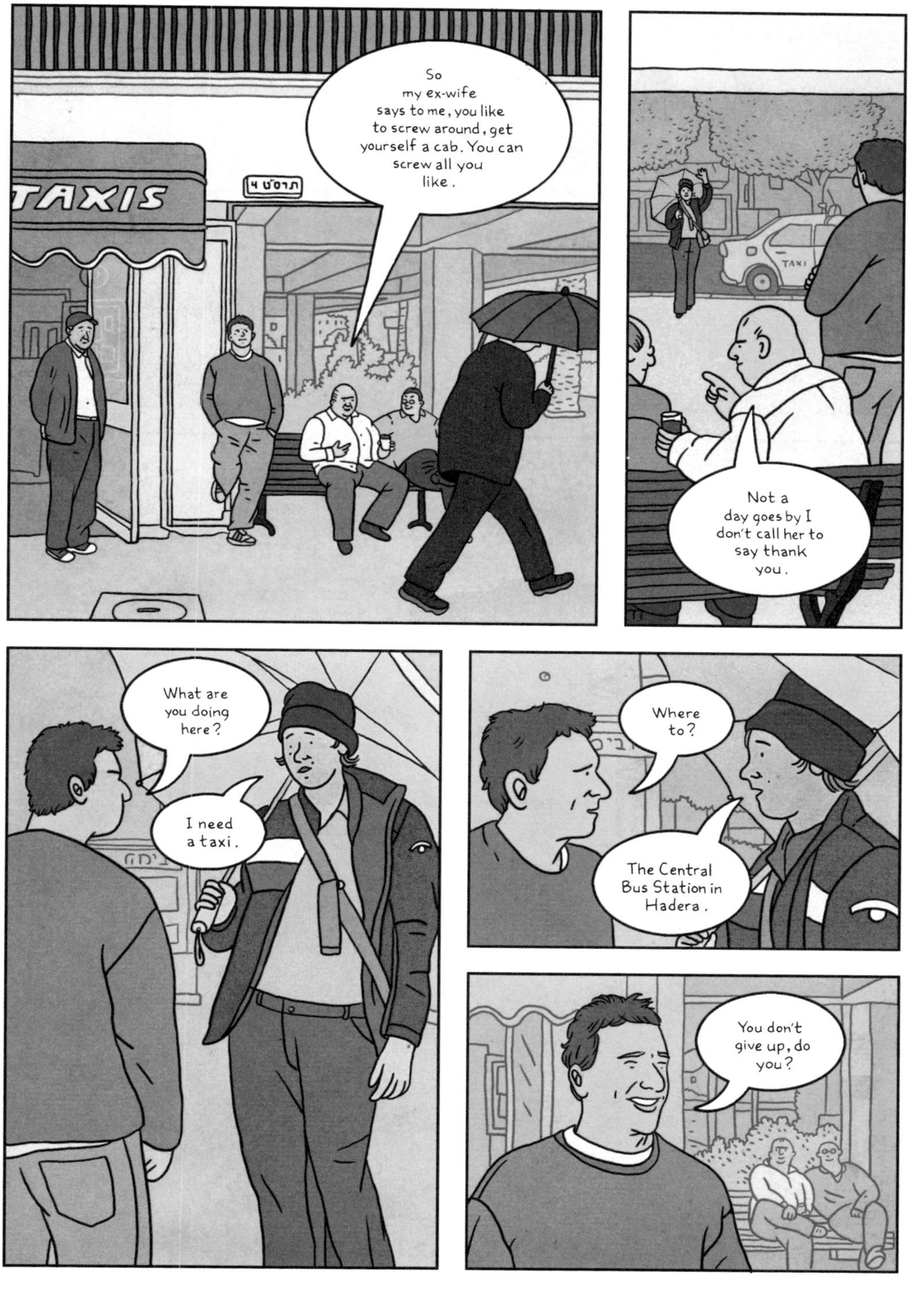
TAXIS
So my ex-wife says to me, you like to screw around, get yourself a cab. You can screw all you like.
Not a day goes by I don't call her to say thank you.
TAXI
What are you doing here?
I need a taxi.
Where to?
The Central Bus Station in Hadera.
You don't give up, do you?

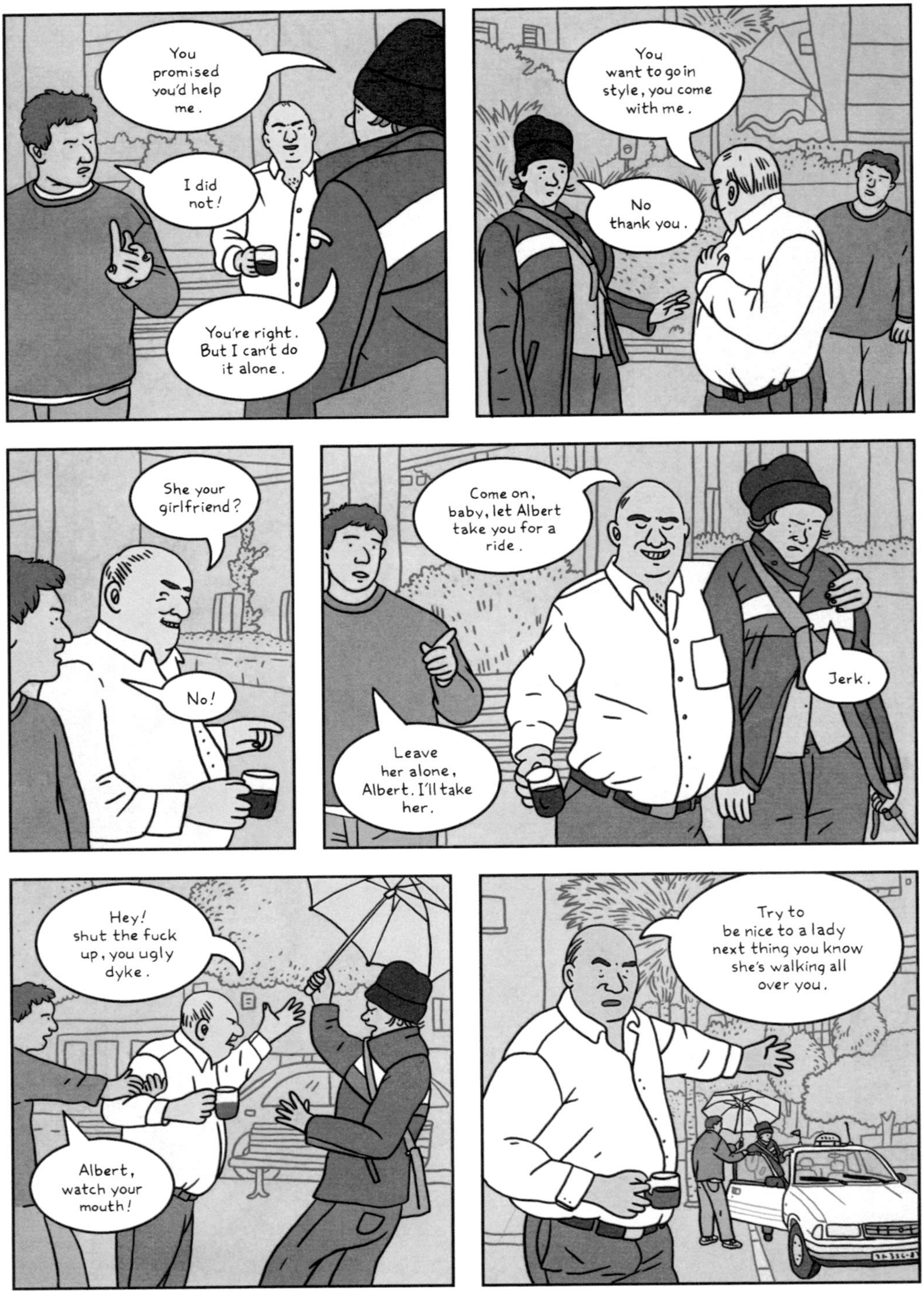
You promised you'd help me.
I did not!
You're right. But I can't do it alone.
You want to go in style, you come with me.
No thank you.
She your girlfriend?
No!
Come on, baby, let Albert take you for a ride.
Jerk.
Leave her alone, Albert. I'll take her.
Hey! shut the fuck up, you ugly dyke.
Albert, watch your mouth!
Try to be nice to a lady next thing you know she's walking all over you.

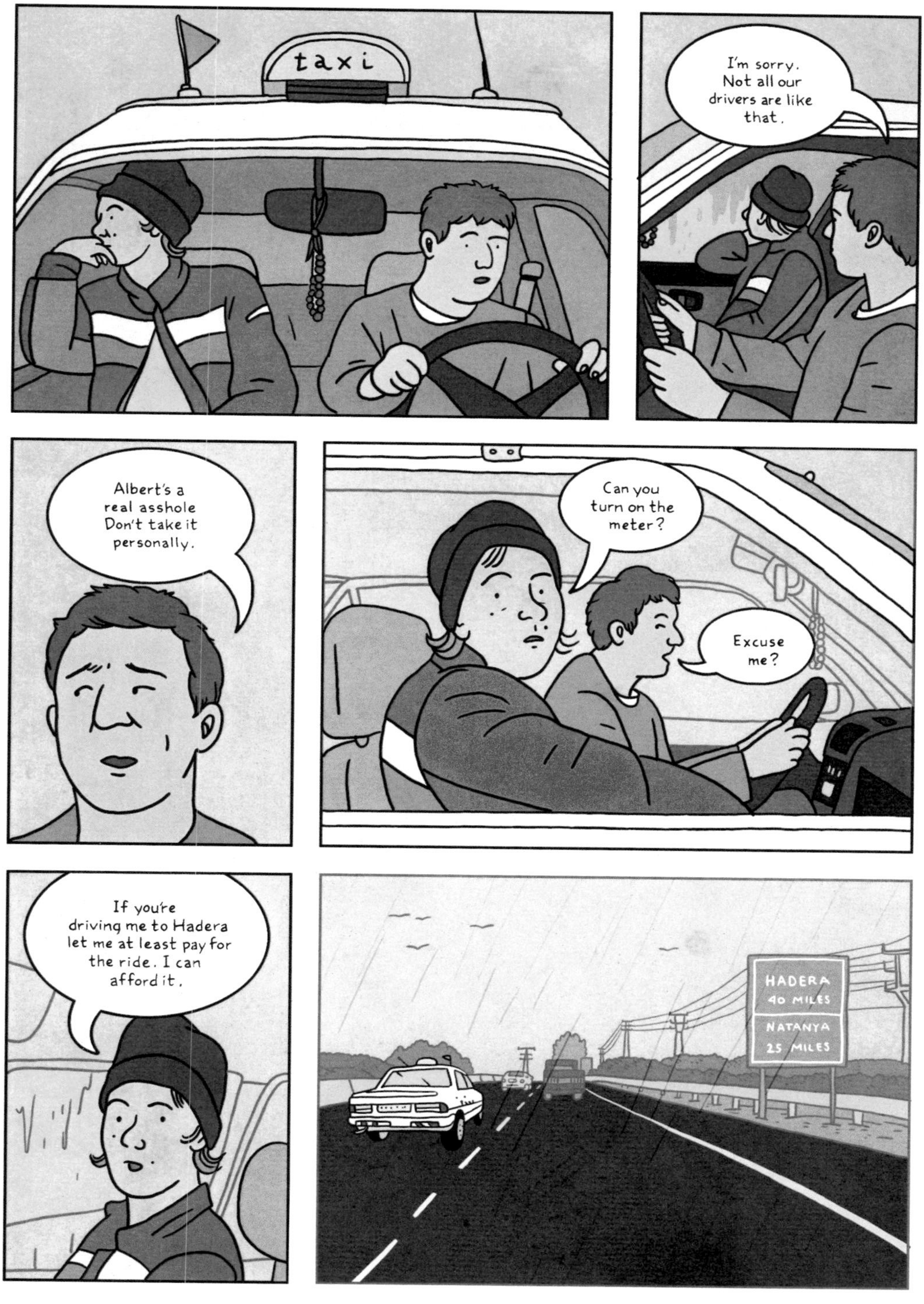
taxi
I'm sorry. Not all our drivers are like that.
Albert's a real asshole Don't take it personally.
Can you turn on the meter?
Excuse me?
If you're driving me to Hadera let me at least pay for the ride. I can afford it.
HADERA 40 MILES
NATANYA 25 MILES

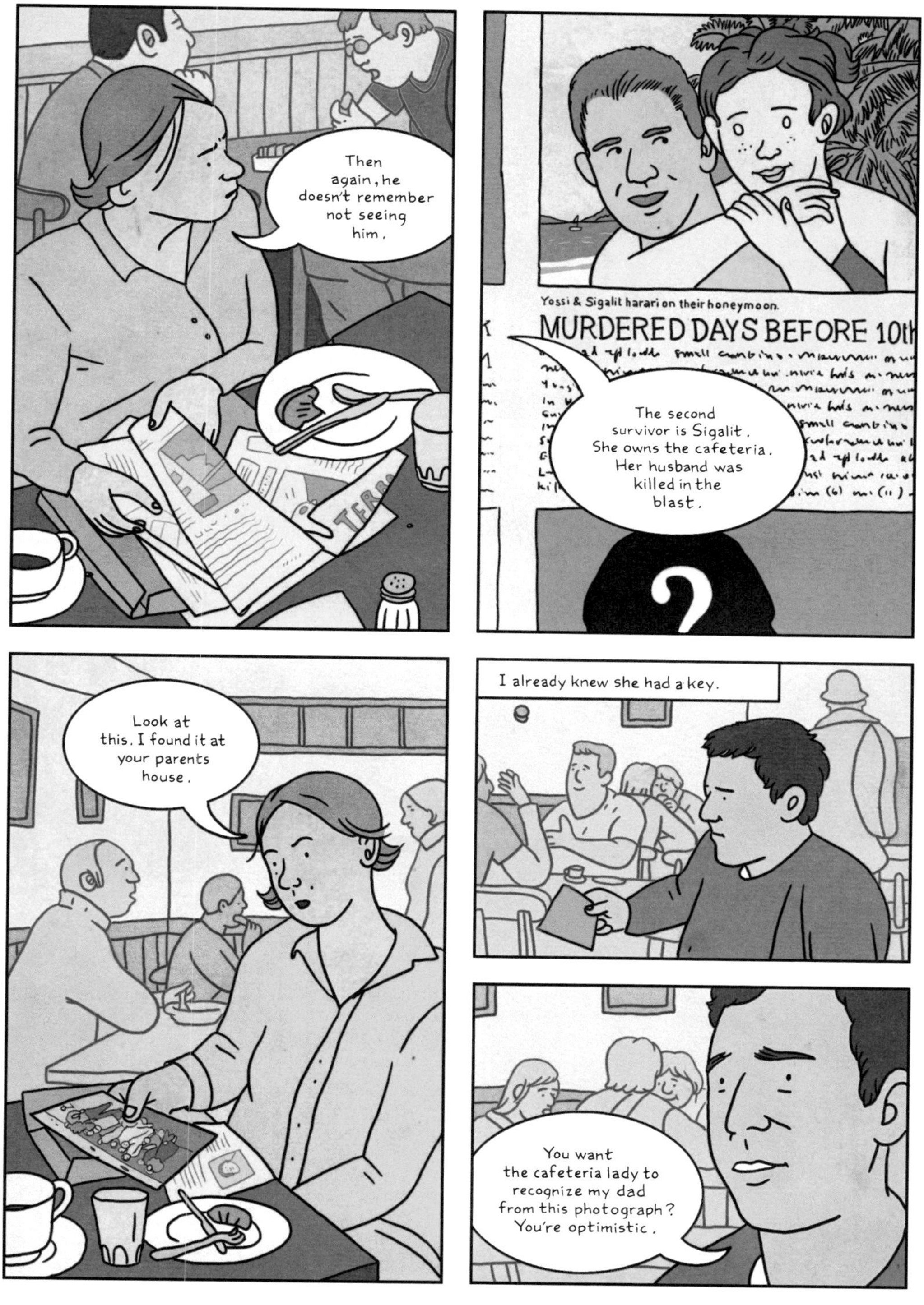

Then again, he doesn't remember not seeing him.
Yossi & Sigalit harari on their honeymoon.
MURDERED DAYS BEFORE 10th
The second survivor is Sigalit. She owns the cafeteria. Her husband was killed in the blast.
Look at this. I found it at your parents house.
I already knew she had a key.
You want the cafeteria lady to recognize my dad from this photograph? You're optimistic.

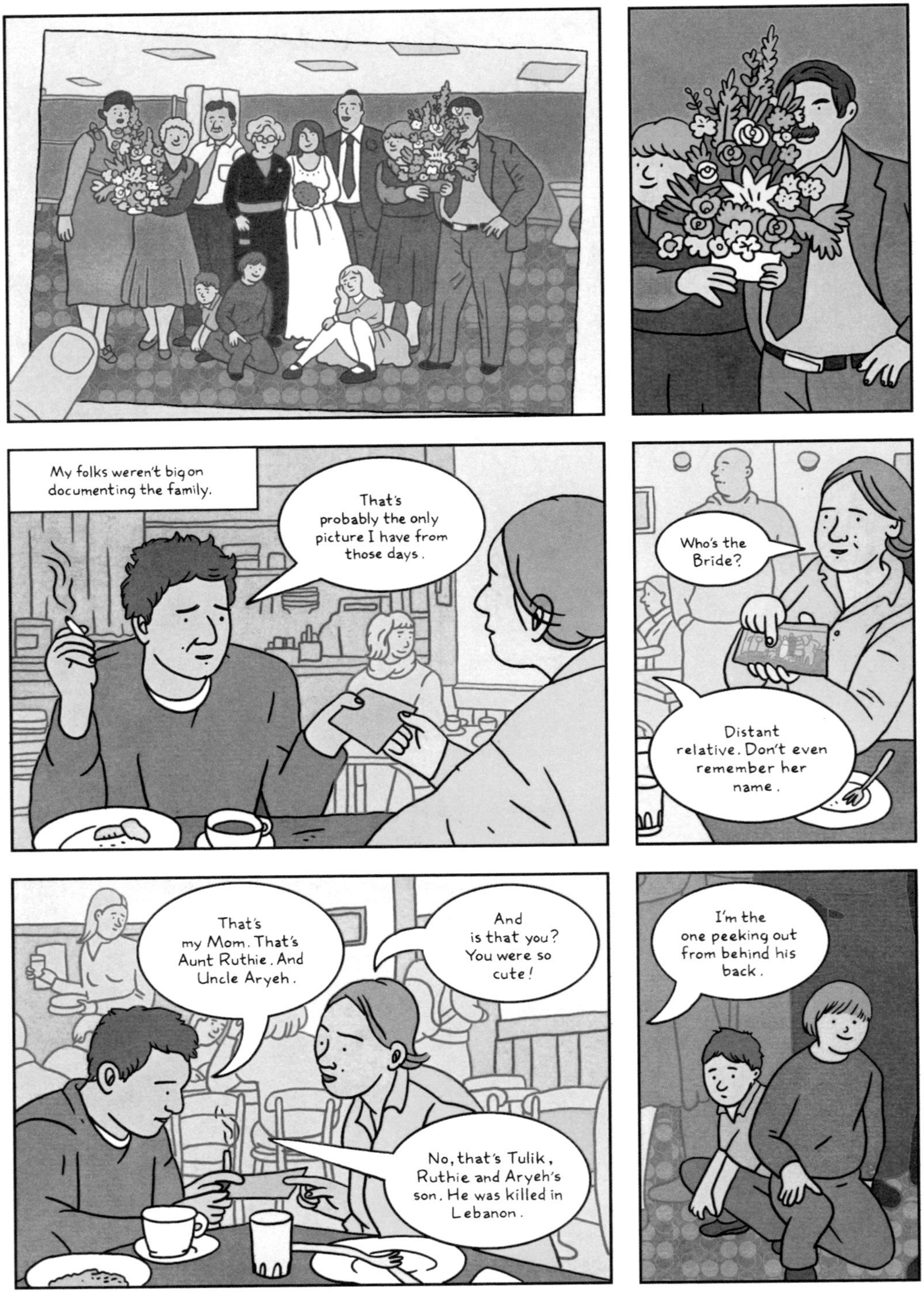

My folks weren't big on documenting the family.
That's probably the only picture I have from those days.
Who's the Bride?
Distant relative. Don't even remember her name.
That's my Mom. That's Aunt Ruthie. And Uncle Aryeh.
And is that you? You were so cute!
No, that's Tulik, Ruthie and Aryeh's son. He was killed in Lebanon.
I'm the one peeking out from behind his back.

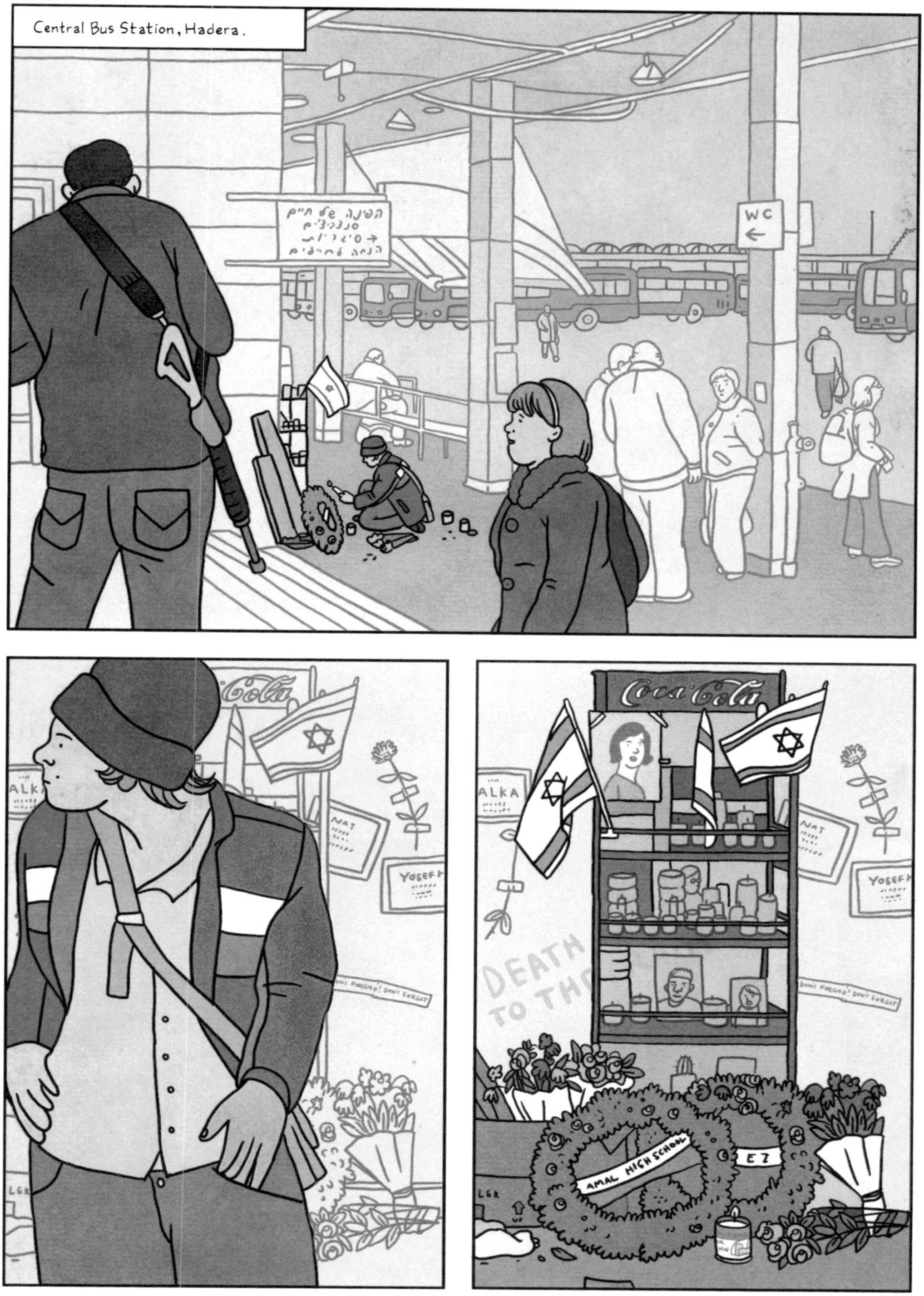

Central Bus Station, Hadera.
WC
Coca-Cola
ALKA
NAT
YOSEF
DON'T FORGIVE! DON'T FORGET
DEATH TO TH
AMAL HIGH SCHOOL
EZ

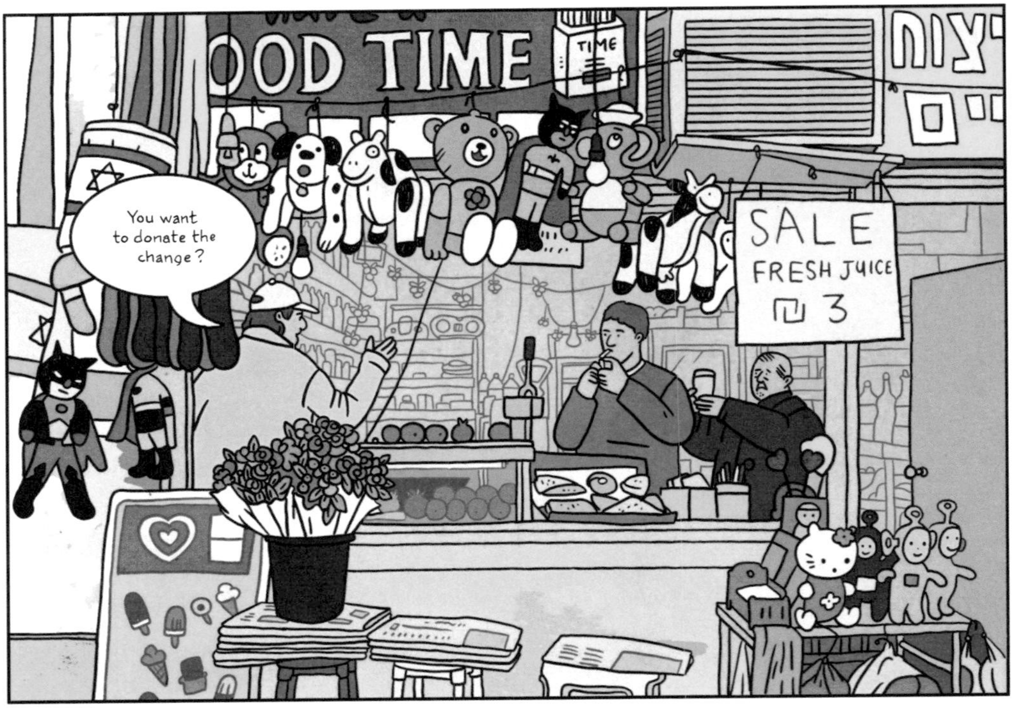
OOD TIME
TIME
You want to donate the change?
SALE
FRESH JUICE
₪ 3

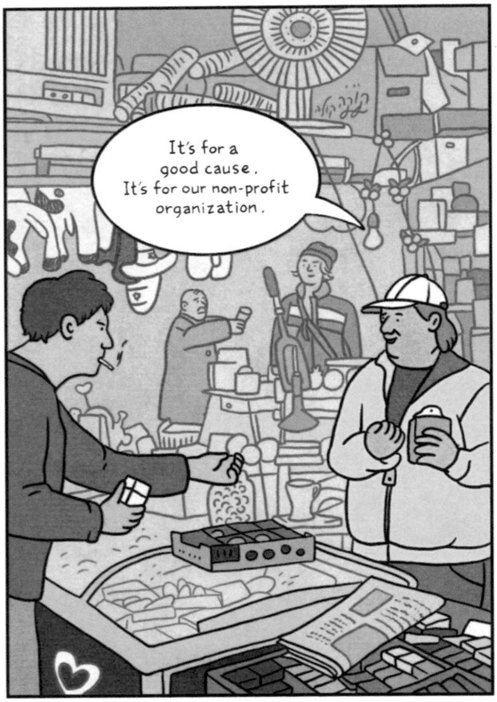
It's for a good cause. It's for our non-profit organization.

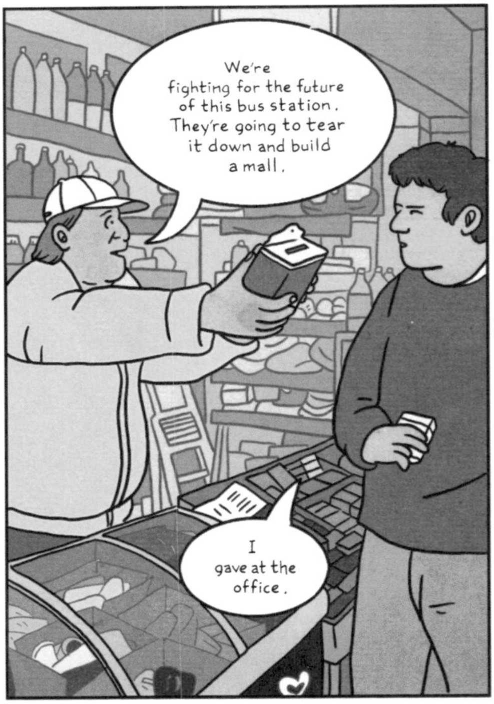
We're fighting for the future of this bus station. They're going to tear it down and build a mall.
I gave at the office.

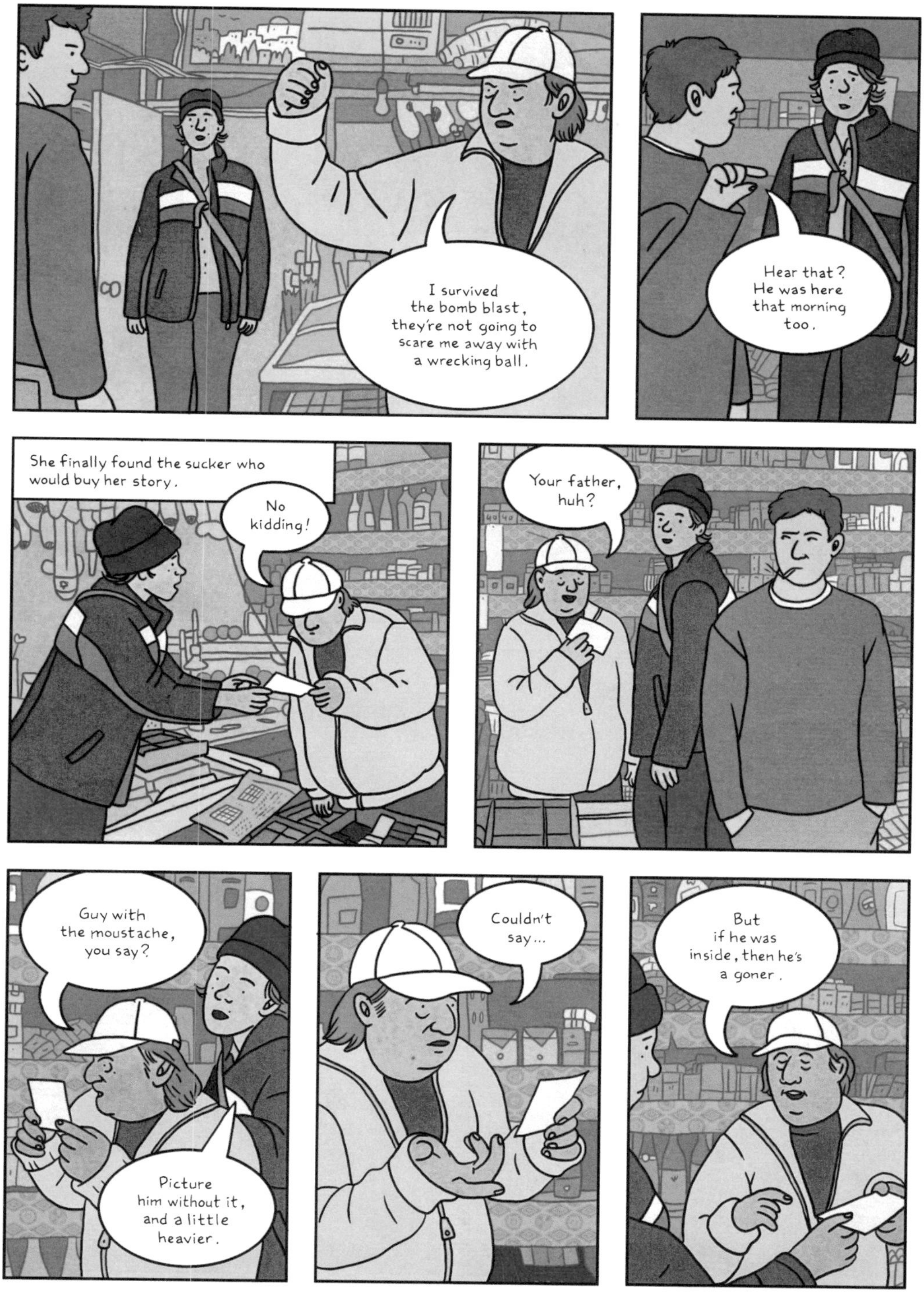
I survived the bomb blast, they're not going to scare me away with a wrecking ball.
Hear that? He was here that morning too.
She finally found the sucker who would buy her story.
No kidding!
Your father, huh?
Guy with the moustache, you say?
Picture him without it, and a little heavier.
Couldn't say...
But if he was inside, then he's a goner.

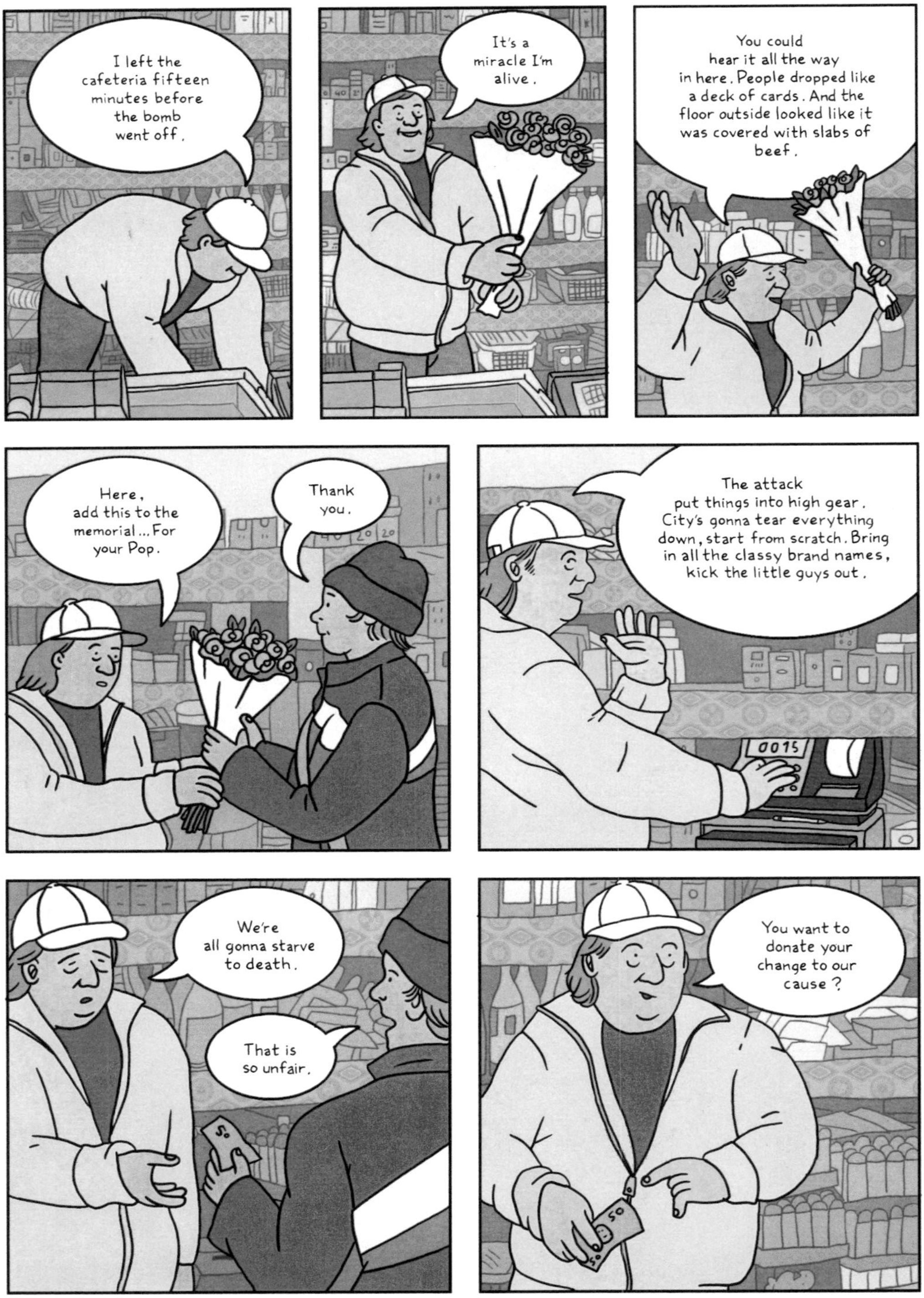

I left the cafeteria fifteen minutes before the bomb went off.
It's a miracle I'm alive.
You could hear it all the way in here. People dropped like a deck of cards. And the floor outside looked like it was covered with slabs of beef.
Here, add this to the memorial... For your Pop.
Thank you.
The attack put things into high gear. City's gonna tear everything down, start from scratch. Bring in all the classy brand names, kick the little guys out.
0015
We're all gonna starve to death.
That is so unfair.
You want to donate your change to our cause?

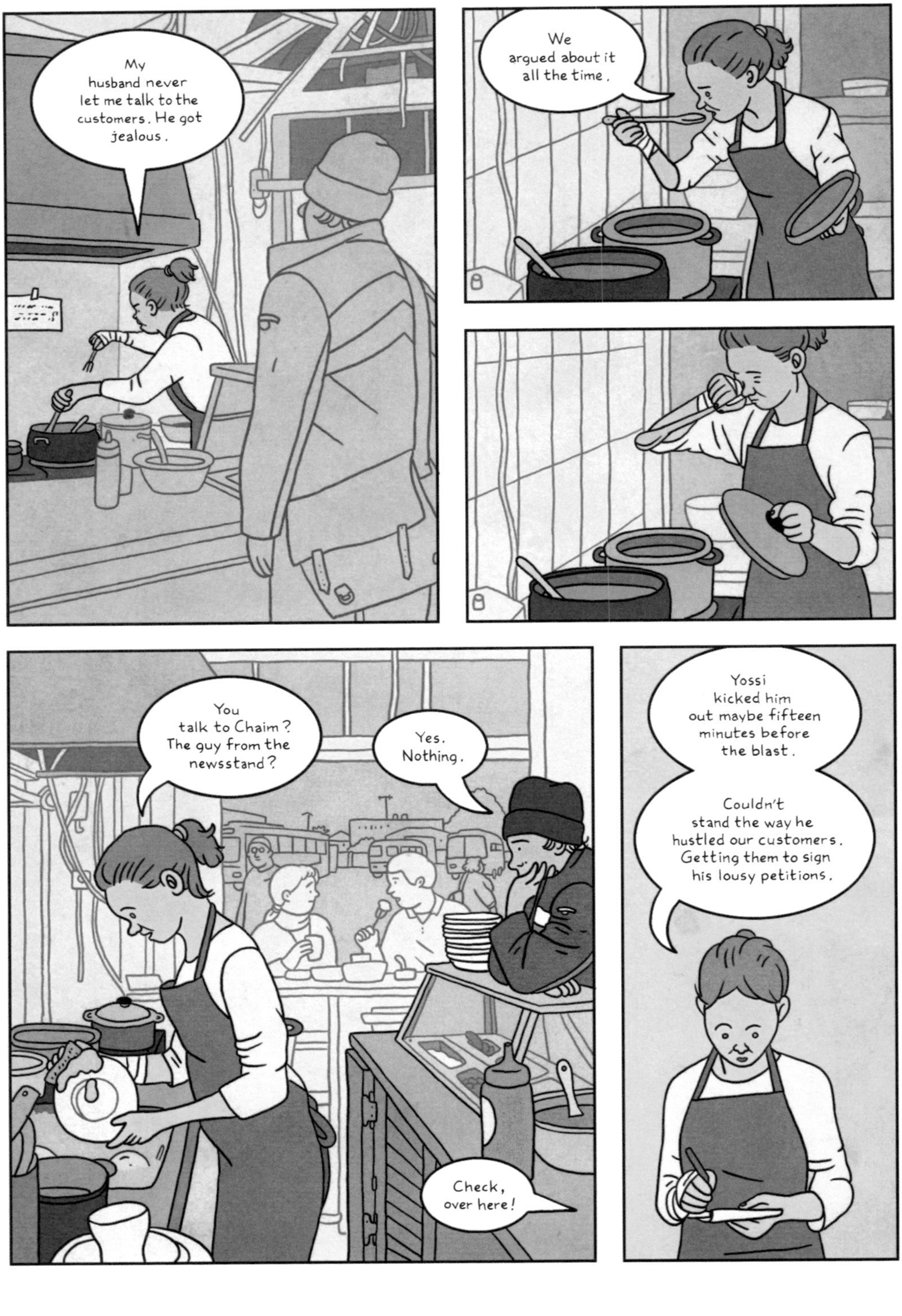
My husband never let me talk to the customers. He got jealous.
We argued about it all the time.
You talk to Chaim? The guy from the newsstand?
Yes. Nothing.
Check, over here!
Yossi kicked him out maybe fifteen minutes before the blast.
Couldn't stand the way he hustled our customers. Getting them to sign his lousy petitions.

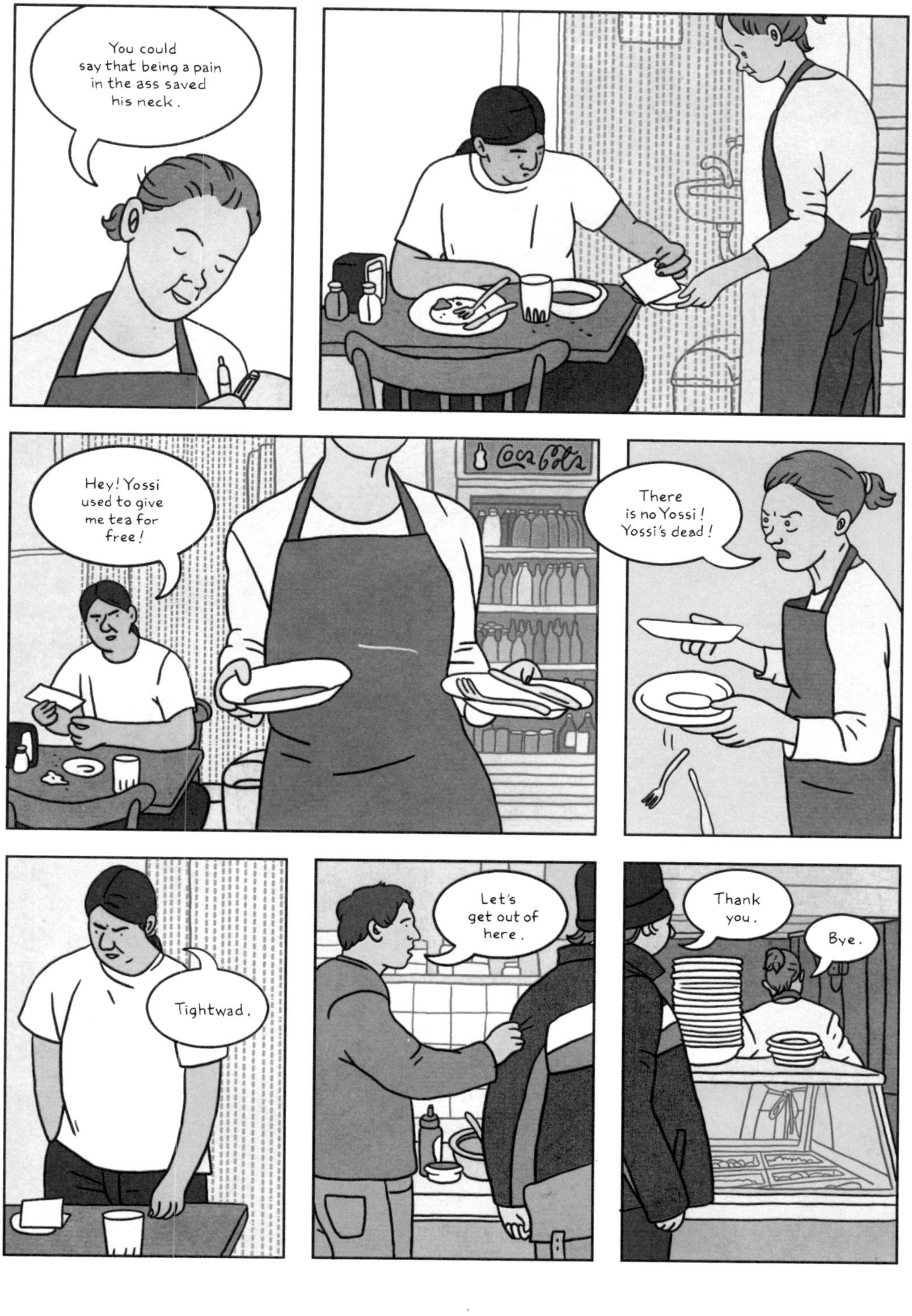
You could say that being a pain in the ass saved his neck.
Hey! Yossi used to give me tea for free!
There is no Yossi! Yossi's dead!
Coca Cola
Tightwad.
Let's get out of here.
Thank you.
Bye.

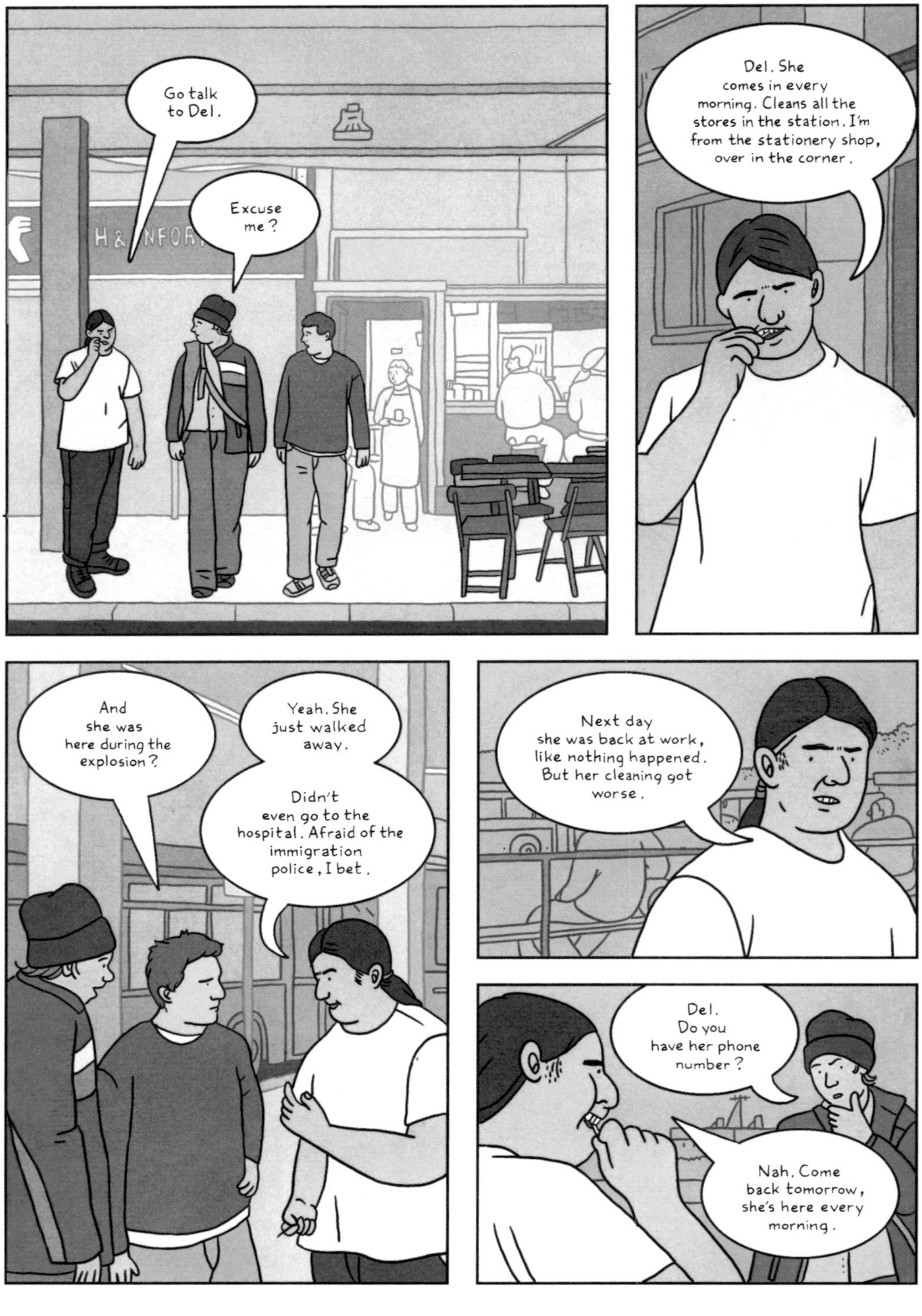
Go talk to Del.
Excuse me?
H & INFOR
Del. She comes in every morning. Cleans all the stores in the station. I'm from the stationery shop, over in the corner.
And she was here during the explosion?
Yeah. She just walked away.
Didn't even go to the hospital. Afraid of the immigration police, I bet.
Next day she was back at work, like nothing happened. But her cleaning got worse.
Del. Do you have her phone number?
Nah. Come back tomorrow, she's here every morning.

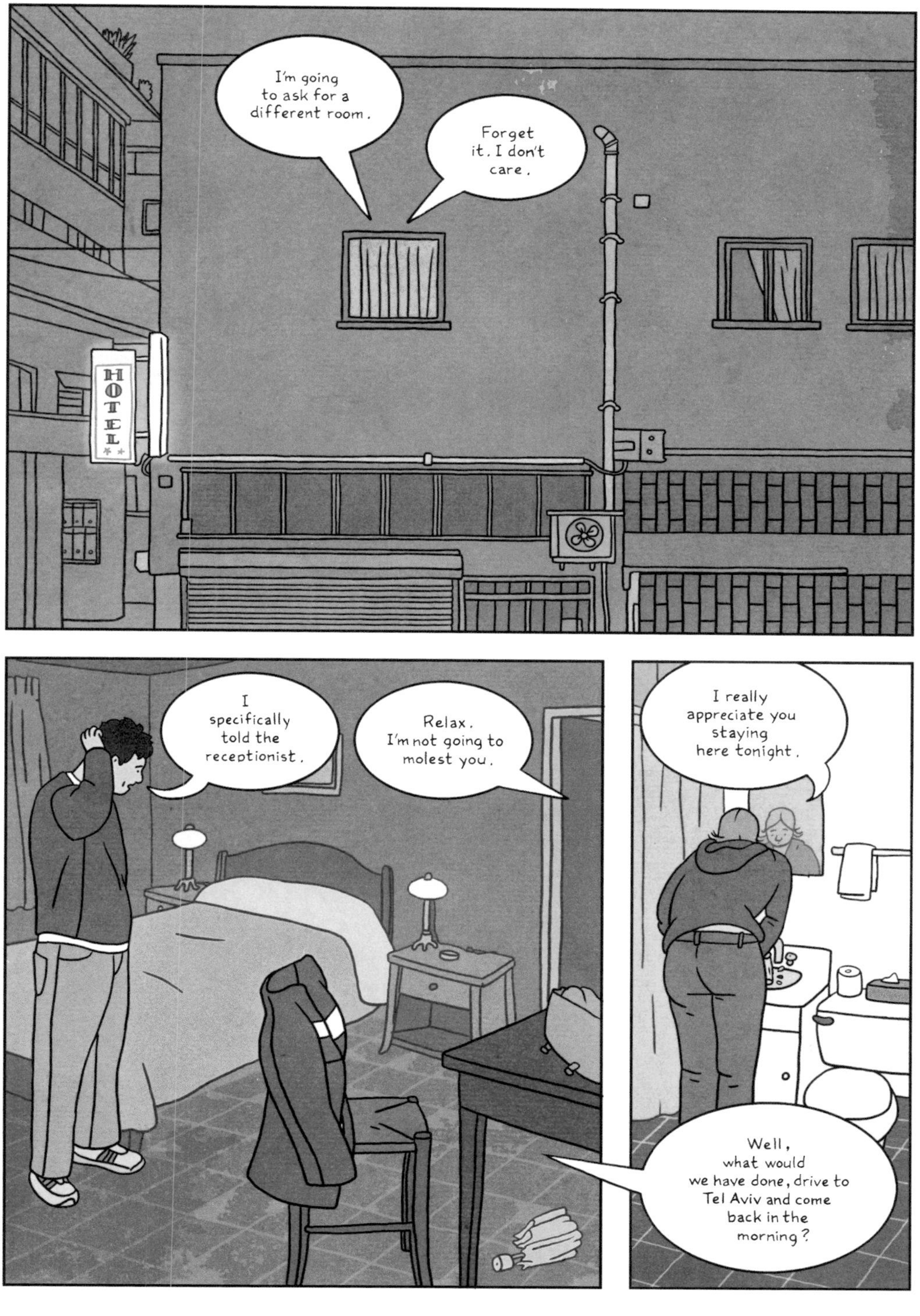
I'm going to ask for a different room.
Forget it. I don't care.
HOTEL
I specifically told the receptionist.
Relax. I'm not going to molest you.
I really appreciate you staying here tonight.
Well, what would we have done, drive to Tel Aviv and come back in the morning?

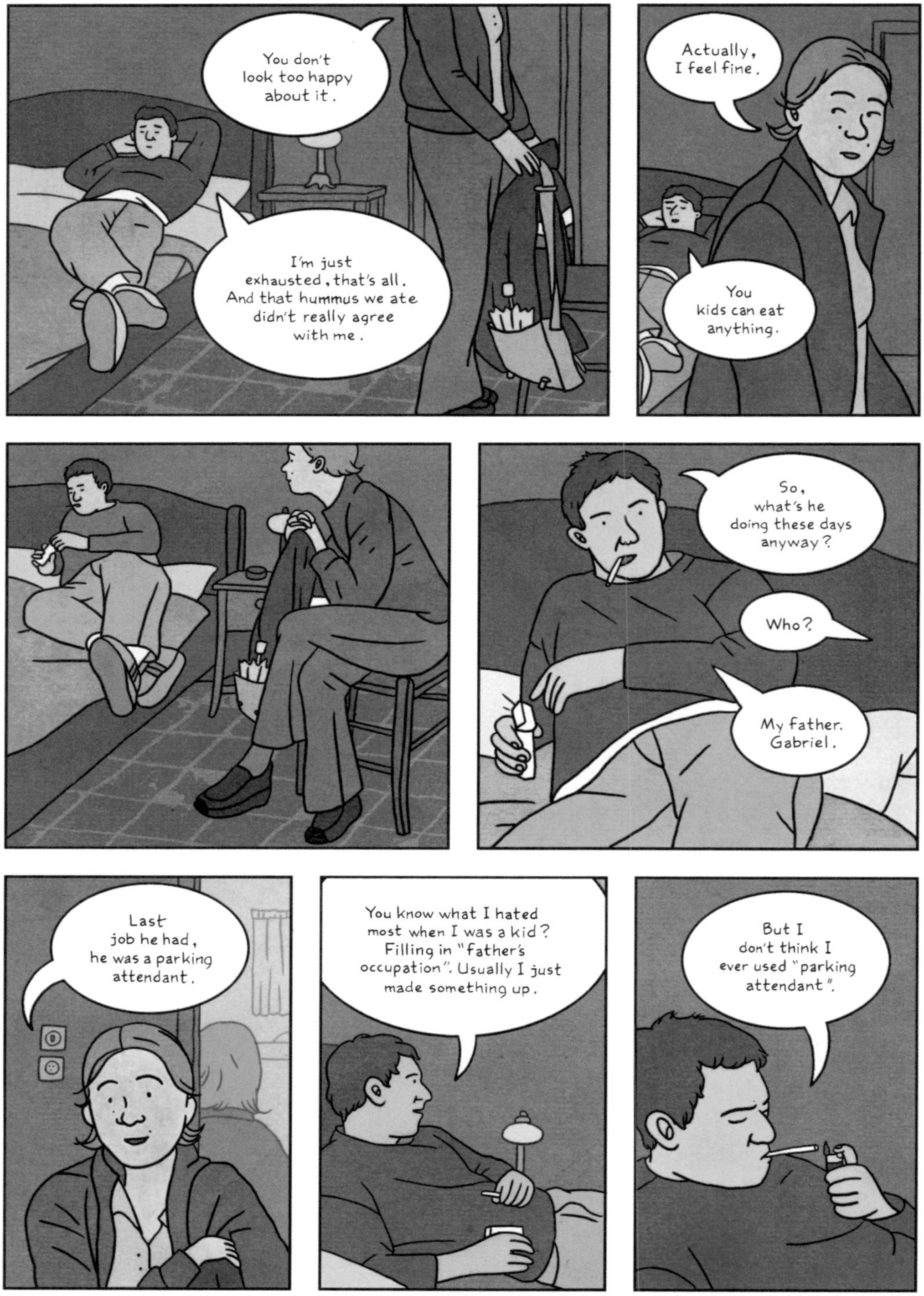
You don't look too happy about it.
I'm just exhausted, that's all. And that hummus we ate didn't really agree with me.
Actually, I feel fine.
You kids can eat anything.
So, what's he doing these days anyway?
Who?
My father. Gabriel.
Last job he had, he was a parking attendant.
You know what I hated most when I was a kid? Filling in "father's occupation". Usually I just made something up.
But I don't think I ever used "parking attendant".

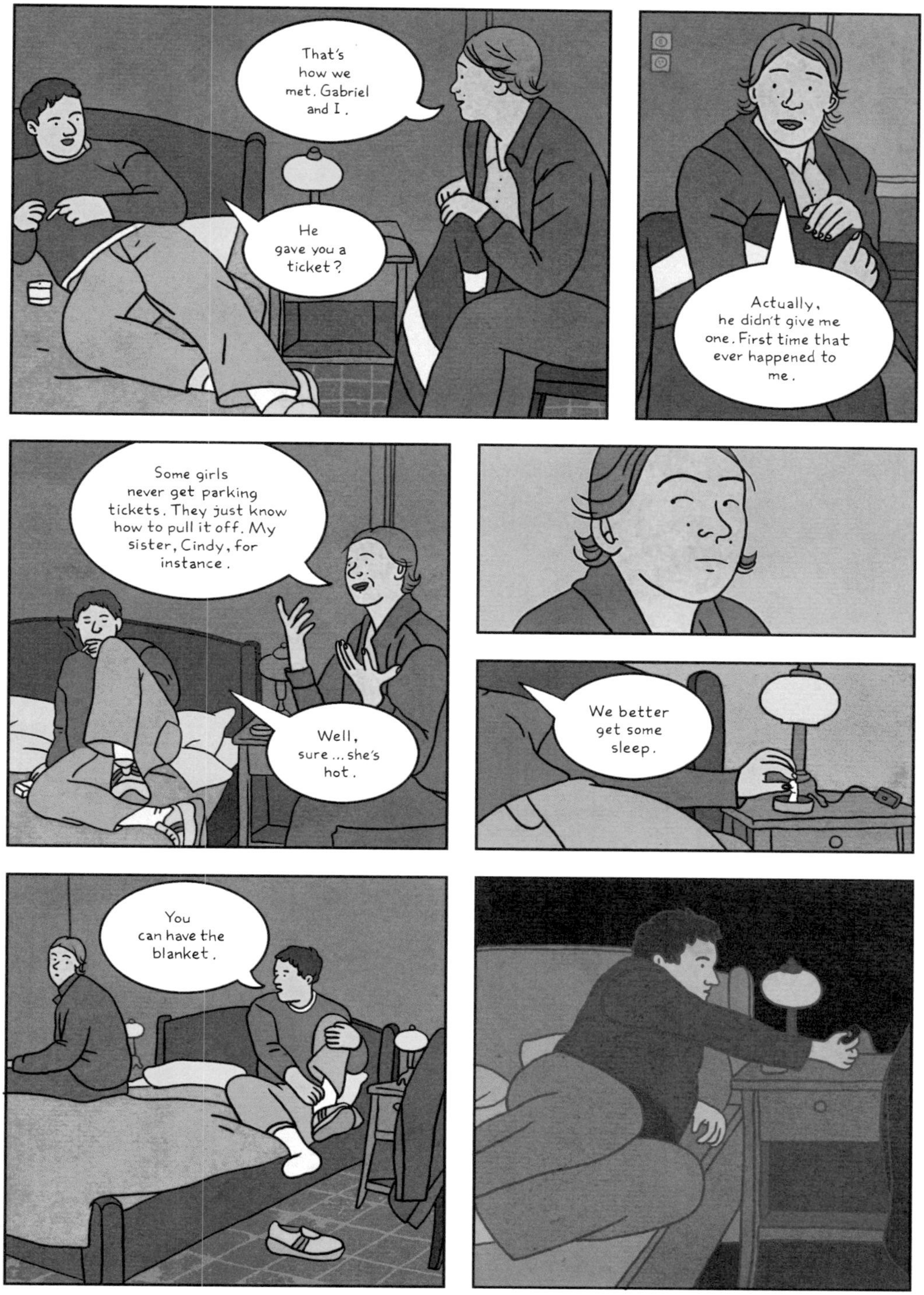
That's how we met. Gabriel and I.
He gave you a ticket?
Actually, he didn't give me one. First time that ever happened to me.
Some girls never get parking tickets. They just know how to pull it off. My sister, Cindy, for instance.
Well, sure ... she's hot.
We better get some sleep.
You can have the blanket.

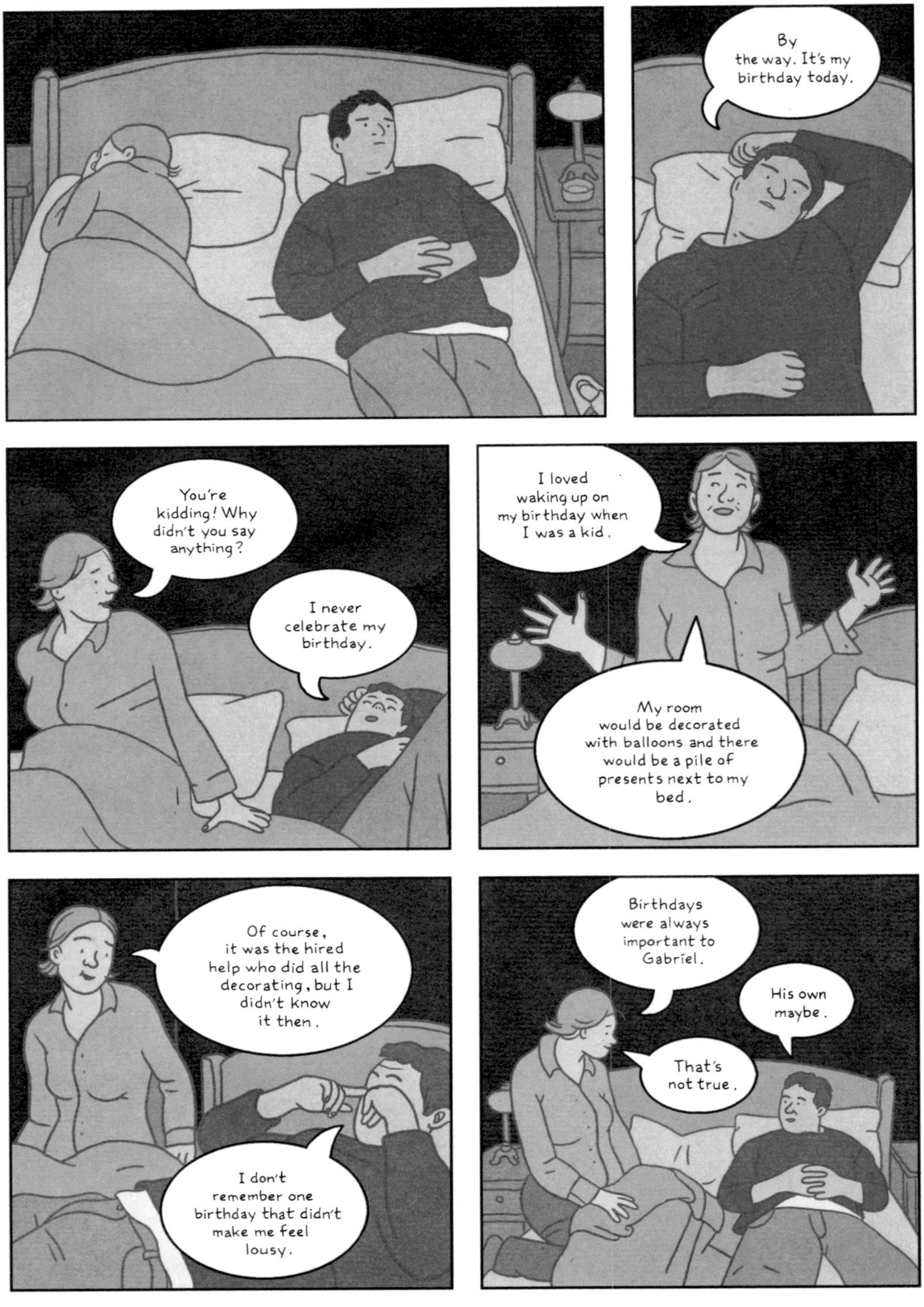

By the way. It's my birthday today.
You're kidding! Why didn't you say anything?
I never celebrate my birthday.
I loved waking up on my birthday when I was a kid.
My room would be decorated with balloons and there would be a pile of presents next to my bed.
Of course, it was the hired help who did all the decorating, but I didn't know it then.
I don't remember one birthday that didn't make me feel lousy.
Birthdays were always important to Gabriel.
His own maybe.
That's not true.

Two weeks before my eleventh birthday. My father starts getting all mysterious.

That's adorable... just like him.

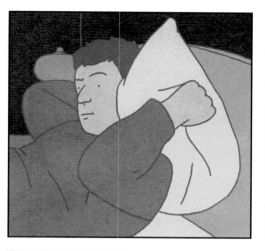
It's the day of my birthday. He takes out a box, tells me to close my eyes. My mother was watching too, all excited.

So? What did he get you?

A Maccabi Tel-Aviv soccer outfit. With the whole team's signatures on the jersey.

That's wonderful!

Right. Only I'm a Ha'Poel fan.

Oh, no! But it's funny, isn't it?

Only a girl could say that.

It sure wasn't funny to me. I was so disappointed I cried.

I was afraid he'd make me wear it to the derby. That's all I needed, for my friends to see me in a Maccabi jersey.

To us kids, Maccabi was worse than satan.

Still, it was a nice gesture.

What's nice about it?

It was so typical. He hardly knew me. He wasn't thinking about me, only about himself.

Why are you yelling at me.

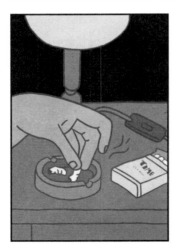

The last time I saw Gabriel was when he took me to the derby.

Yeah?

He said if he could explain it to me i'd see what a brilliant game it was.

And?

I was bored out of my skull.

You see?

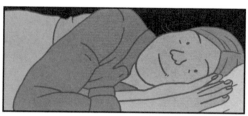

But I enjoyed watching him. He actually cried when Maccabi won. Real tears!

Afterwards we went trampoline jumping.

My father went trampoline jumping?

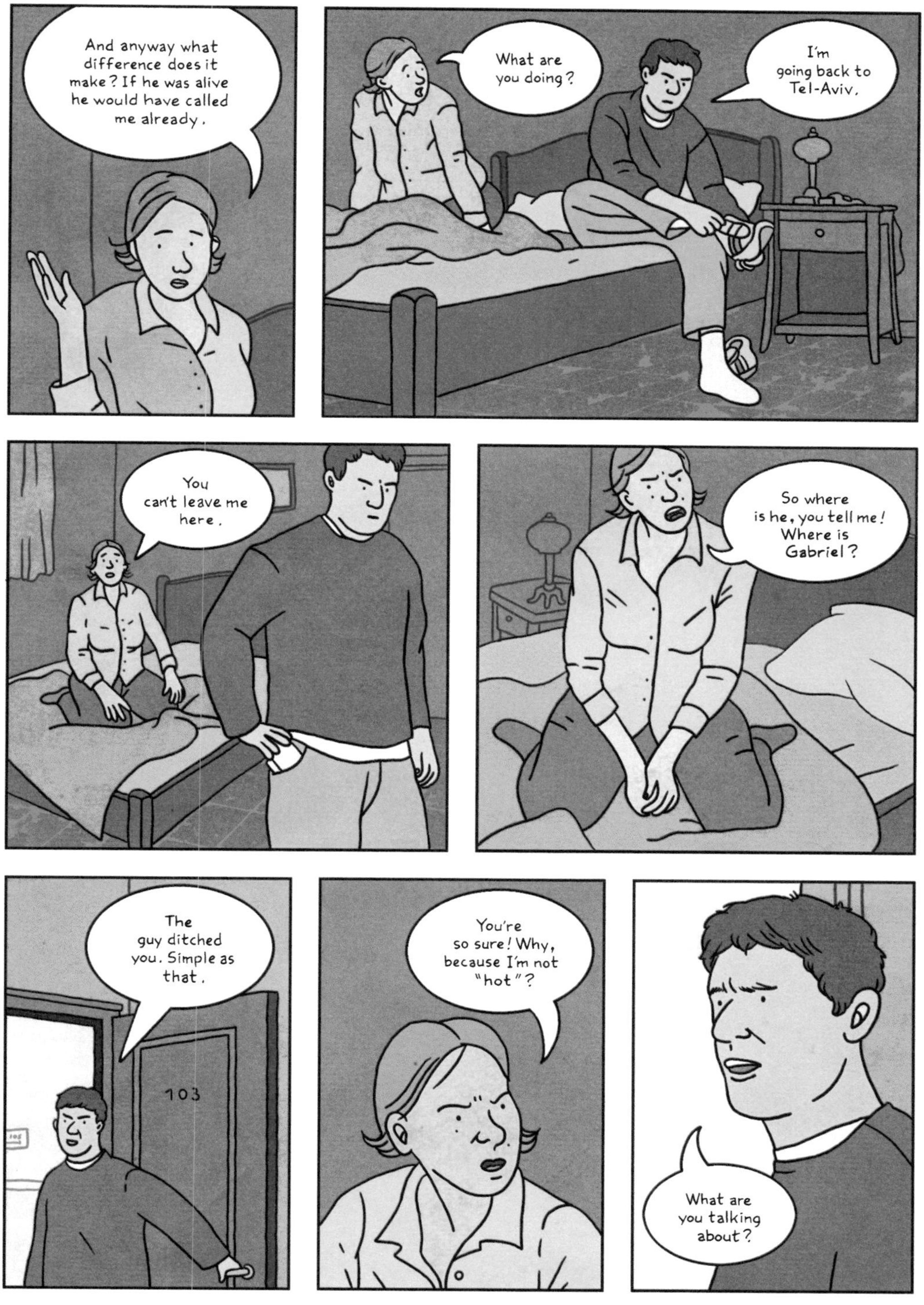
And anyway what difference does it make? If he was alive he would have called me already.
What are you doing?
I'm going back to Tel-Aviv.
You can't leave me here.
So where is he, you tell me! Where is Gabriel?
The guy ditched you. Simple as that.
103
You're so sure! Why, because I'm not "hot"?
What are you talking about?

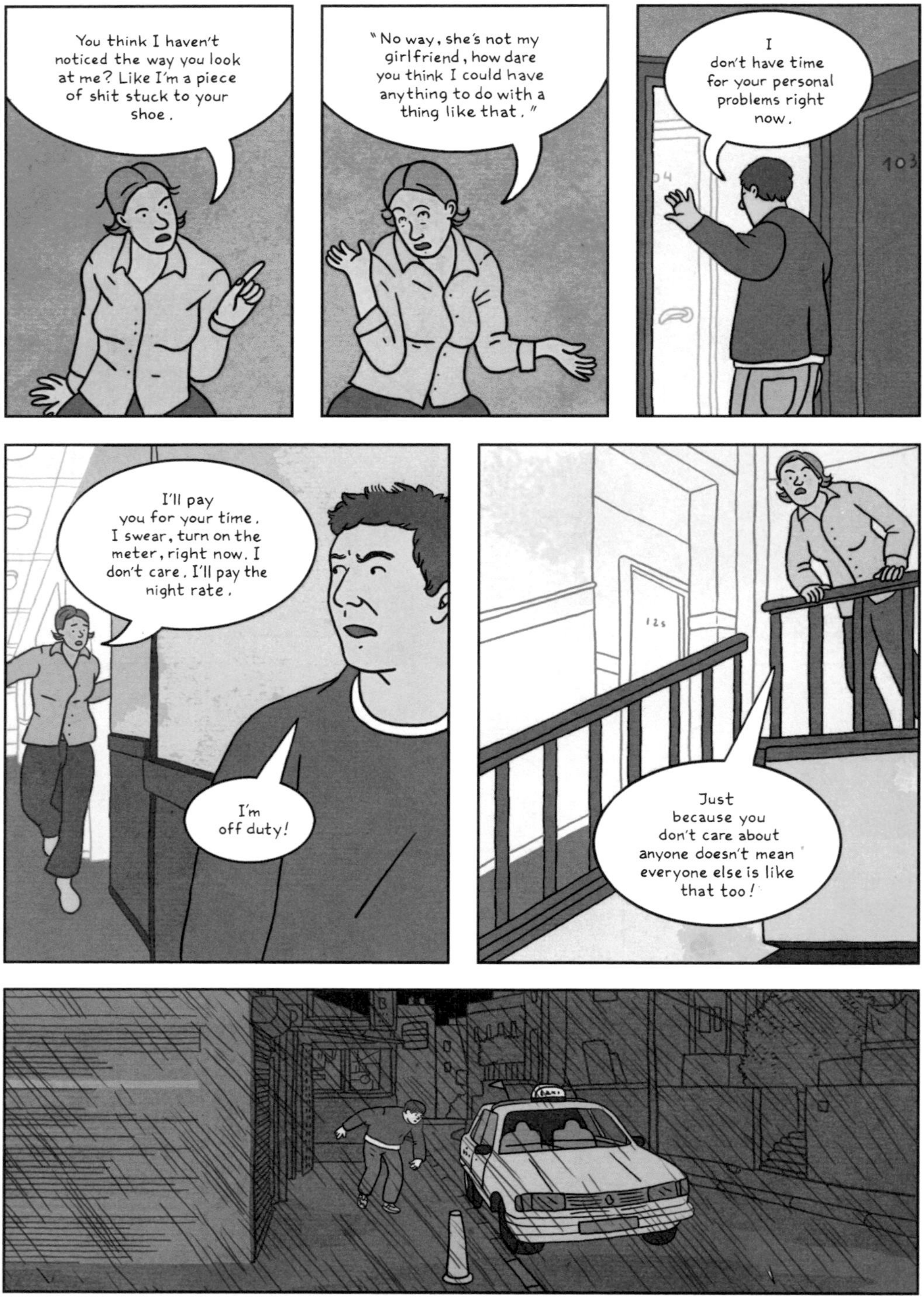
You think I haven't noticed the way you look at me? Like I'm a piece of shit stuck to your shoe.
"No way, she's not my girlfriend, how dare you think I could have anything to do with a thing like that."
I don't have time for your personal problems right now.
I'll pay you for your time. I swear, turn on the meter, right now. I don't care. I'll pay the night rate.
I'm off duty!
Just because you don't care about anyone doesn't mean everyone else is like that too!

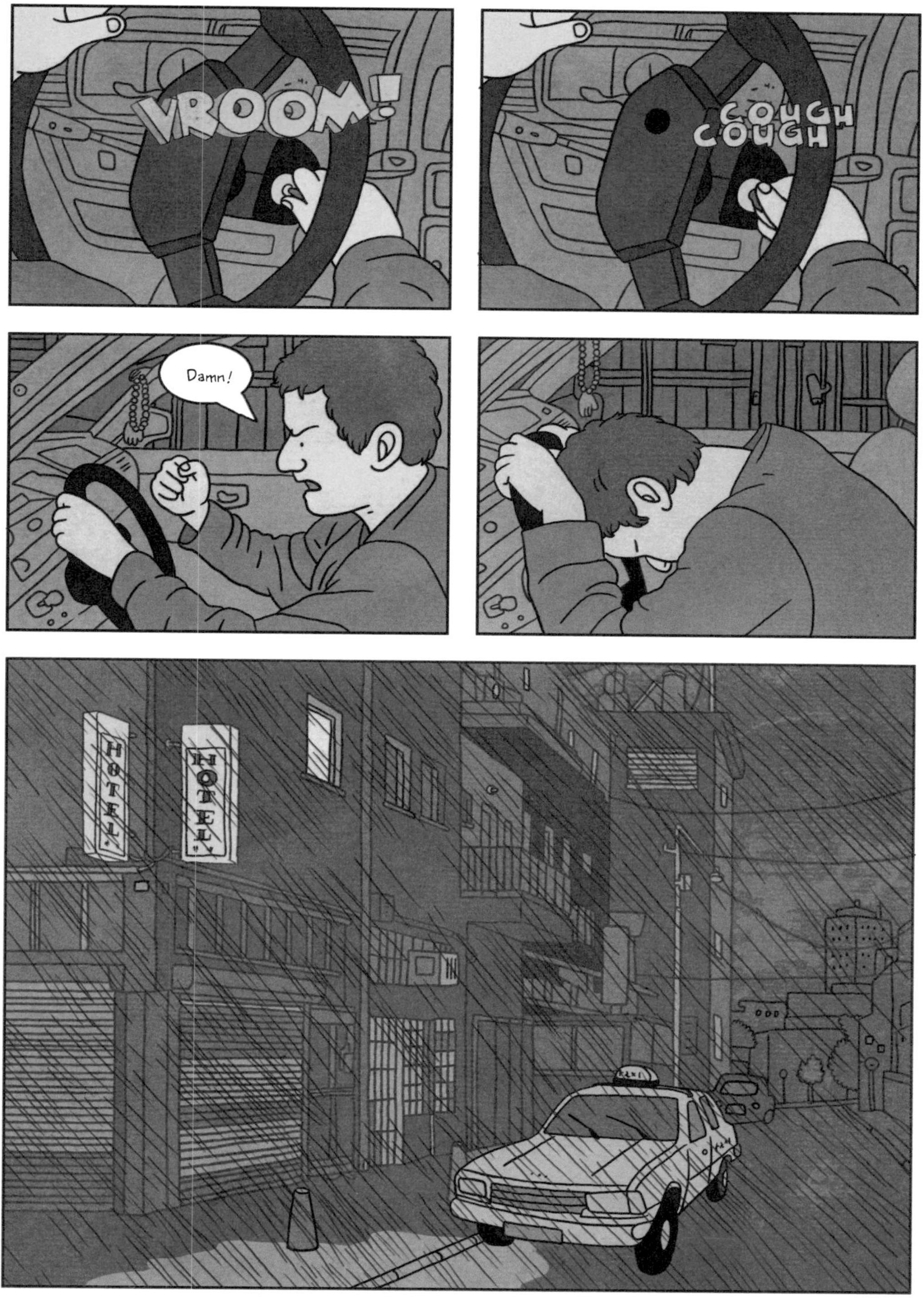
VROOM!
COUGH COUGH
Damn!
HOTEL
HOTEL

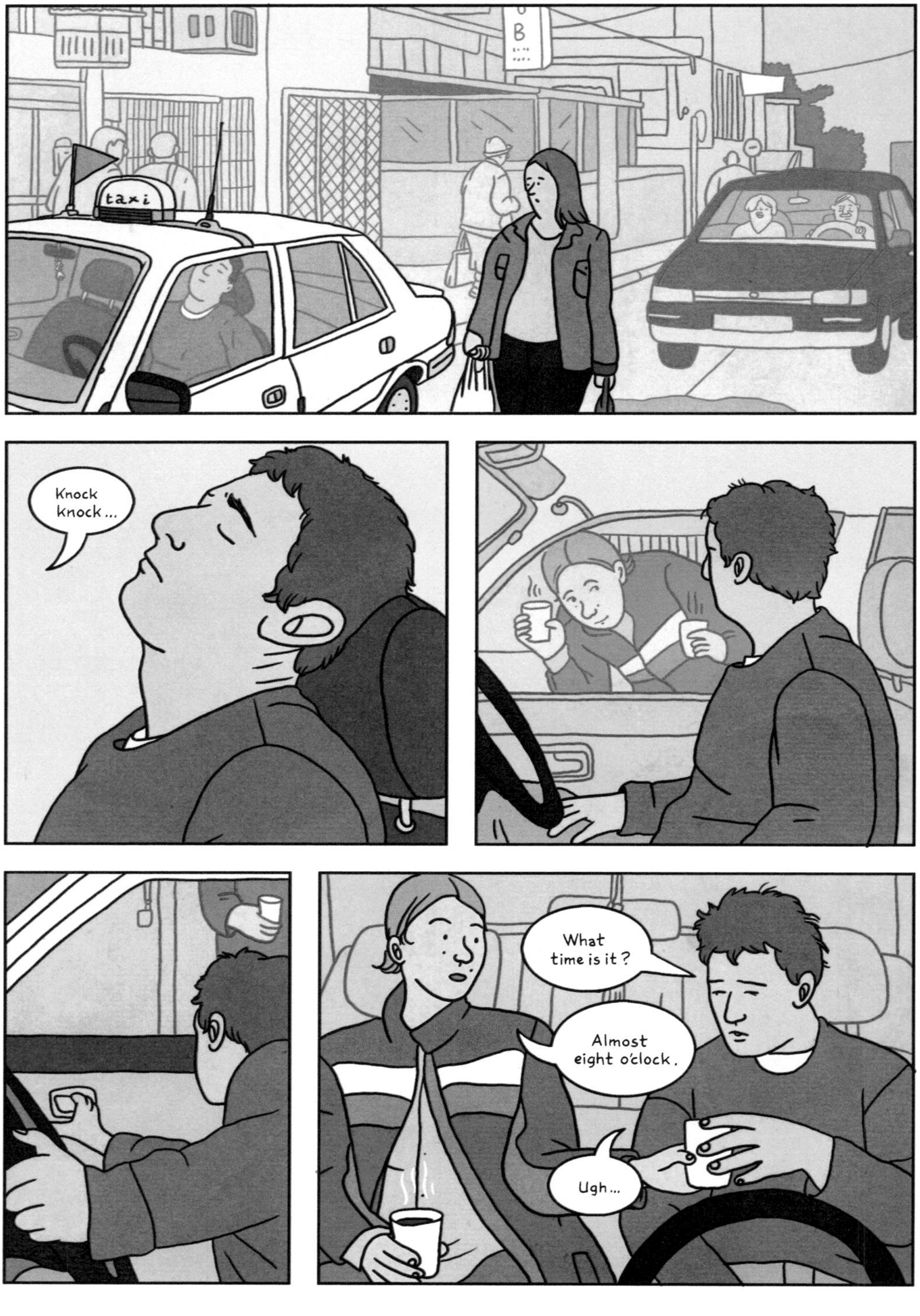
taxi
Knock knock...
What time is it?
Almost eight o'clock.
Ugh...

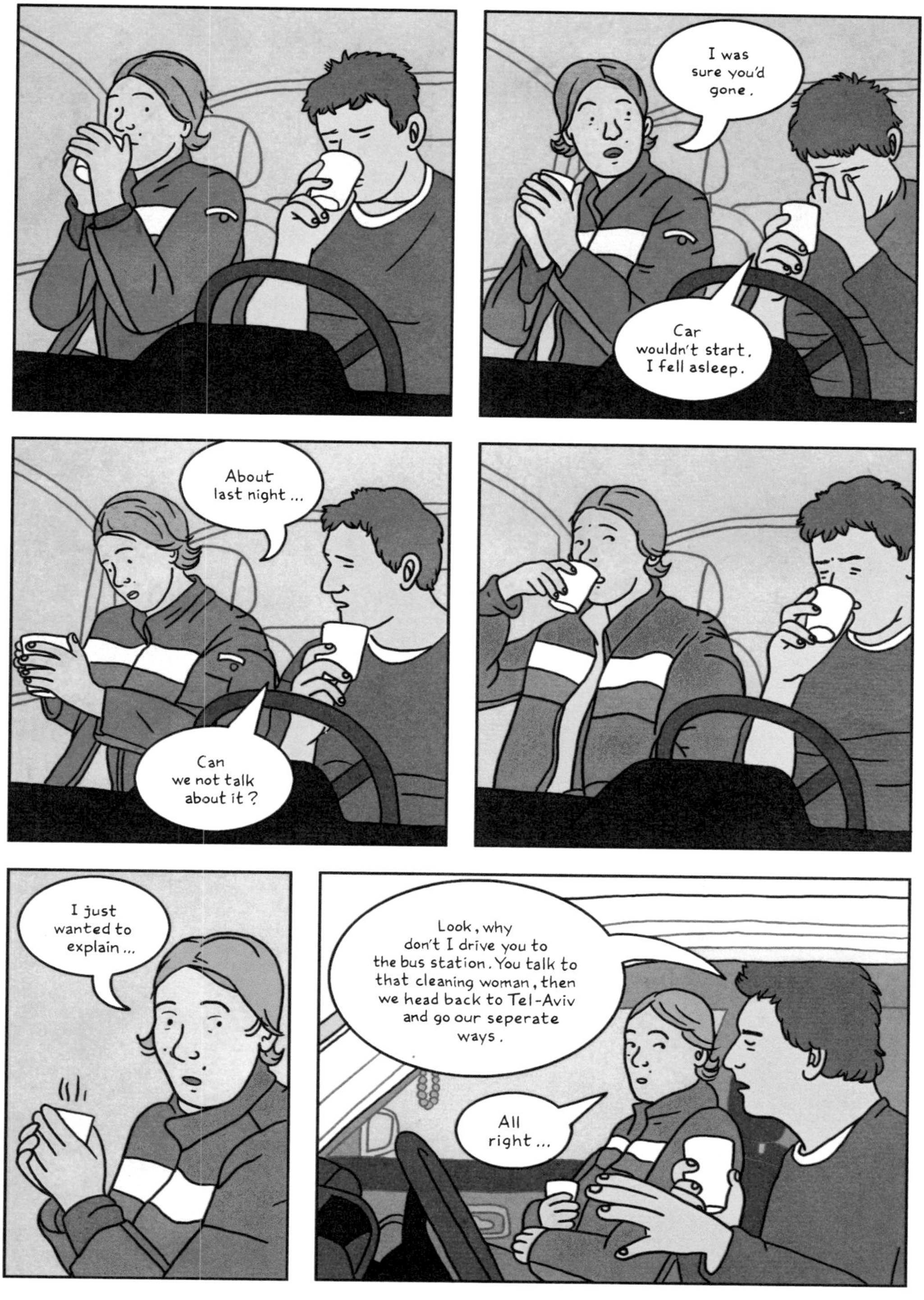
I was sure you'd gone.
Car wouldn't start. I fell asleep.
About last night ...
Can we not talk about it?
I just wanted to explain ...
Look, why don't I drive you to the bus station. You talk to that cleaning woman, then we head back to Tel-Aviv and go our seperate ways.
All right ...

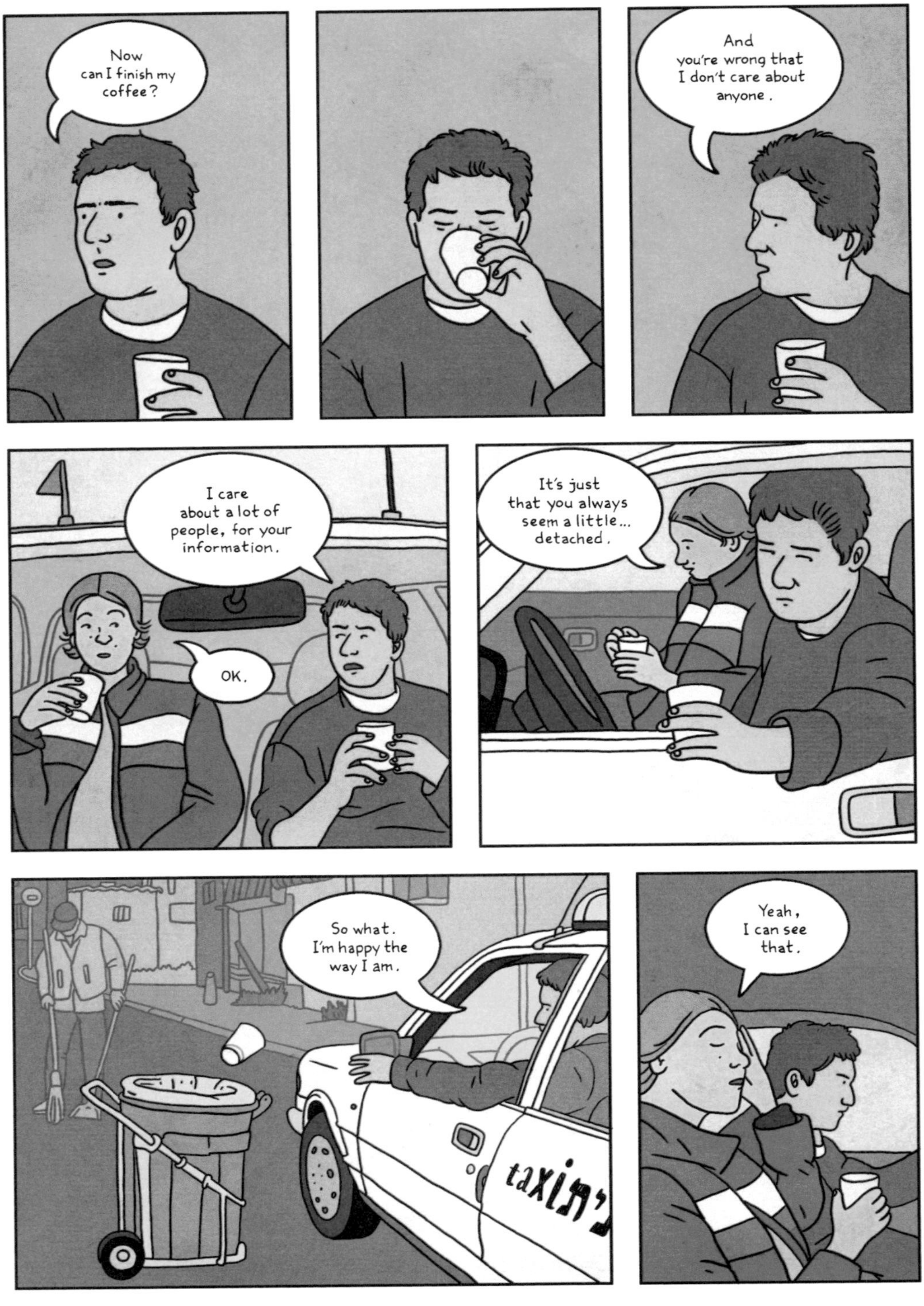
Now can I finish my coffee?
And you're wrong that I don't care about anyone.
I care about a lot of people, for your information.
OK.
It's just that you always seem a little... detached.
So what. I'm happy the way I am.
taxi
Yeah, I can see that.

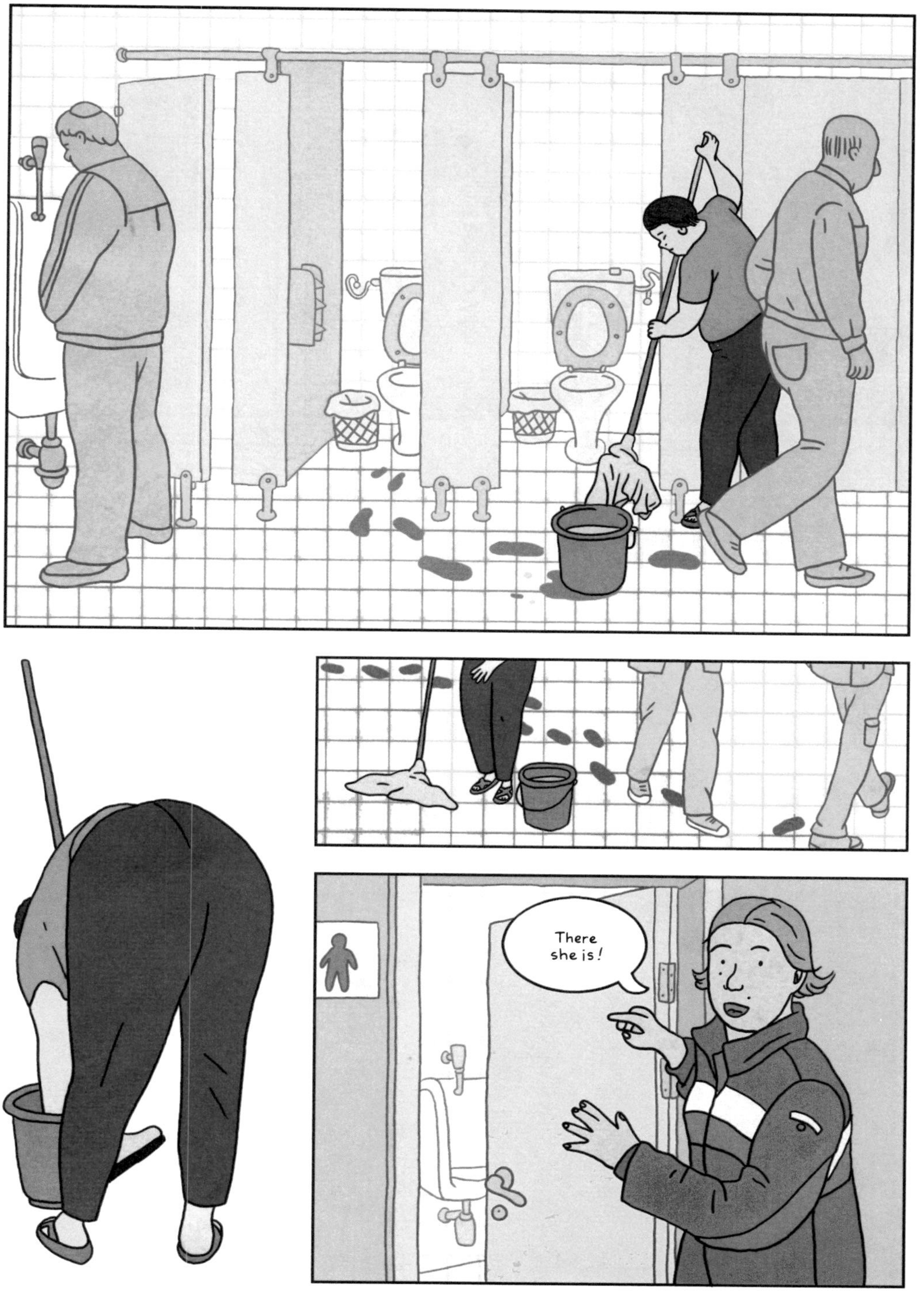
There she is!

Del?

Can we talk to you?

I not Del. I Nora.

Where is Del?

She go back to Philipines.

When?

After the bomb. She has a baby... She got scared.

But the guy from the shop... he said she still works here.

We switch. He not notice.

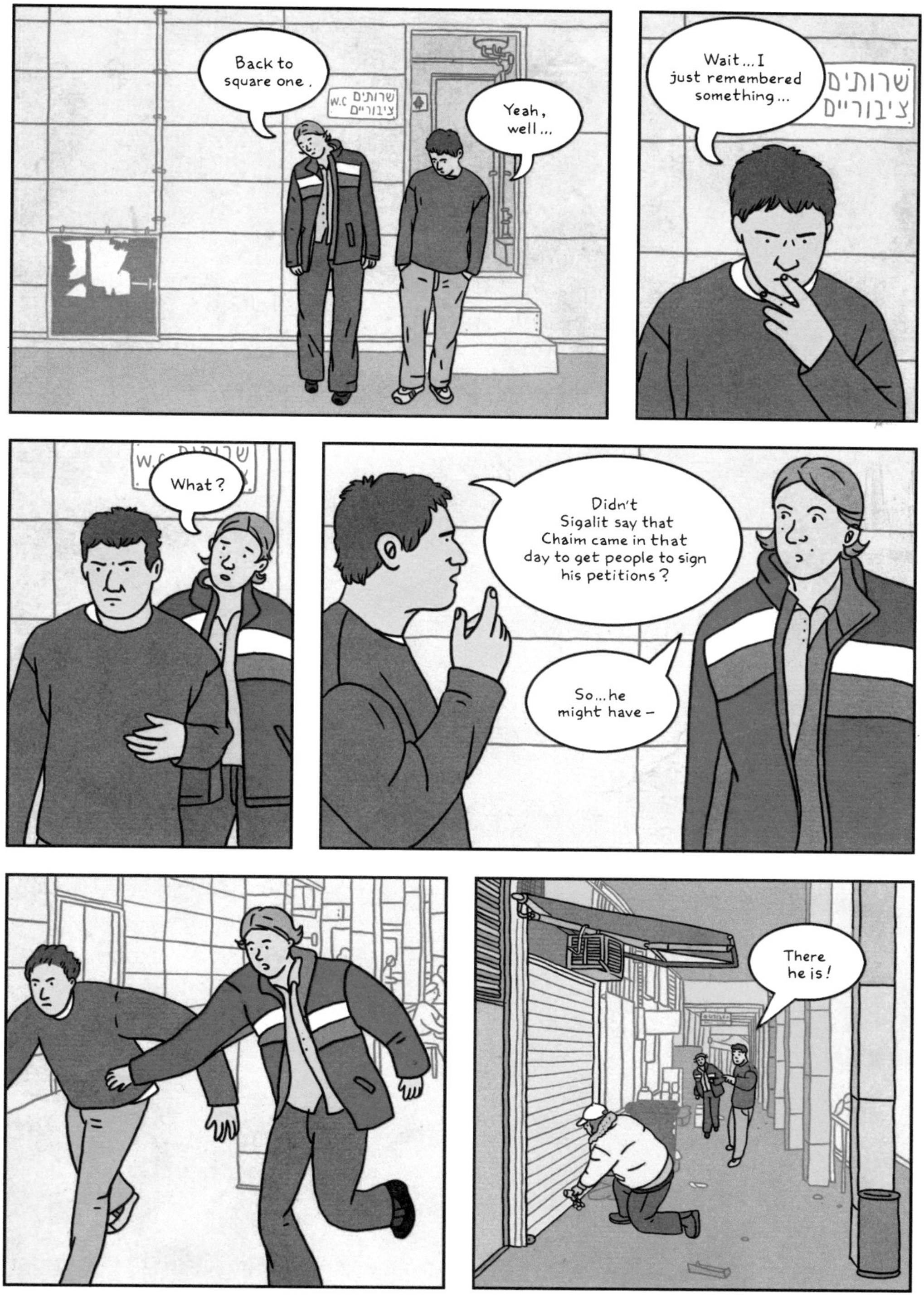
Back to square one.
שרותים
W.C
ציבוריים
Yeah, well...
Wait... I just remembered something...
שרותים
ציבוריים
What?
Didn't Sigalit say that Chaim came in that day to get people to sign his petitions?
So... he might have –
There he is!

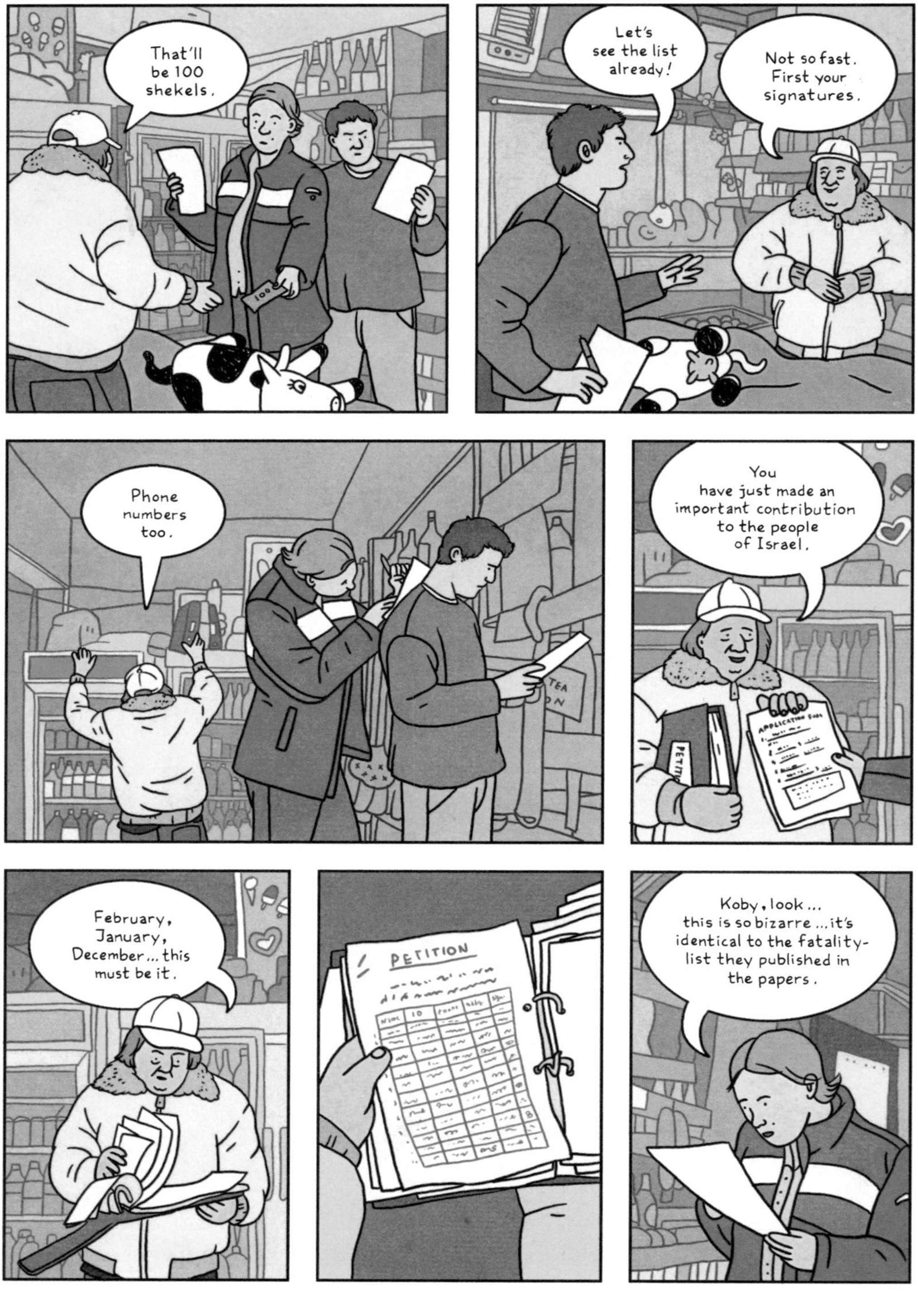
That'll be 100 shekels.
Let's see the list already!
Not so fast. First your signatures.
Phone numbers too.
You have just made an important contribution to the people of Israel.
February, January, December... this must be it.
PETITION
Koby, look... this is so bizarre... it's identical to the fatality-list they published in the papers.

Excuse me there's no law against using the names of the deceased if they signed just before they died! I consulted a lawyer!

I don't see my father's name.

No.

Yossi, the guy from the cafeteria, he didn't have time to sign, either...poor bastard.

Koby, look... who's that?

Atara Dayan...no idea. Why?

She's not on any of my lists.

So?

Everyone on this petition was present at the time of the attack.

The old lady that was killed...That soldier...Arik Dabush.

Even Del is listed here!

So this Atara Dayan must have been in the cafeteria too...

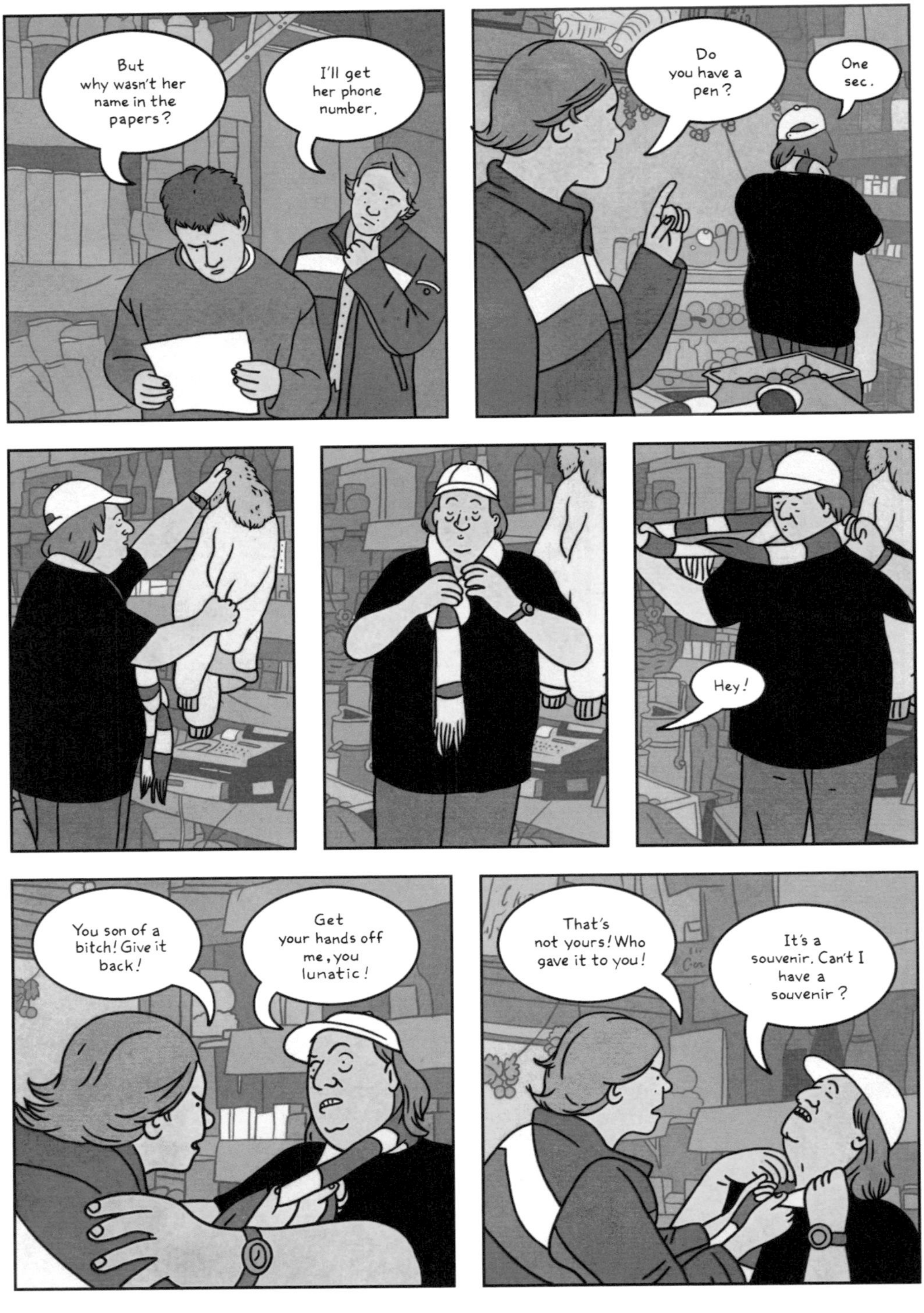
But why wasn't her name in the papers?
I'll get her phone number.
Do you have a pen?
One sec.
Hey!
You son of a bitch! Give it back!
Get your hands off me, you lunatic!
That's not yours! Who gave it to you!
It's a souvenir. Can't I have a souvenir?

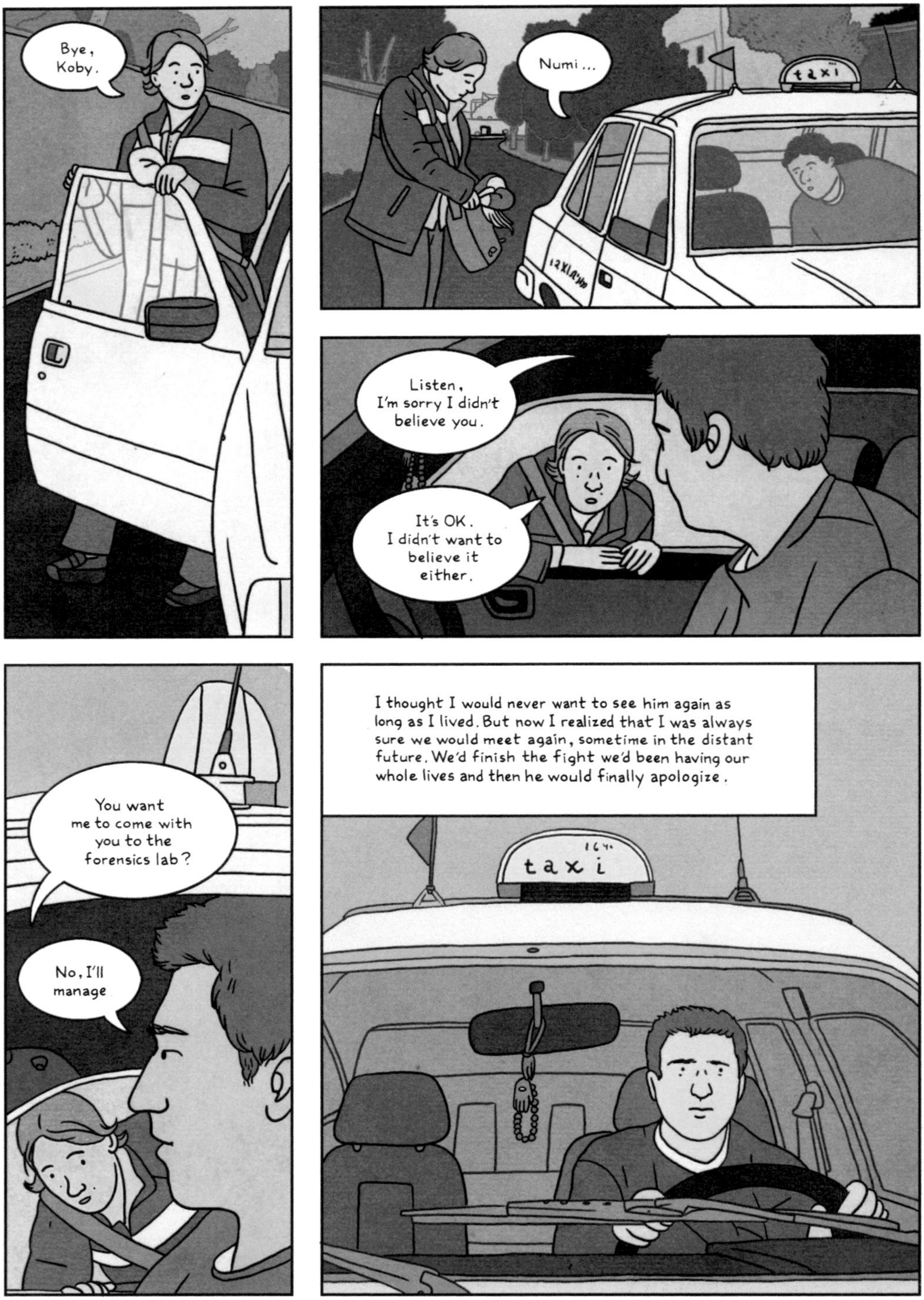
Bye, Koby.
Numi...
Listen, I'm sorry I didn't believe you.
It's OK. I didn't want to believe it either.
You want me to come with you to the forensics lab?
No, I'll manage
I thought I would never want to see him again as long as I lived. But now I realized that I was always sure we would meet again, sometime in the distant future. We'd finish the fight we'd been having our whole lives and then he would finally apologize.
taxi

chapter three
riding the waves

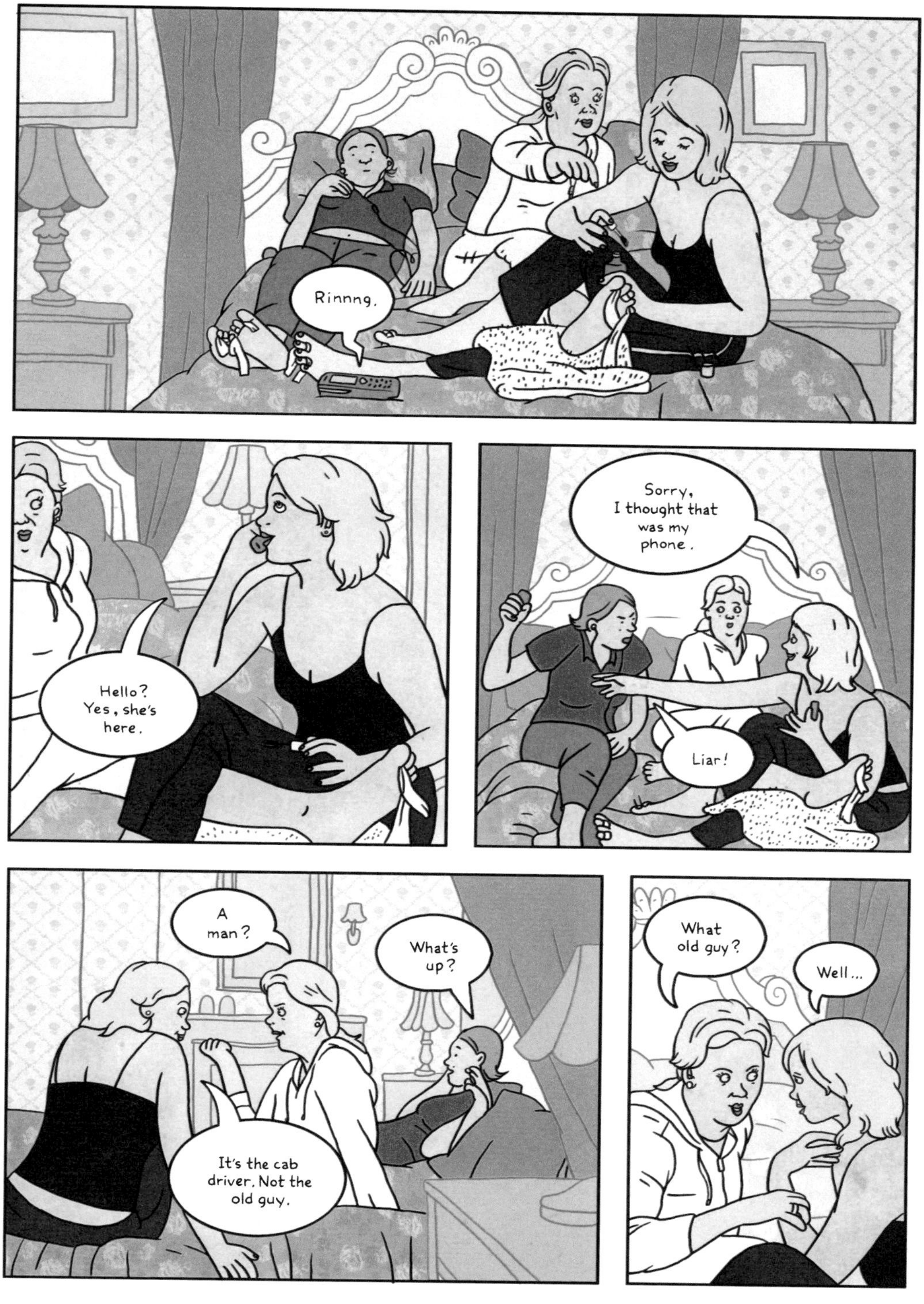
Rinnng.
Hello? Yes, she's here.
Sorry, I thought that was my phone.
Liar!
A man?
What's up?
It's the cab driver. Not the old guy.
What old guy?
Well...

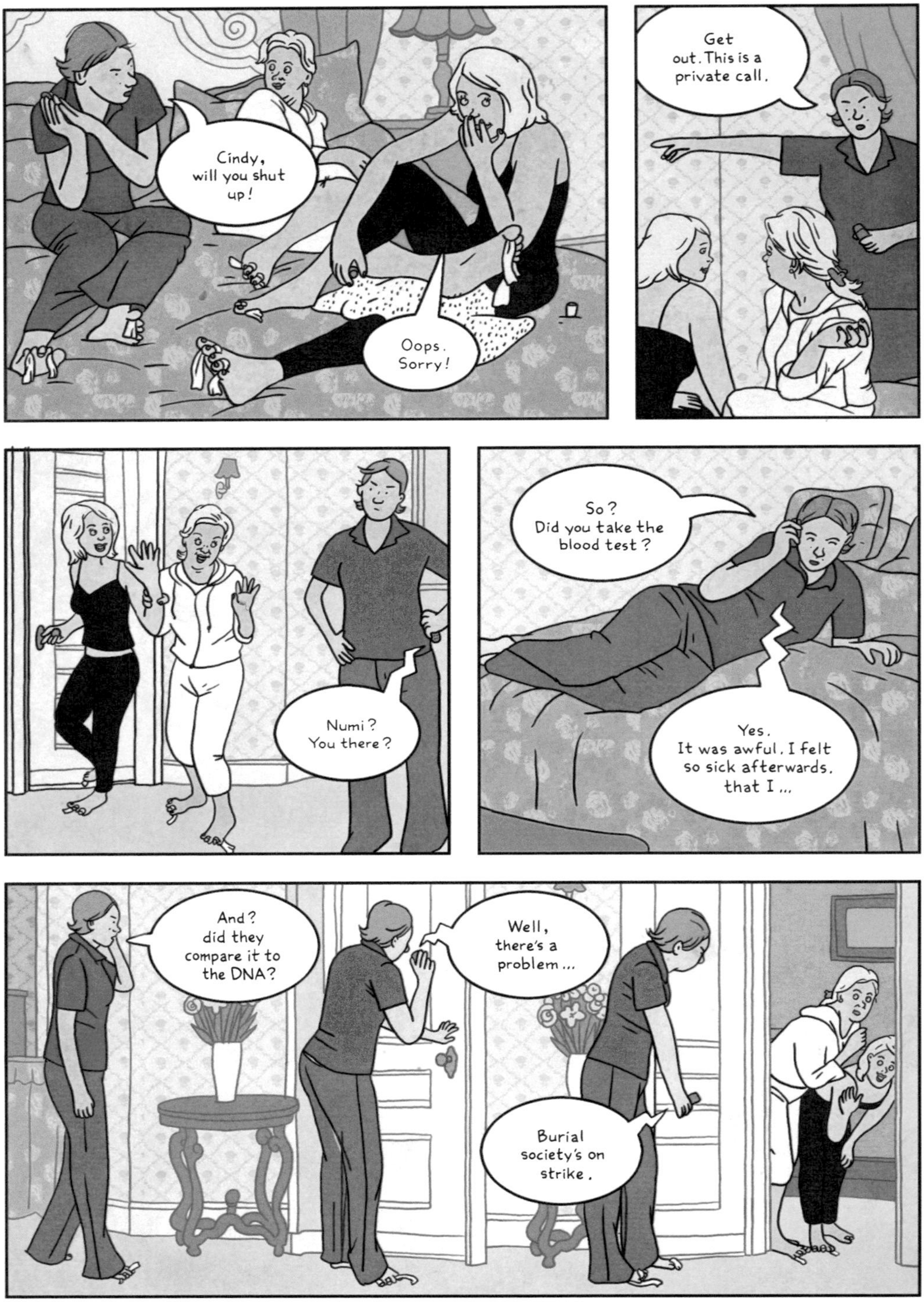
Cindy, will you shut up!
Oops. Sorry!
Get out. This is a private call.
Numi? You there?
So? Did you take the blood test?
Yes. It was awful. I felt so sick afterwards, that I...
And? did they compare it to the DNA?
Well, there's a problem...
Burial society's on strike.

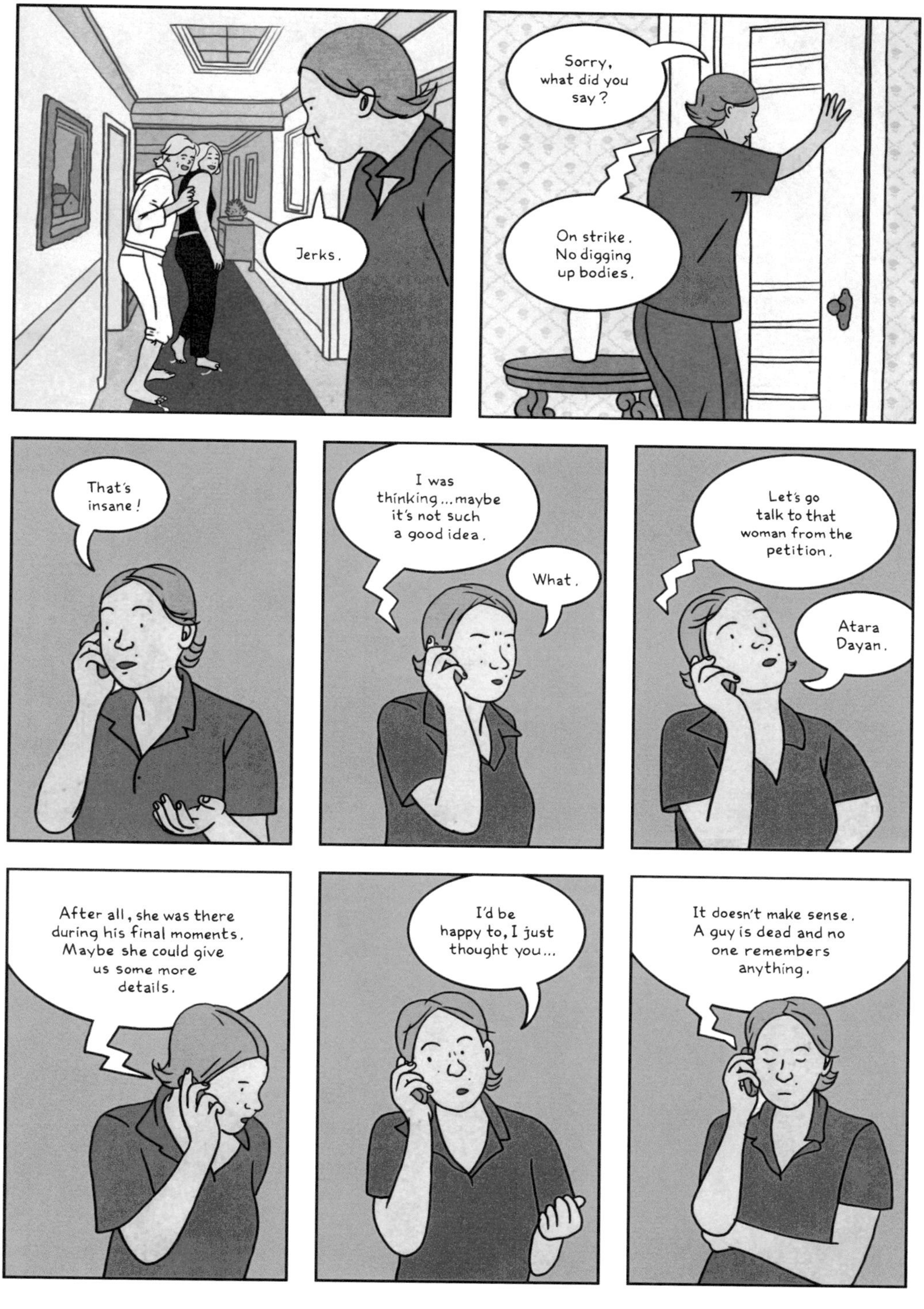
Jerks.
Sorry, what did you say?
On strike. No digging up bodies.
That's insane!
I was thinking... maybe it's not such a good idea.
What.
Let's go talk to that woman from the petition.
Atara Dayan.
After all, she was there during his final moments. Maybe she could give us some more details.
I'd be happy to, I just thought you...
It doesn't make sense. A guy is dead and no one remembers anything.

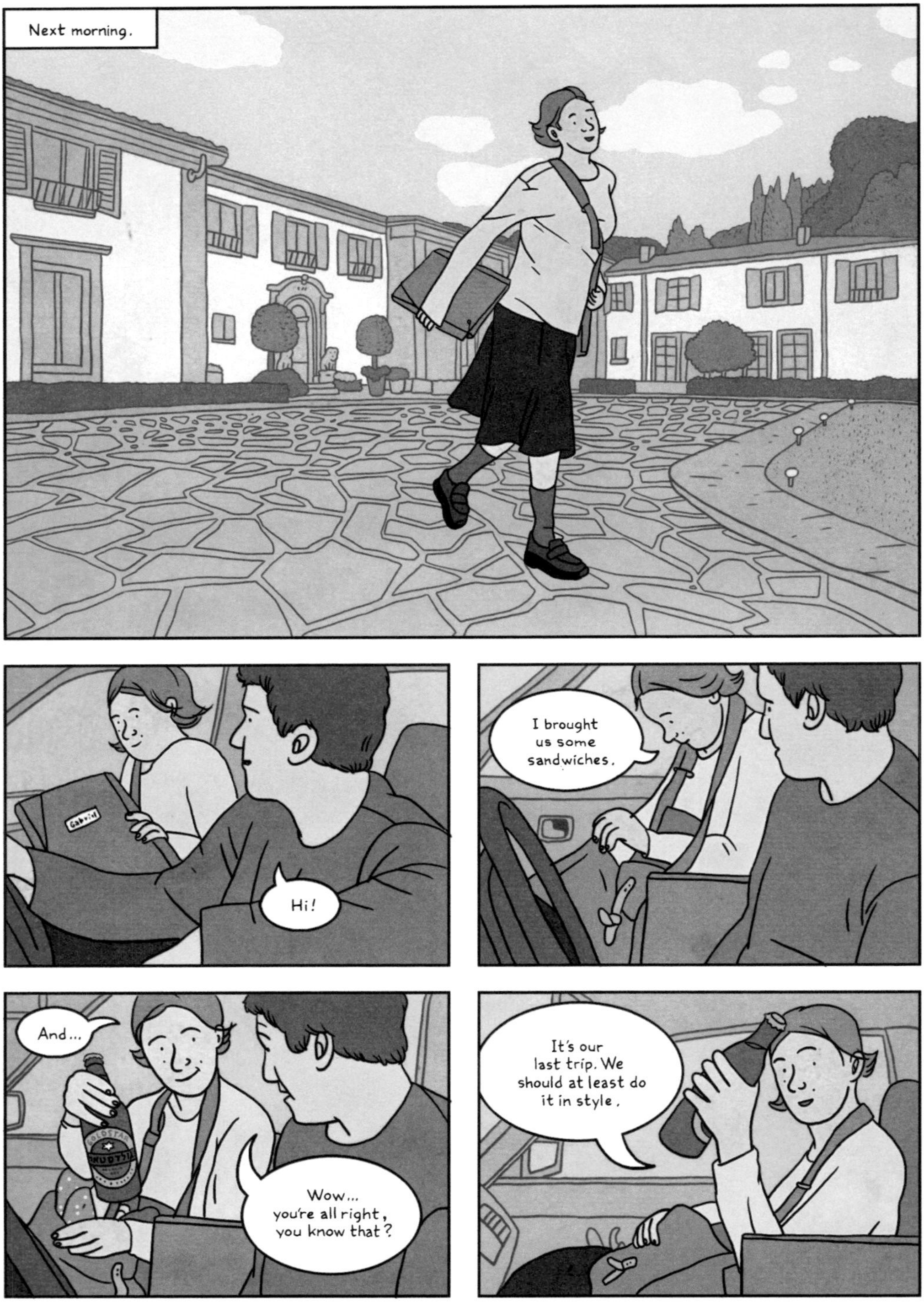
Next morning.
Hi!
I brought us some sandwiches.
And...
Wow... you're all right, you know that?
It's our last trip. We should at least do it in style.

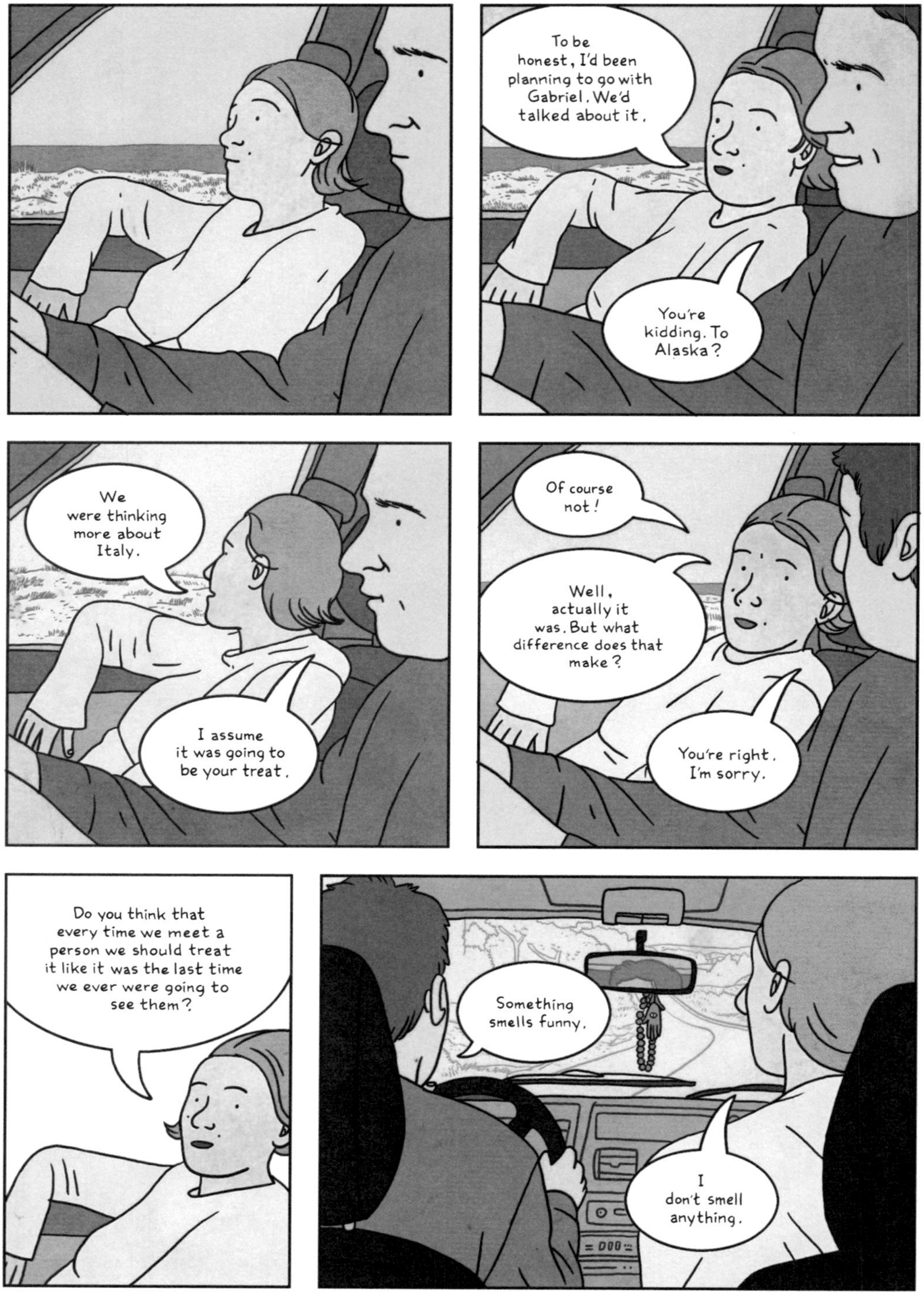
To be honest, I'd been planning to go with Gabriel. We'd talked about it.
You're kidding. To Alaska?
We were thinking more about Italy.
I assume it was going to be your treat.
Of course not!
Well, actually it was. But what difference does that make?
You're right. I'm sorry.
Do you think that every time we meet a person we should treat it like it was the last time we ever were going to see them?
Something smells funny.
I don't smell anything.

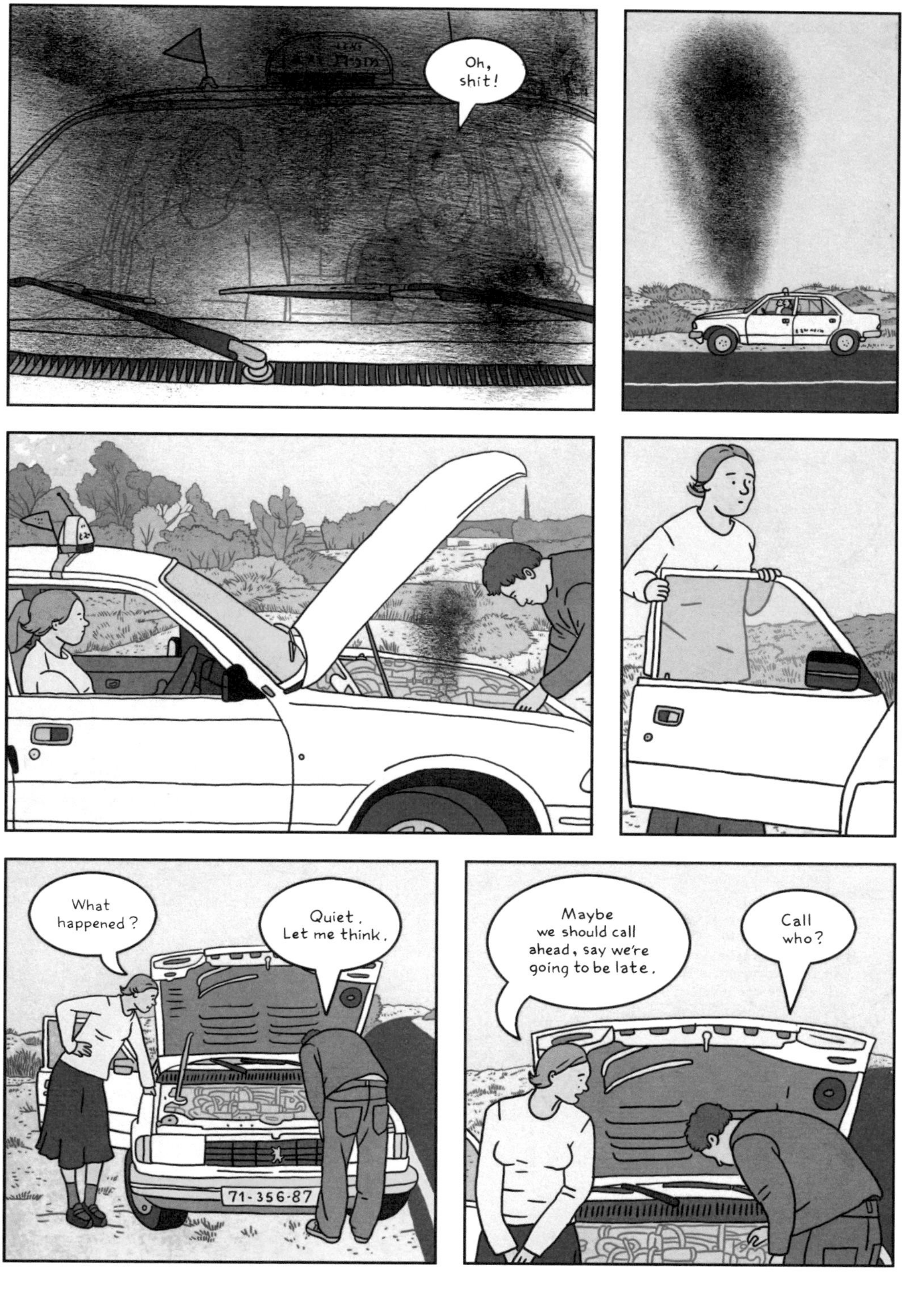
Oh, shit!
What happened?
Quiet. Let me think.
Maybe we should call ahead, say we're going to be late.
Call who?

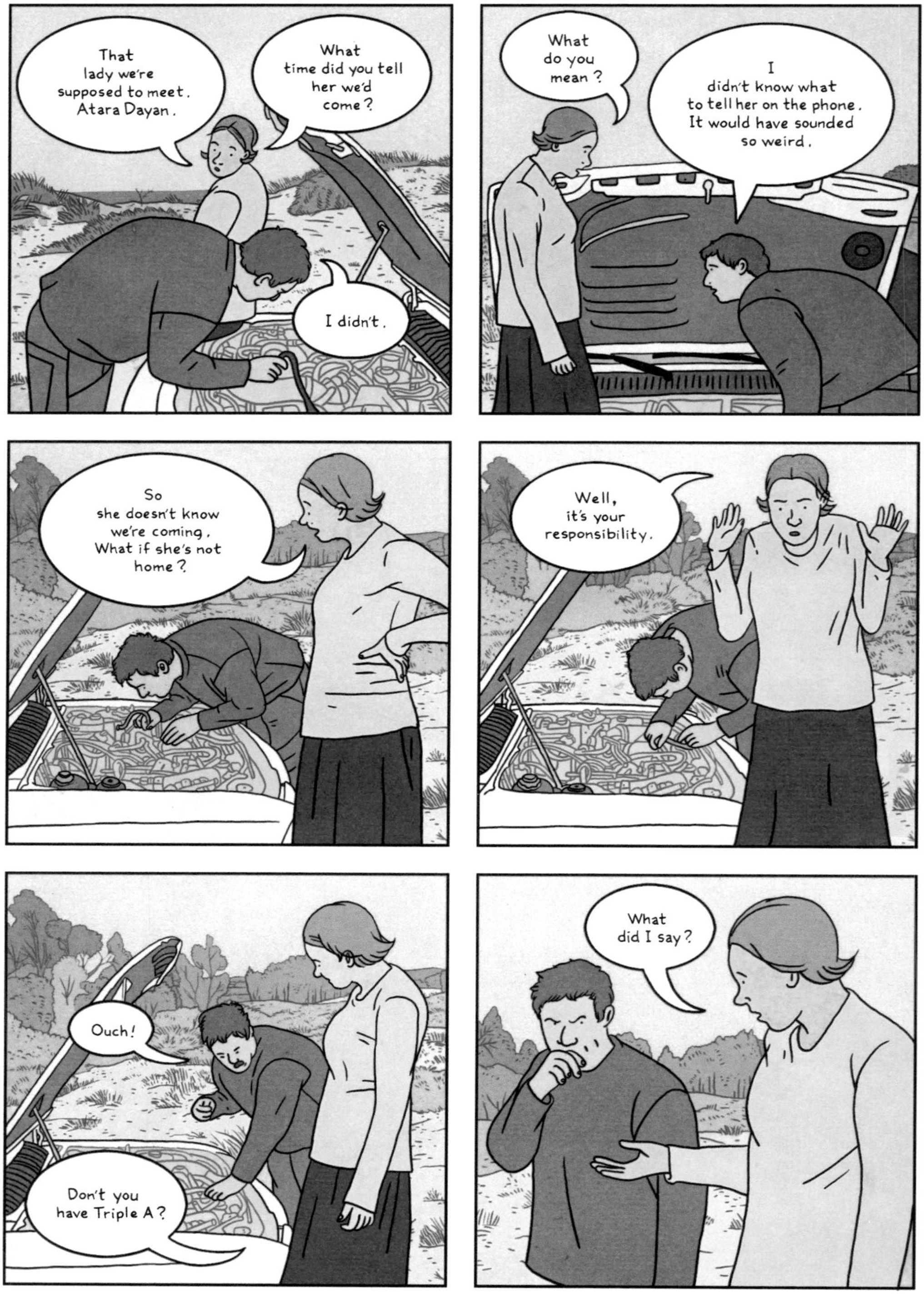
That lady we're supposed to meet. Atara Dayan.
What time did you tell her we'd come?
I didn't.
What do you mean?
I didn't know what to tell her on the phone. It would have sounded so weird.
So she doesn't know we're coming. What if she's not home?
Well, it's your responsibility.
Ouch!
Don't you have Triple A?
What did I say?

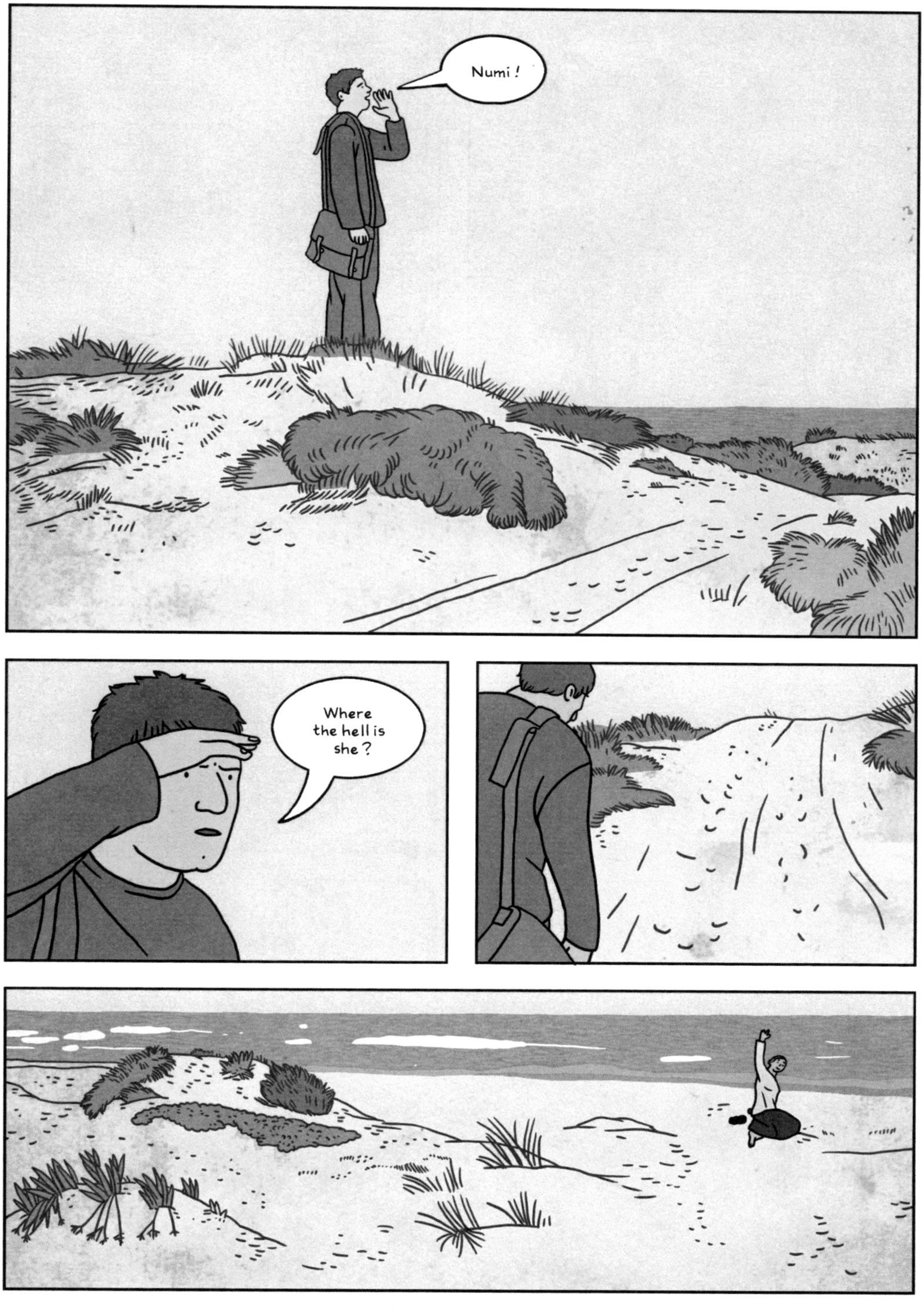
Numi !
Where the hell is she ?

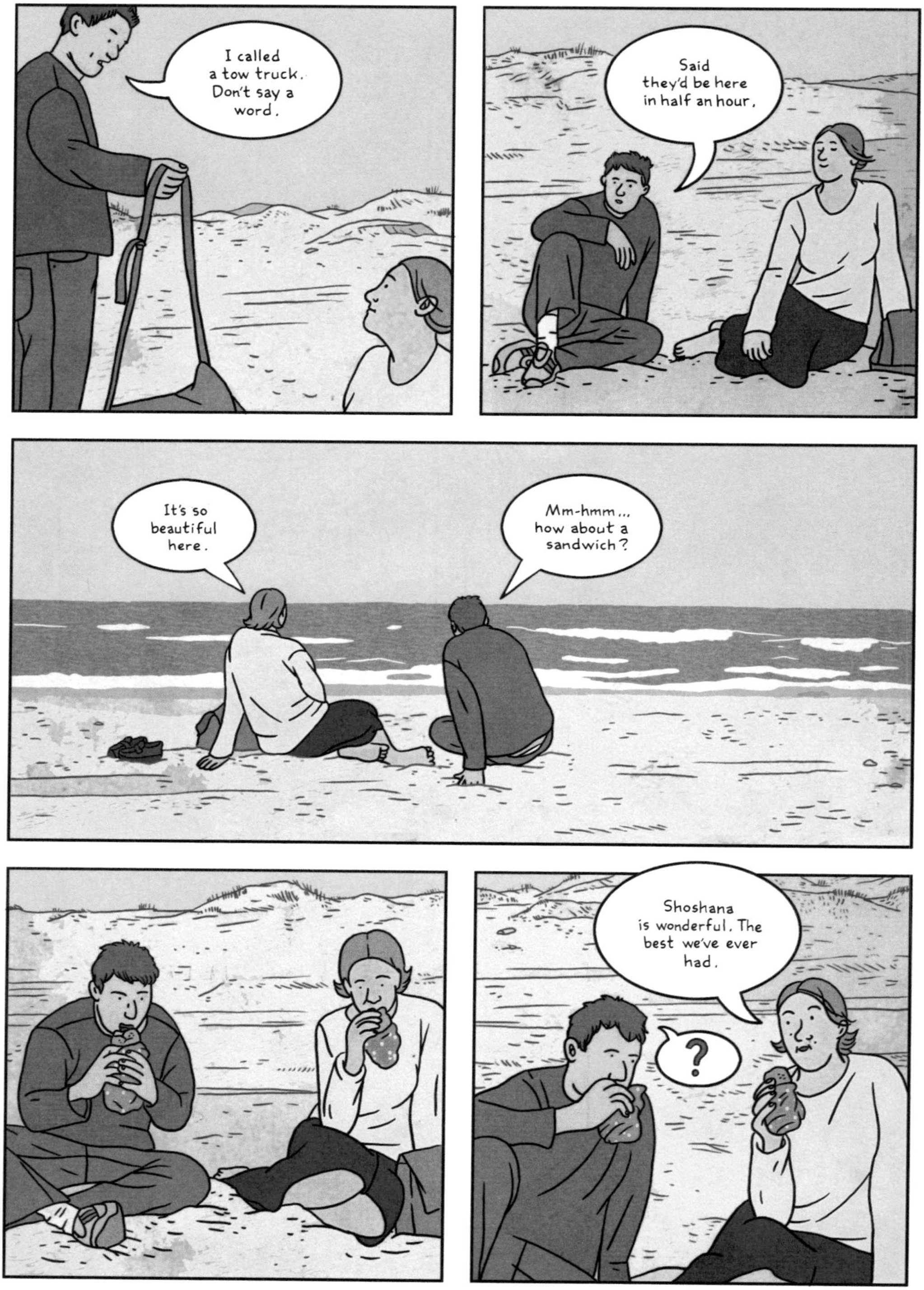
I called a tow truck. Don't say a word.
Said they'd be here in half an hour.
It's so beautiful here.
Mm-hmm... how about a sandwich?
Shoshana is wonderful. The best we've ever had.
?

Brrr...
How is it?
It's great! Come on in!
Don't look!
Liar! It's freezing!
Start swimming, you'll warm up.
Yeah, right.

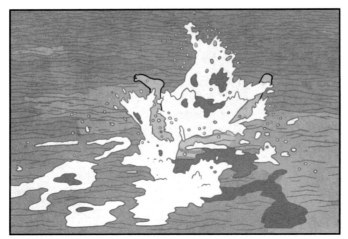

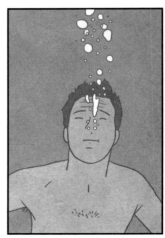

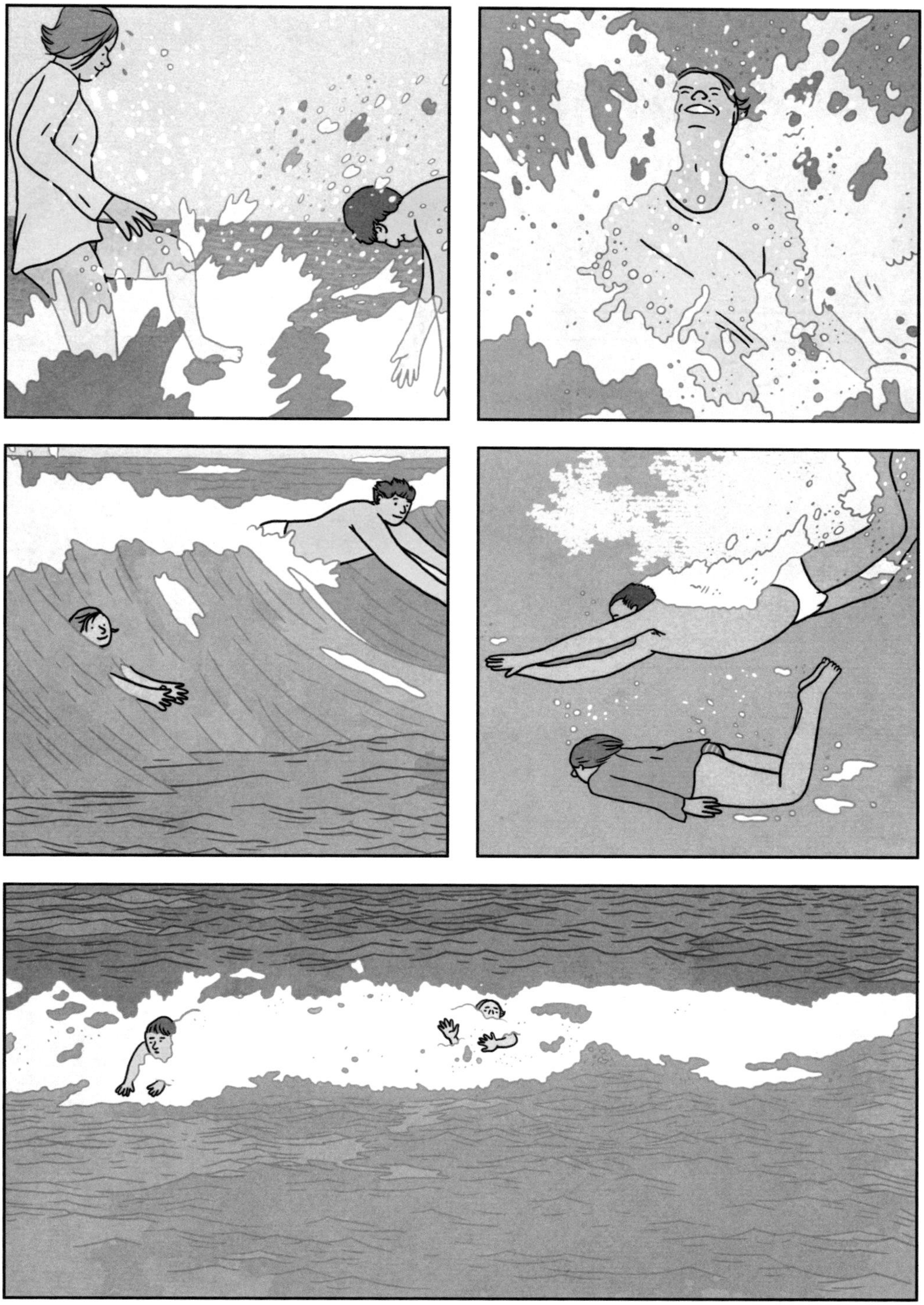

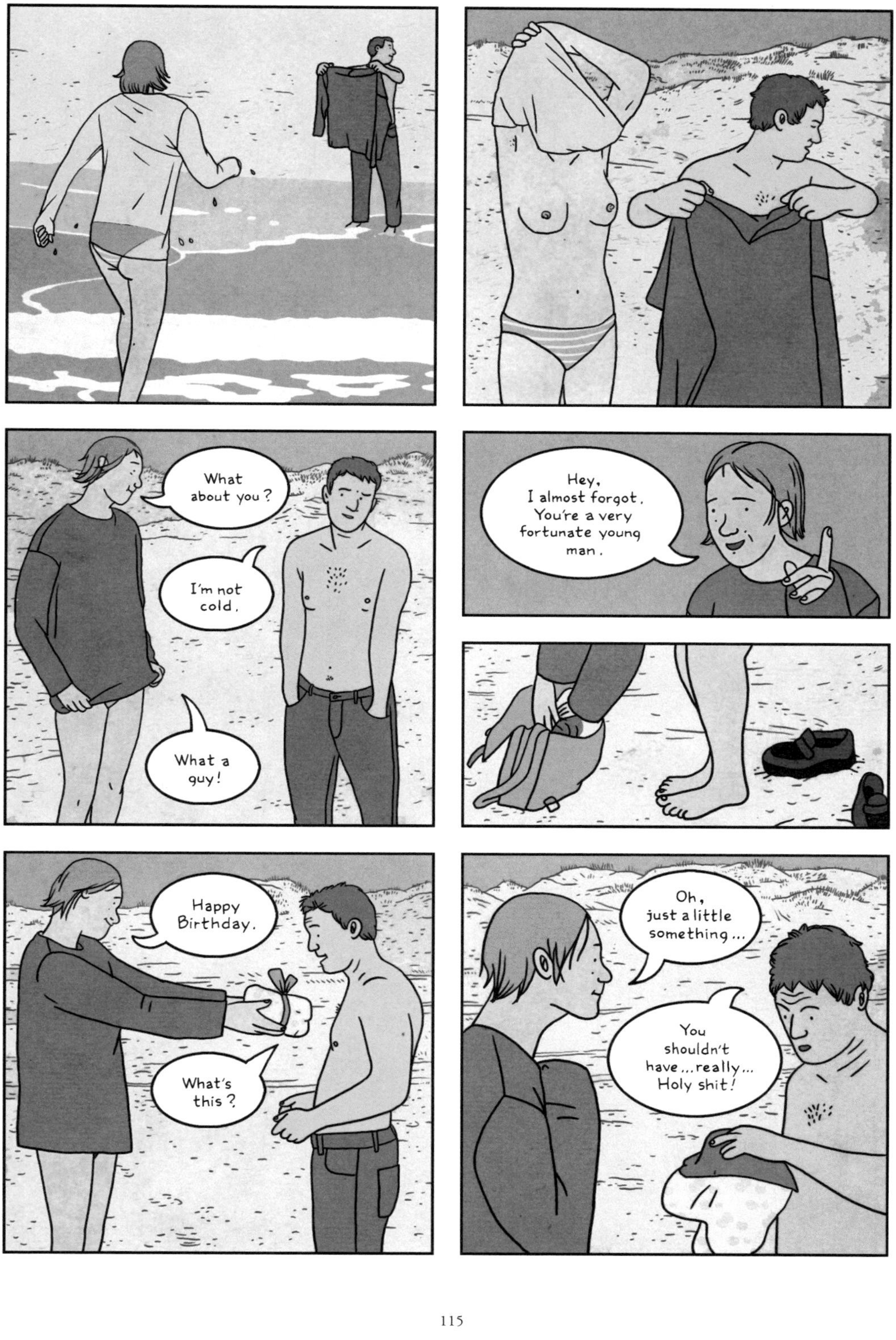
What about you?
I'm not cold.
What a guy!
Hey, I almost forgot. You're a very fortunate young man.
Happy Birthday.
What's this?
Oh, just a little something...
You shouldn't have...really... Holy shit!

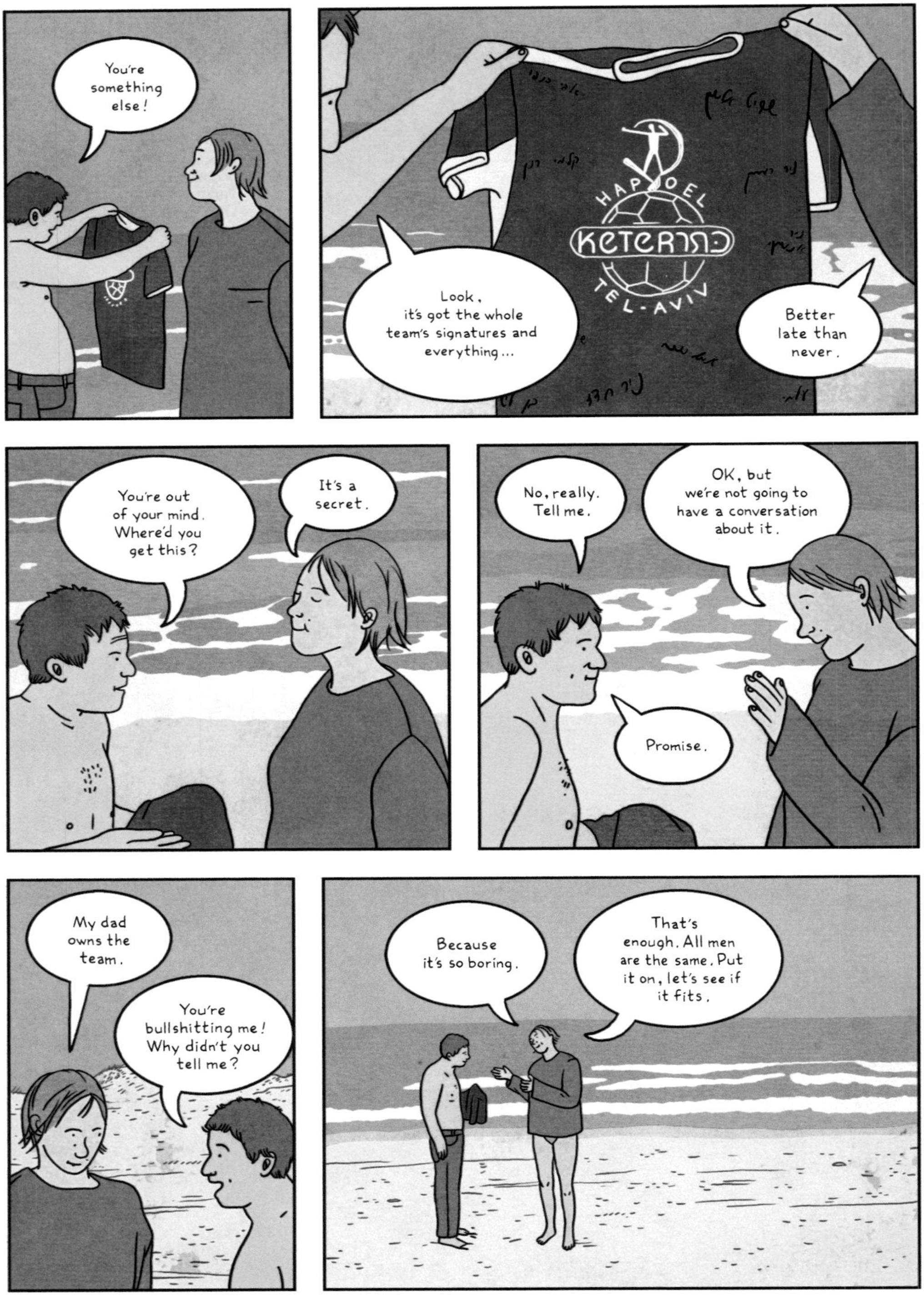
You're something else!
HAPOEL
KETER
TEL-AVIV
Look, it's got the whole team's signatures and everything...
Better late than never.
You're out of your mind. Where'd you get this?
It's a secret.
No, really. Tell me.
OK, but we're not going to have a conversation about it.
Promise.
My dad owns the team.
You're bullshitting me! Why didn't you tell me?
Because it's so boring.
That's enough. All men are the same. Put it on, let's see if it fits.

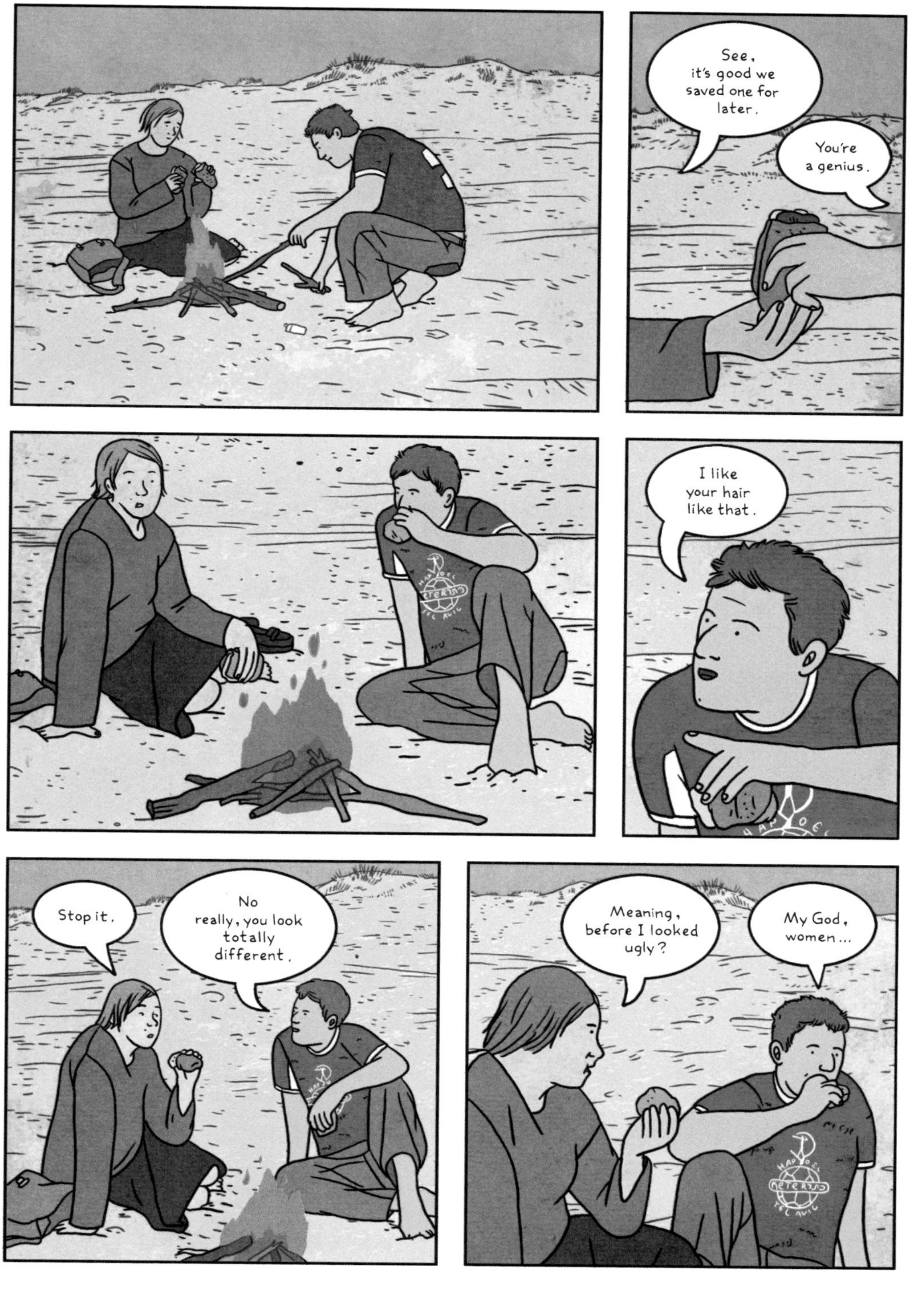
See, it's good we saved one for later.
You're a genius.
I like your hair like that.
Stop it.
No really, you look totally different.
Meaning, before I looked ugly?
My God, women...

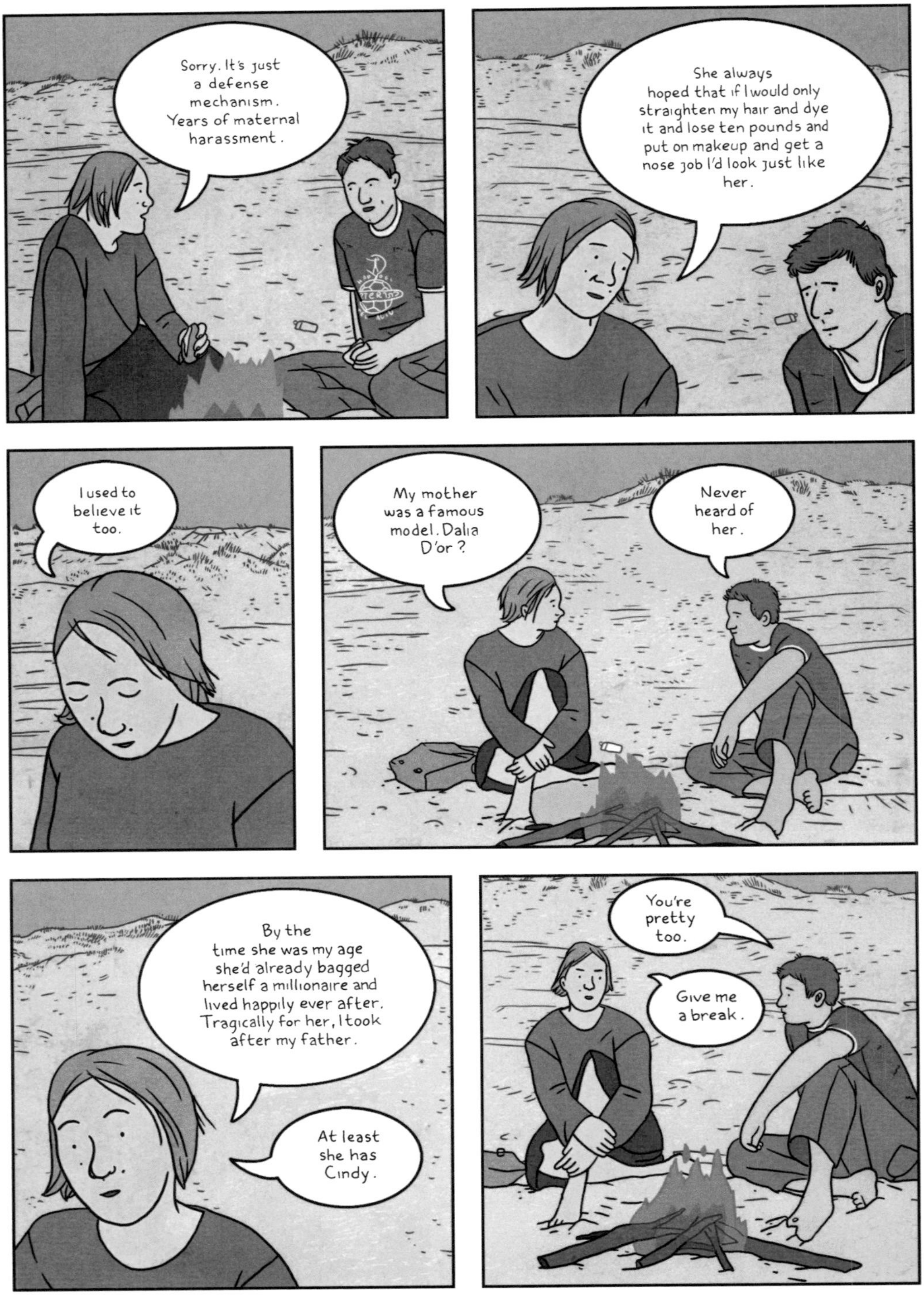
Sorry. It's just a defense mechanism. Years of maternal harassment.
She always hoped that if I would only straighten my hair and dye it and lose ten pounds and put on makeup and get a nose job I'd look just like her.
I used to believe it too.
My mother was a famous model. Dalia D'or?
Never heard of her.
By the time she was my age she'd already bagged herself a millionaire and lived happily ever after. Tragically for her, I took after my father.
At least she has Cindy.
You're pretty too.
Give me a break.

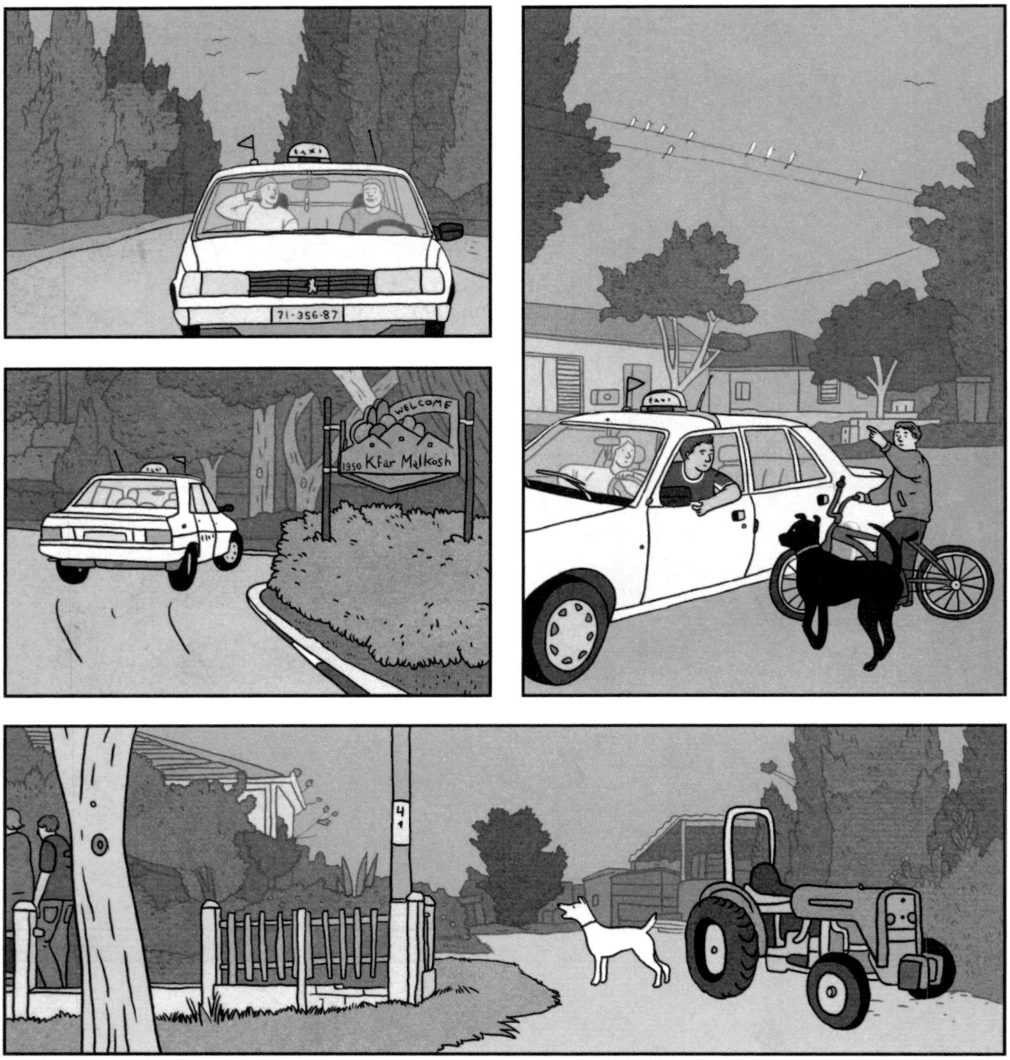
71-356-87
WELCOME
1950 Kfar Malkosh
DAYAN
Good evening.

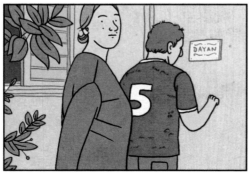

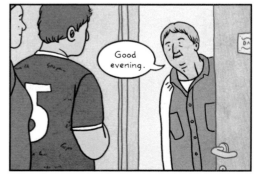

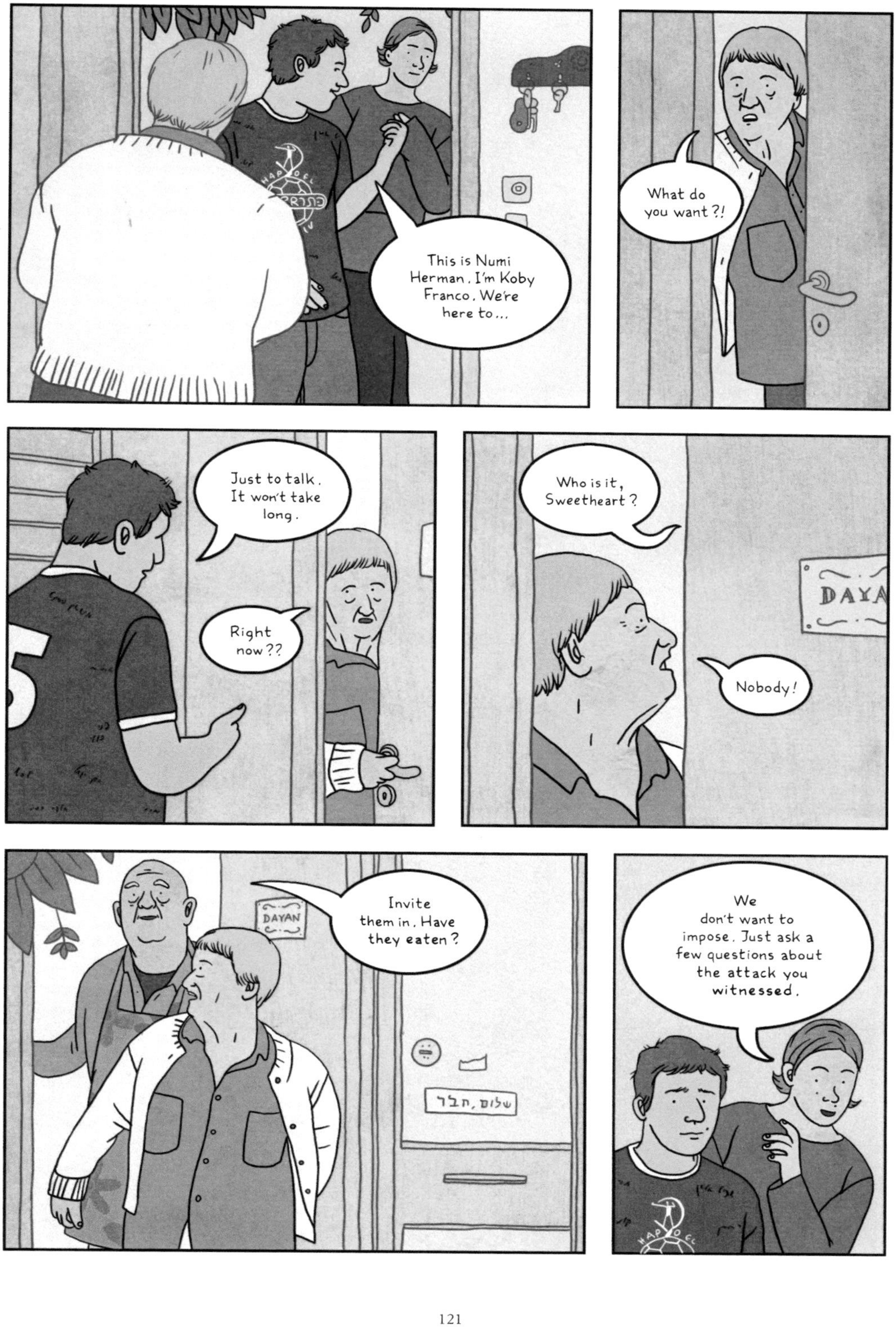
This is Numi Herman. I'm Koby Franco. We're here to...
What do you want?!
Just to talk. It won't take long.
Right now??
Who is it, Sweetheart?
Nobody!
DAYAN
Invite them in. Have they eaten?
שלום, חבר
We don't want to impose. Just ask a few questions about the attack you witnessed.

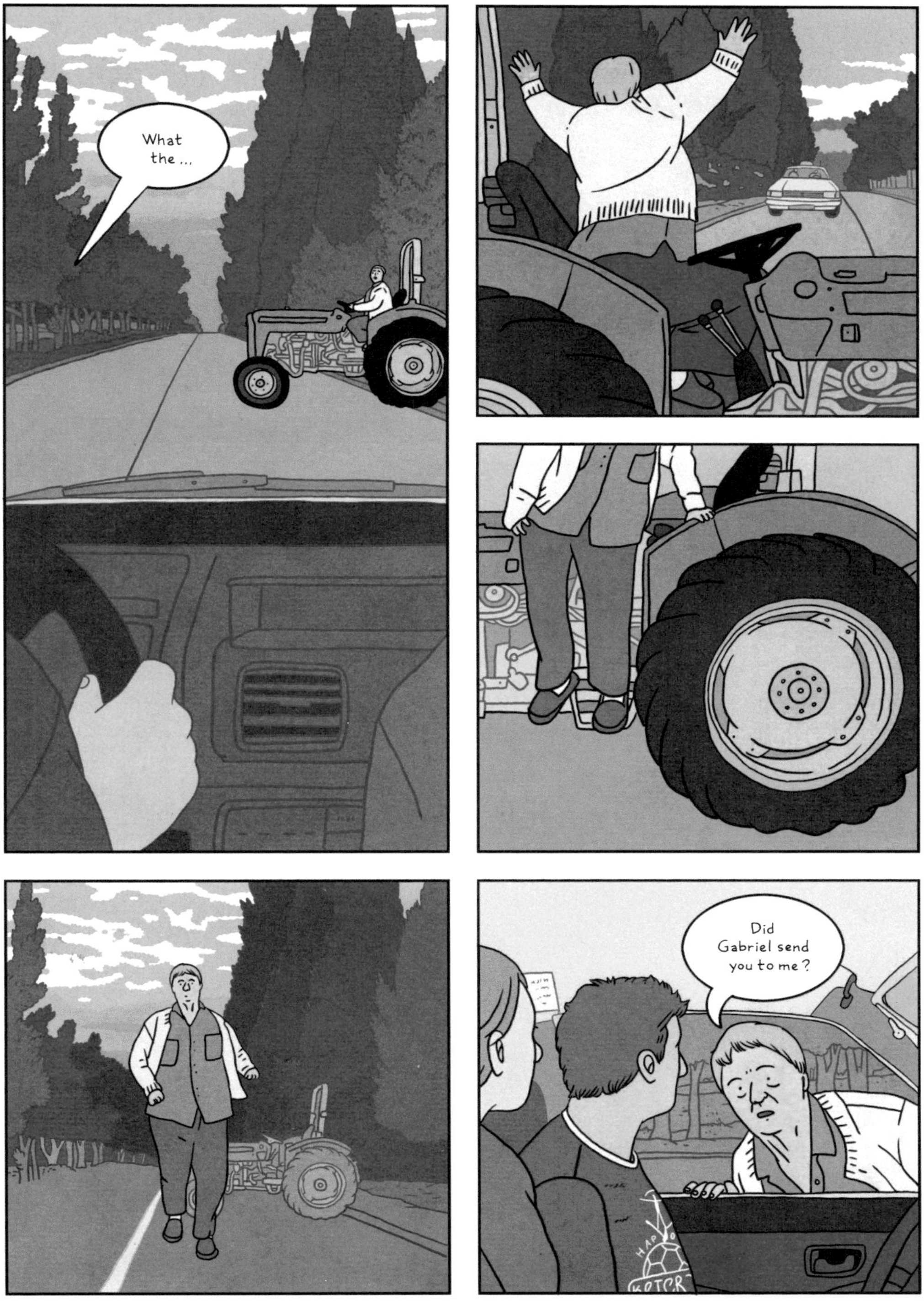
What the ...
Did Gabriel send you to me?

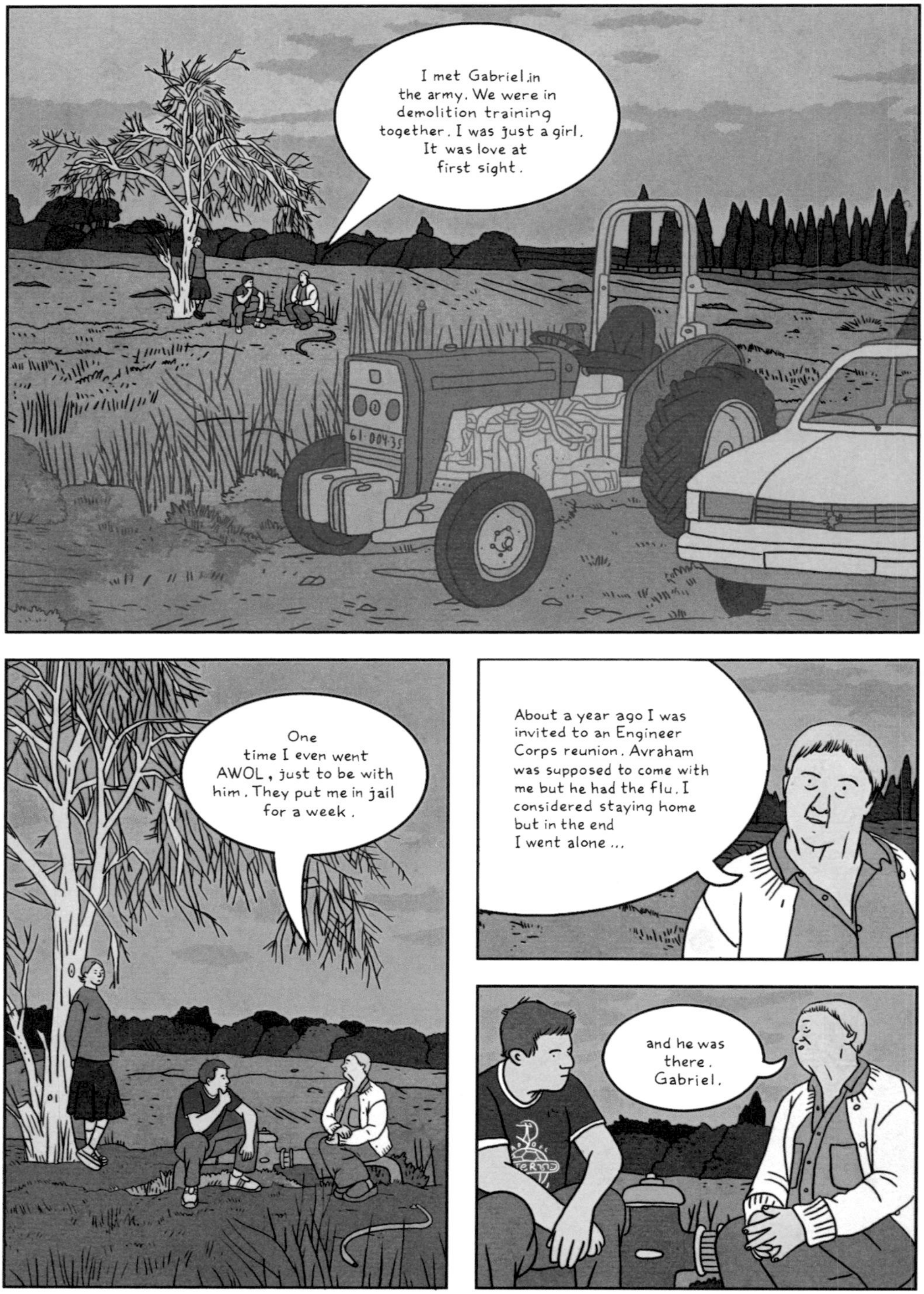
I met Gabriel in the army. We were in demolition training together. I was just a girl. It was love at first sight.
61-004-35
One time I even went AWOL, just to be with him. They put me in jail for a week.
About a year ago I was invited to an Engineer Corps reunion. Avraham was supposed to come with me but he had the flu. I considered staying home but in the end I went alone...
and he was there. Gabriel.

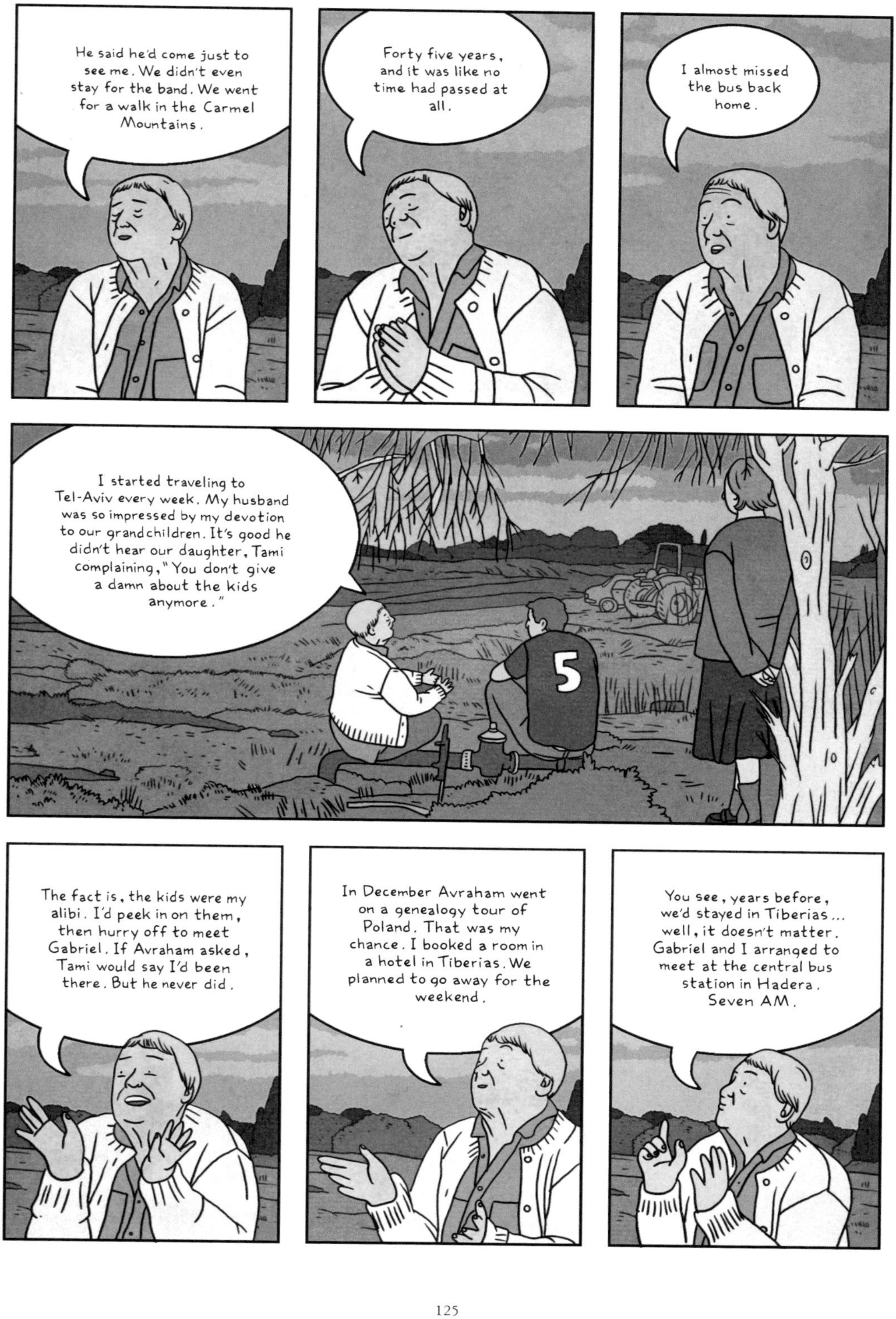
He said he'd come just to see me. We didn't even stay for the band. We went for a walk in the Carmel Mountains.
Forty five years, and it was like no time had passed at all.
I almost missed the bus back home.
I started traveling to Tel-Aviv every week. My husband was so impressed by my devotion to our grandchildren. It's good he didn't hear our daughter, Tami complaining, "You don't give a damn about the kids anymore."
5
The fact is, the kids were my alibi. I'd peek in on them, then hurry off to meet Gabriel. If Avraham asked, Tami would say I'd been there. But he never did.
In December Avraham went on a genealogy tour of Poland. That was my chance. I booked a room in a hotel in Tiberias. We planned to go away for the weekend.
You see, years before, we'd stayed in Tiberias... well, it doesn't matter. Gabriel and I arranged to meet at the central bus station in Hadera. Seven AM.

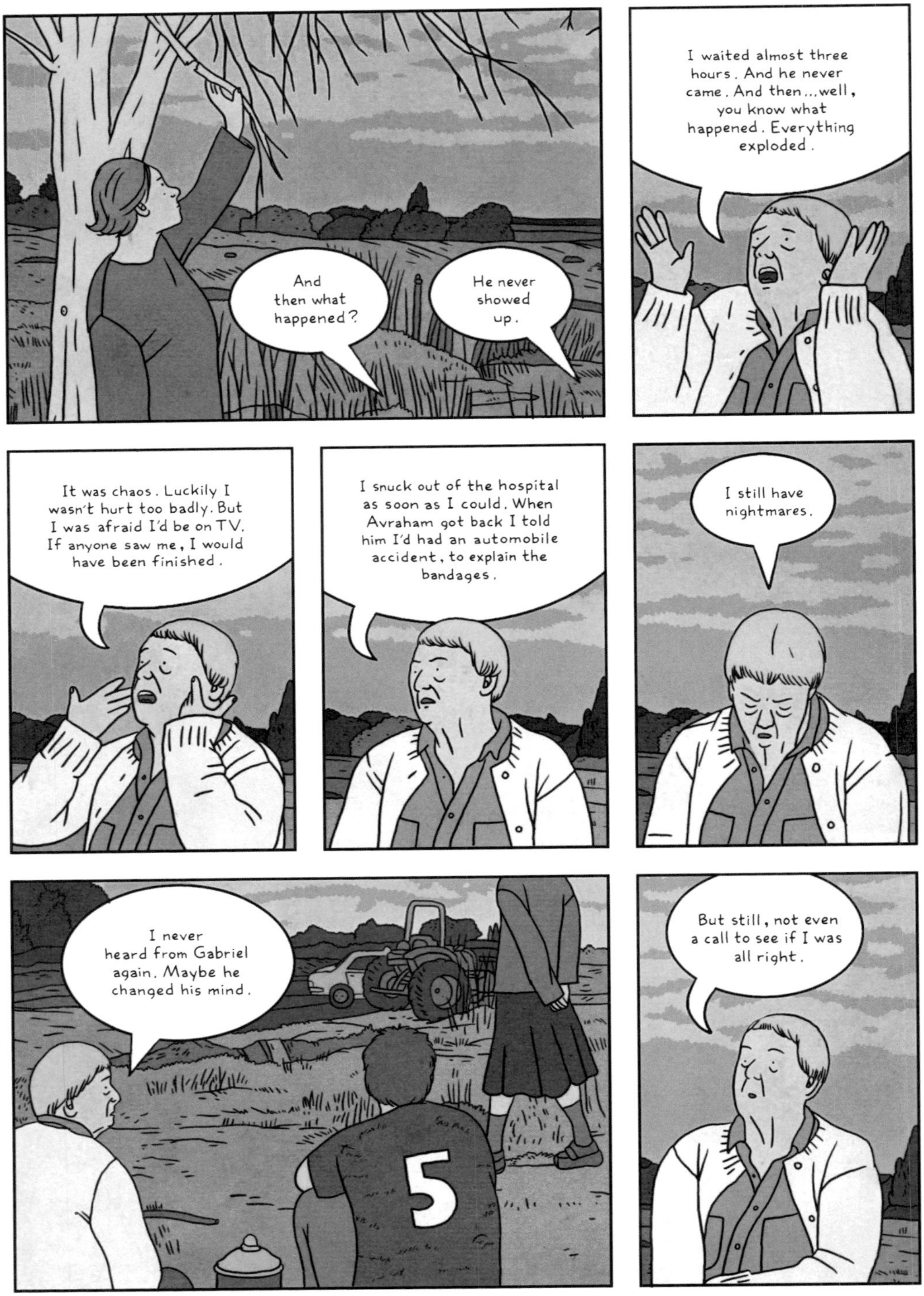
And then what happened?
He never showed up.
I waited almost three hours. And he never came. And then...well, you know what happened. Everything exploded.
It was chaos. Luckily I wasn't hurt too badly. But I was afraid I'd be on TV. If anyone saw me, I would have been finished.
I snuck out of the hospital as soon as I could. When Avraham got back I told him I'd had an automobile accident, to explain the bandages.
I still have nightmares.
I never heard from Gabriel again. Maybe he changed his mind.
5
But still, not even a call to see if I was all right.

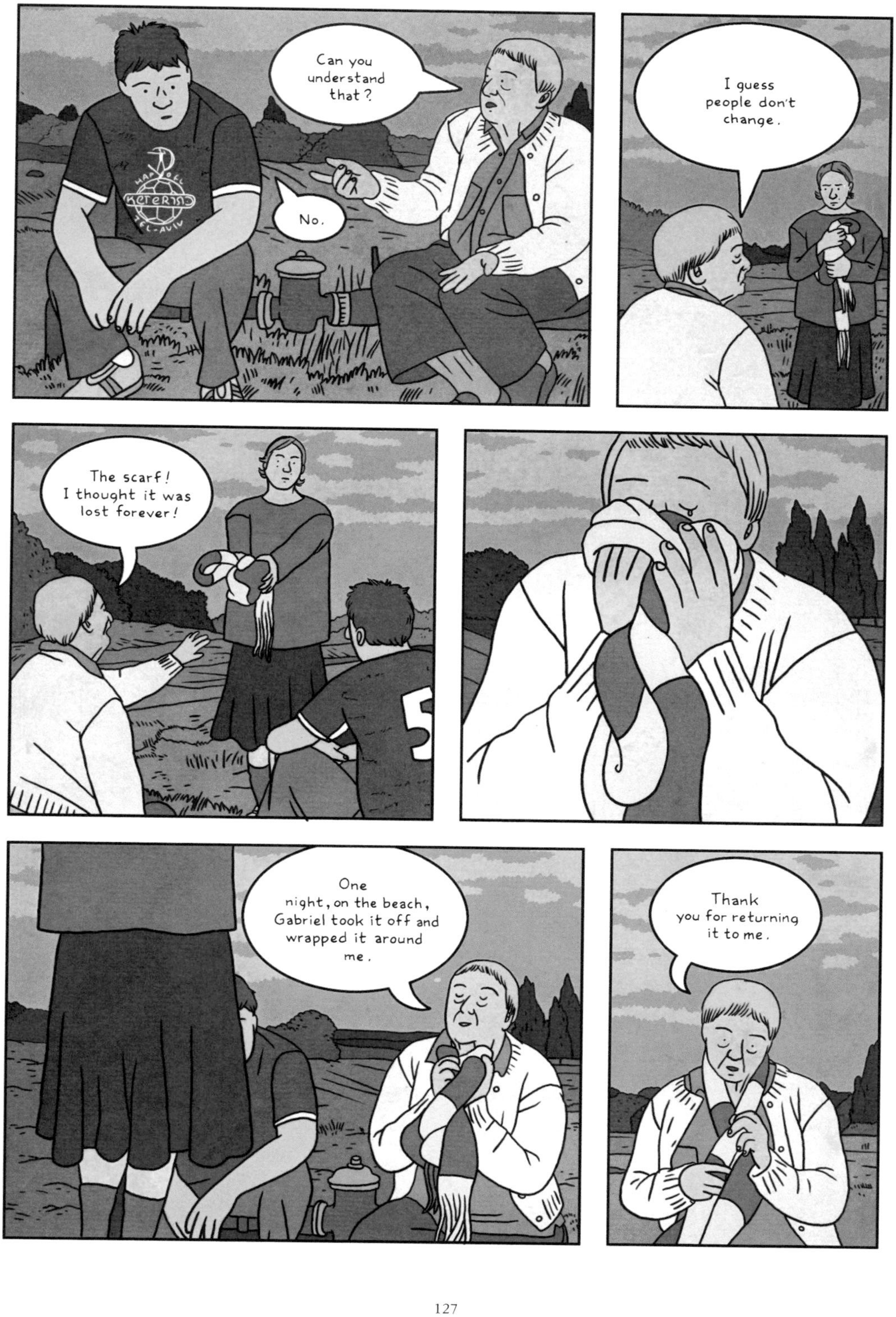
Can you understand that?
No.
I guess people don't change.
The scarf! I thought it was lost forever!
One night, on the beach, Gabriel took it off and wrapped it around me.
Thank you for returning it to me.

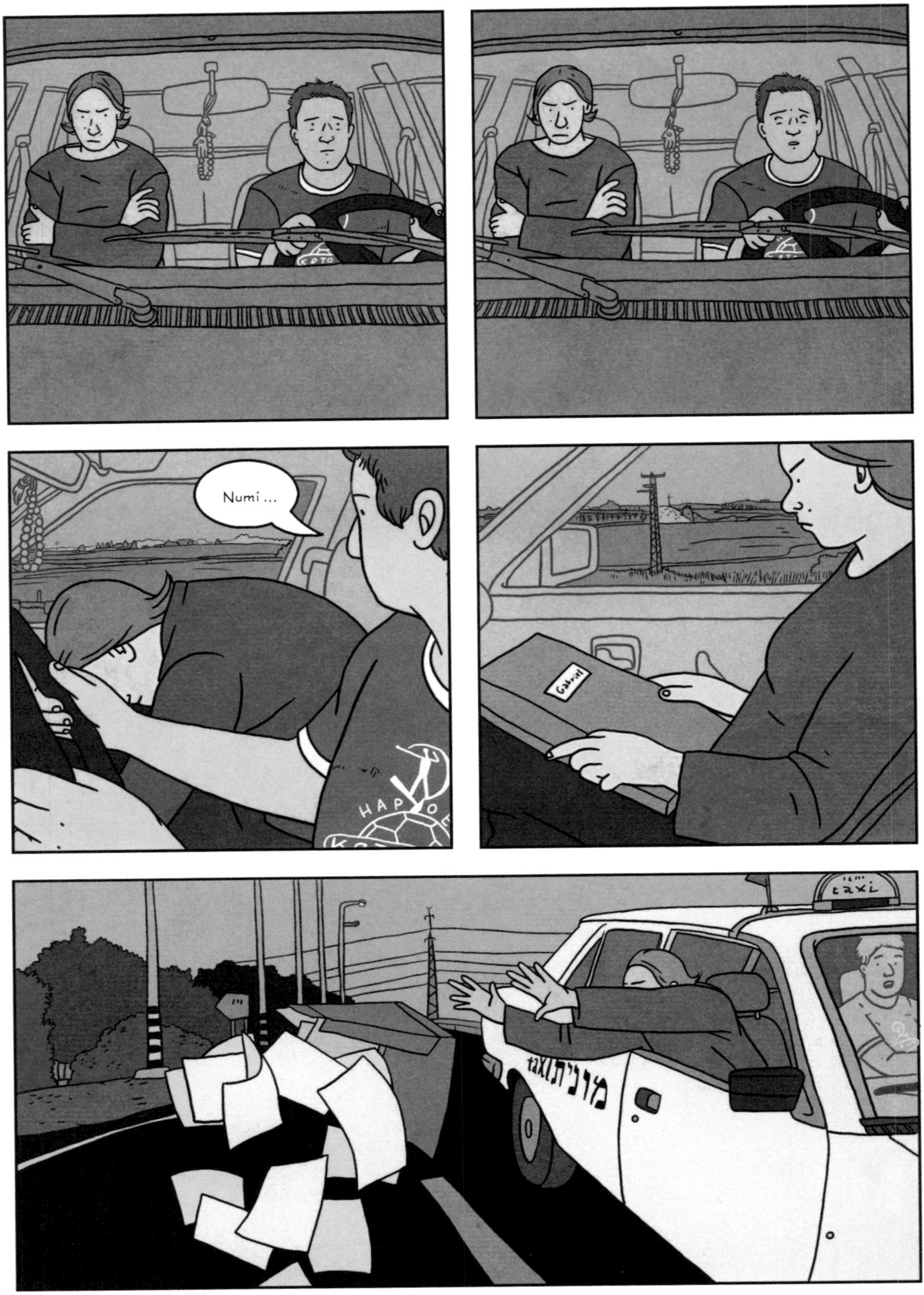
Numi ...
Gabriel
taxi
מונית taxi

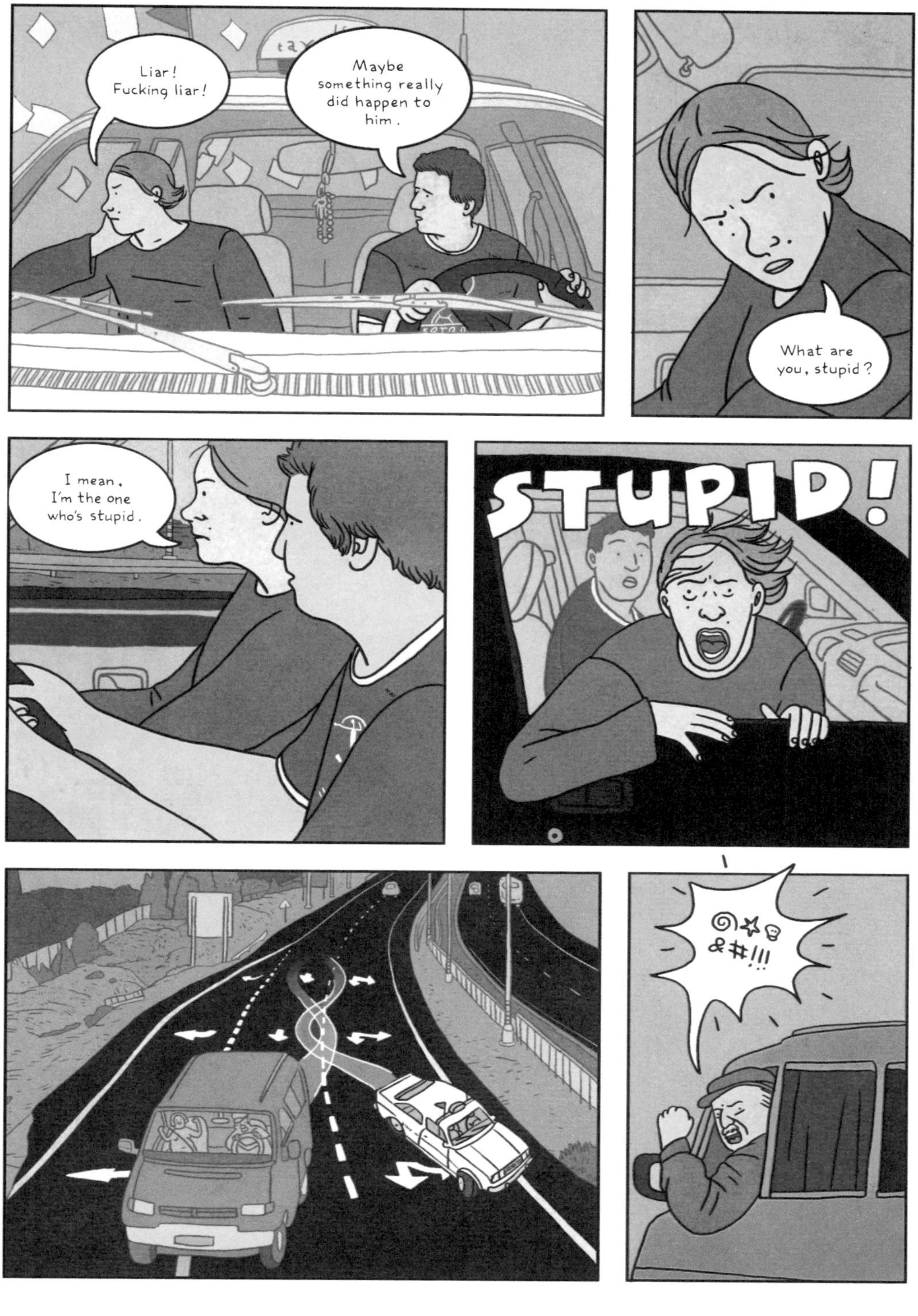
Liar! Fucking liar!
Maybe something really did happen to him.
What are you, stupid?
I mean, I'm the one who's stupid.
STUPID!
&#!!!

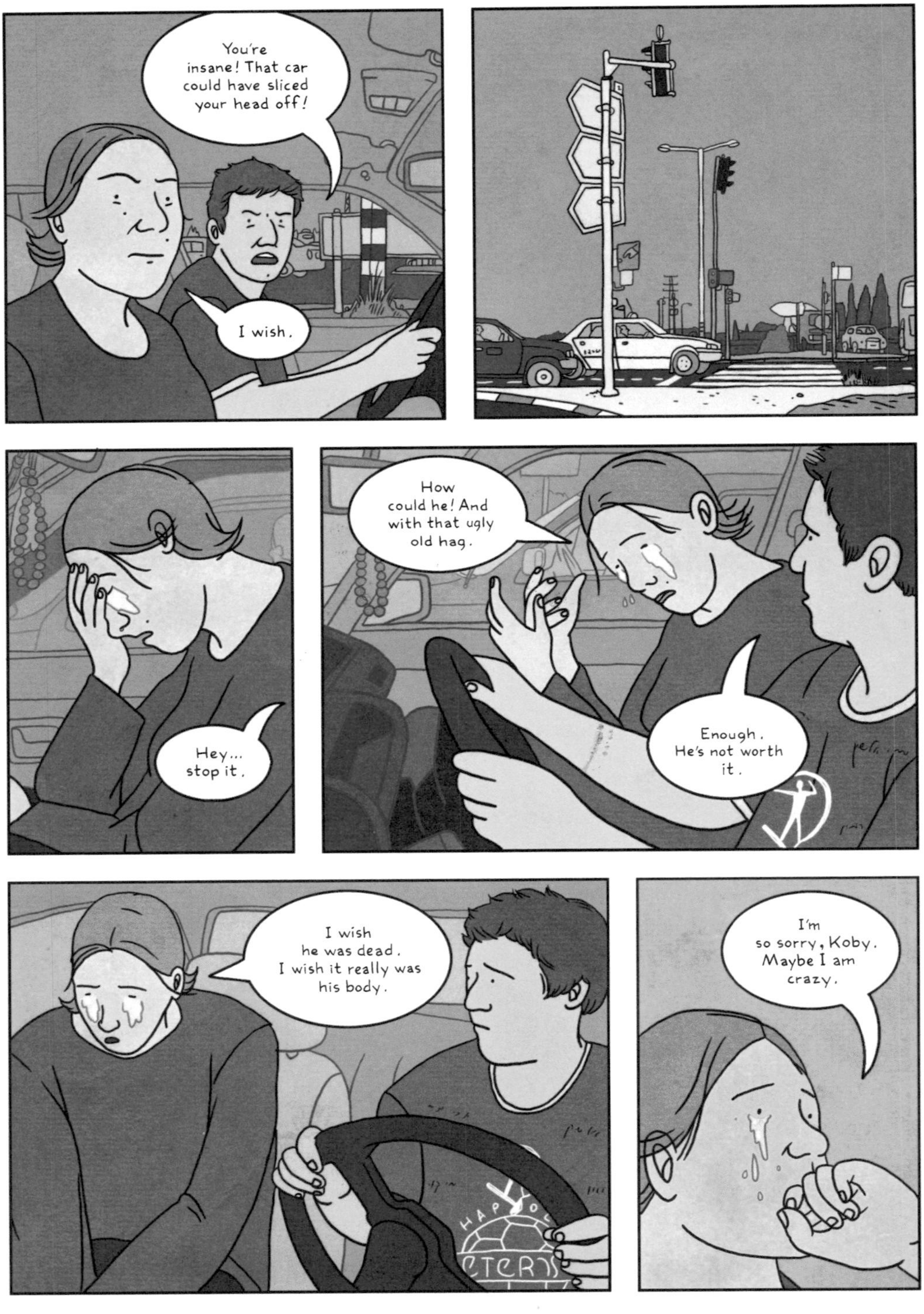
You're insane! That car could have sliced your head off!
I wish.
Hey... stop it.
How could he! And with that ugly old hag.
Enough. He's not worth it.
I wish he was dead. I wish it really was his body.
I'm so sorry, Koby. Maybe I am crazy.

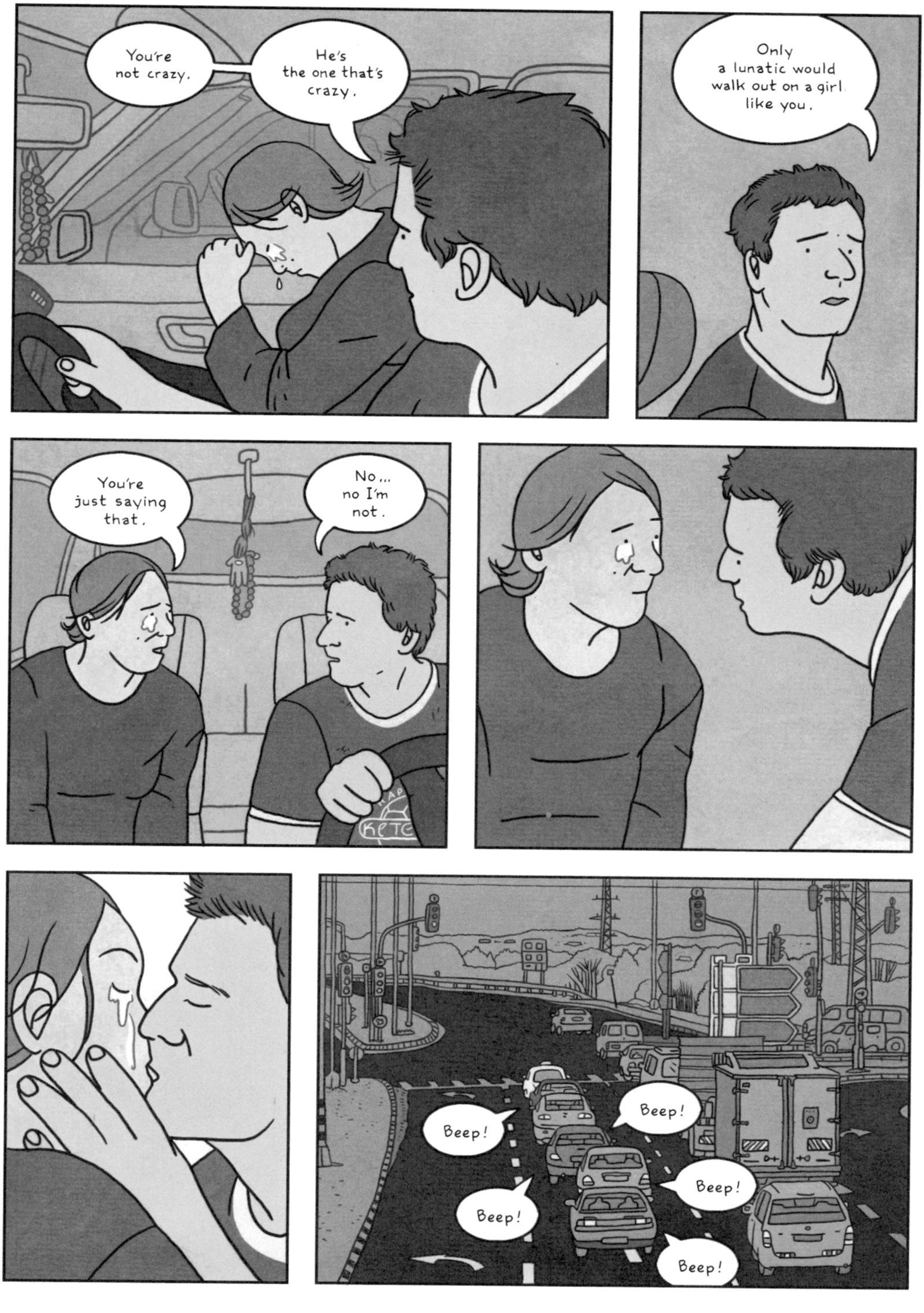
You're not crazy.
He's the one that's crazy.
Only a lunatic would walk out on a girl like you.
You're just saying that.
No... no I'm not.
Beep!
Beep!
Beep!
Beep!
Beep!

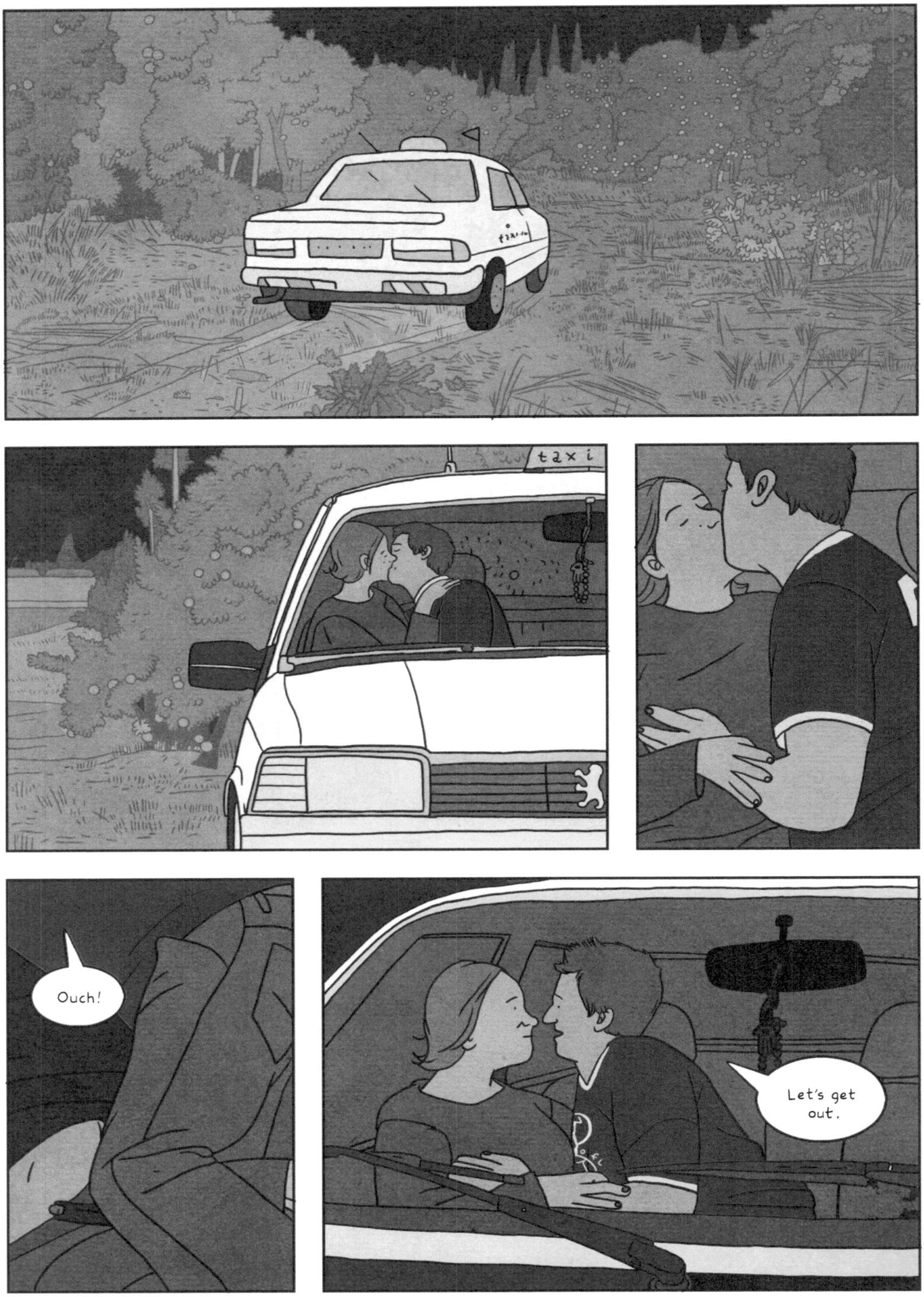
taxi
Ouch!
Let's get out.

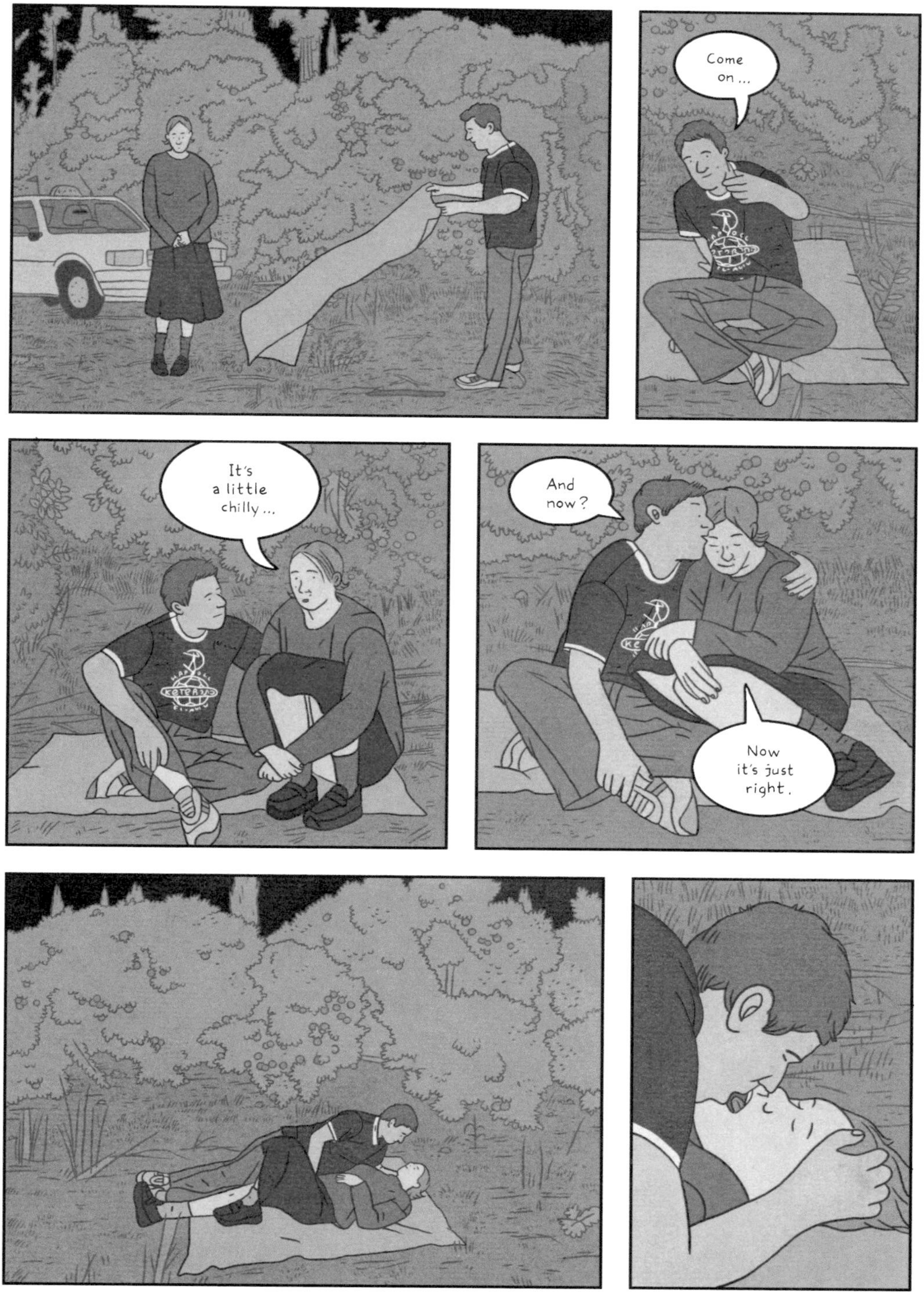
Come on ...
It's a little chilly ...
And now?
Now it's just right.

It's like being fifteen again ... doing it with your clothes on.
Stop ... don't look.

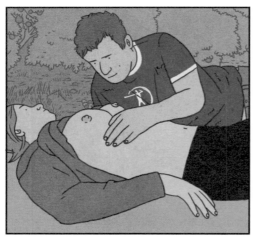

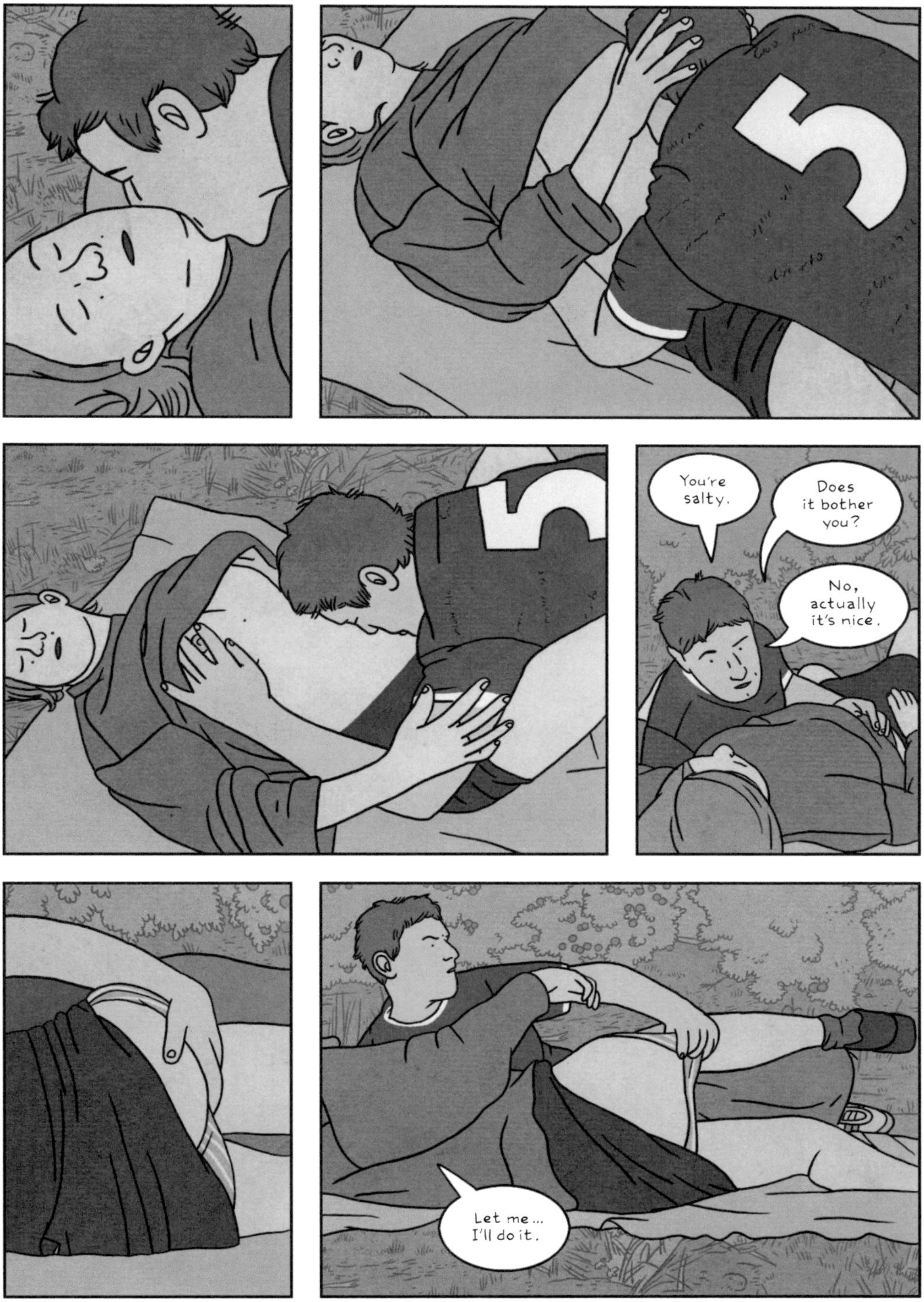
You're salty.
Does it bother you?
No, actually it's nice.
Let me... I'll do it.

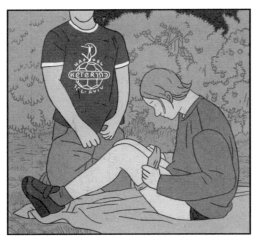

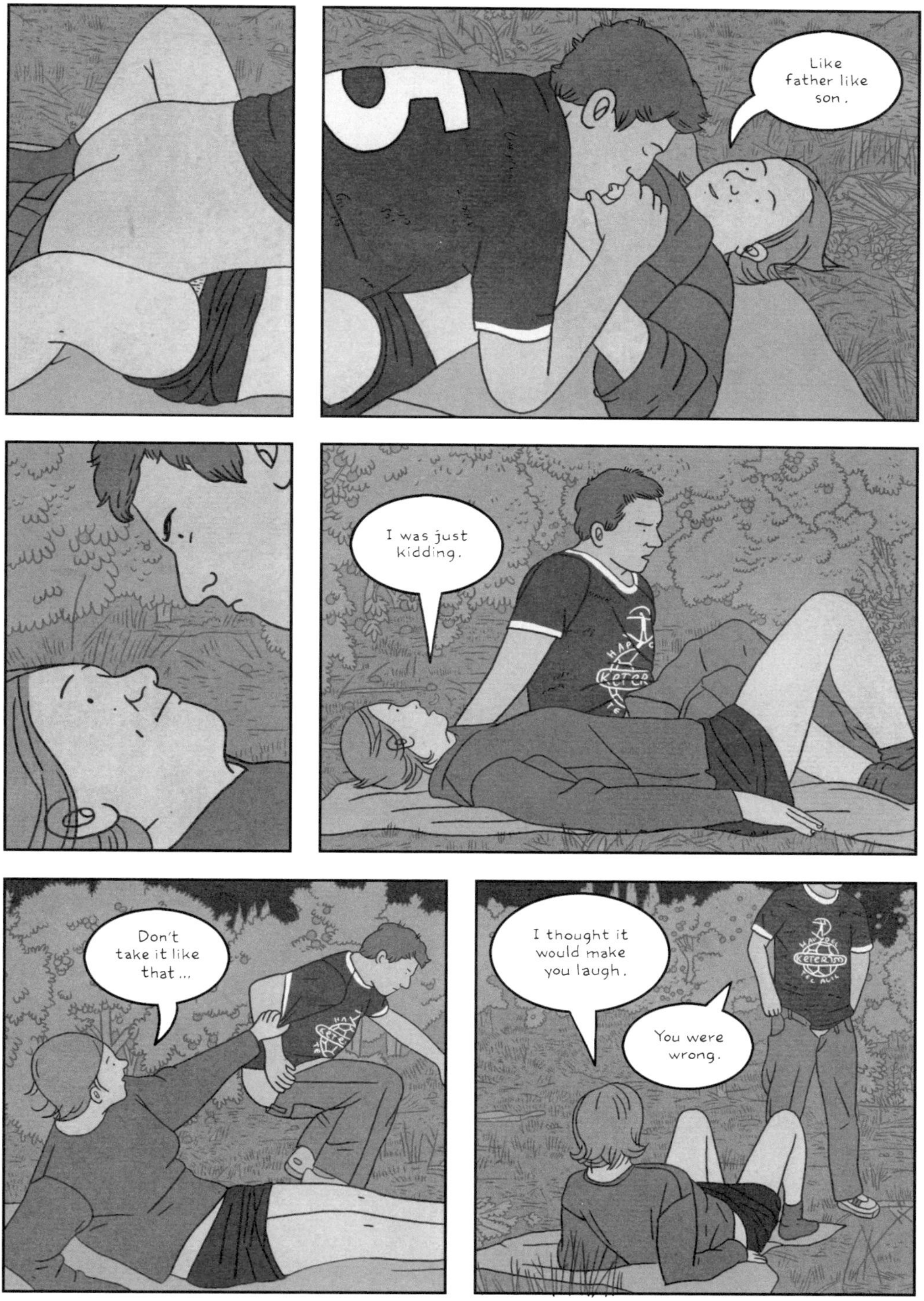

Like father like son.
I was just kidding.
Don't take it like that...
I thought it would make you laugh.
You were wrong.

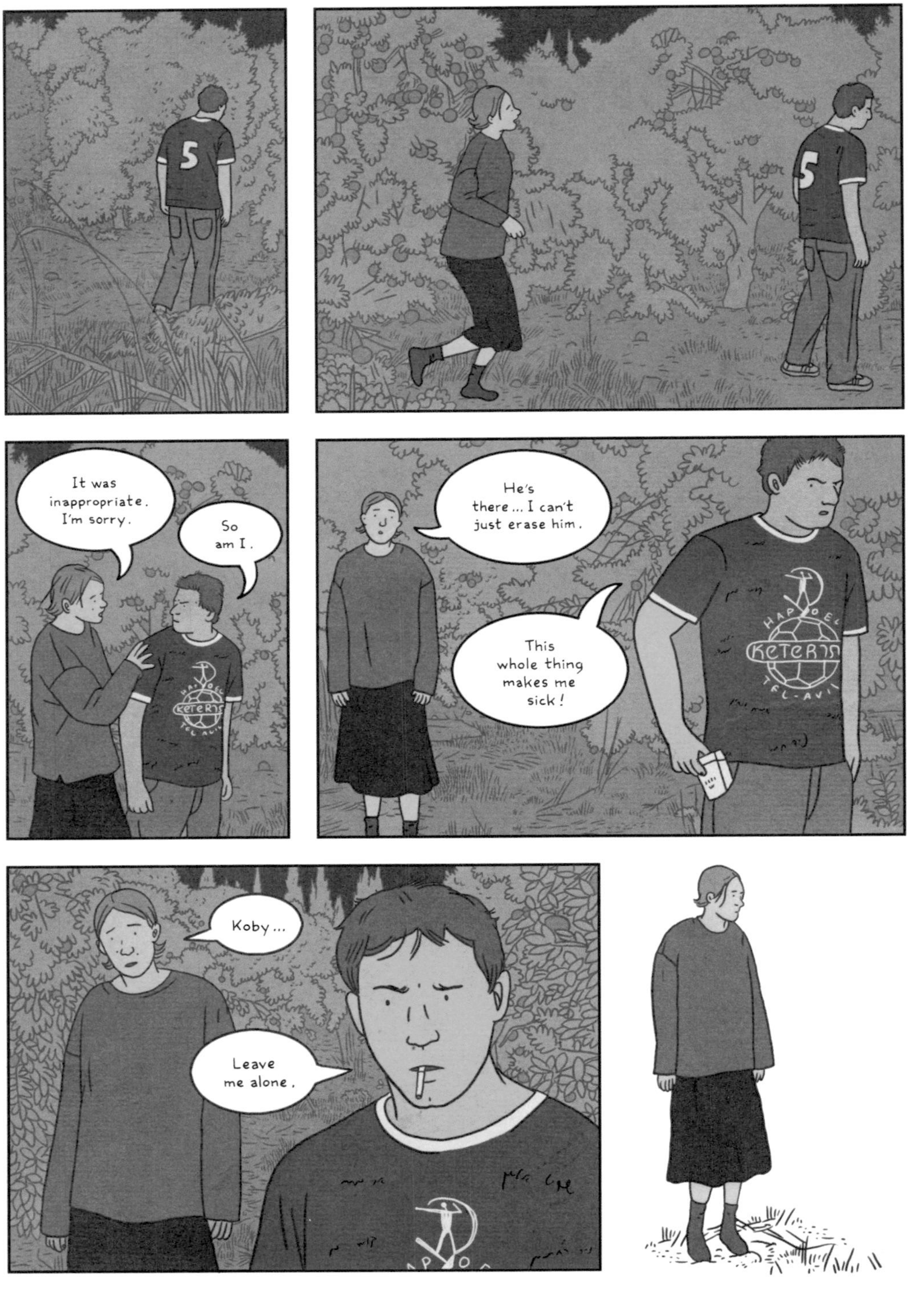
It was inappropriate. I'm sorry.
So am I.
He's there... I can't just erase him.
This whole thing makes me sick!
Koby...
Leave me alone.

HAPOEL

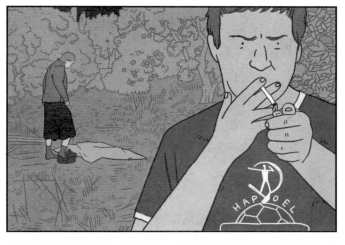

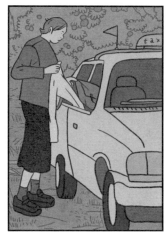

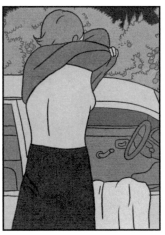

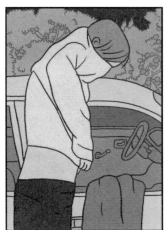

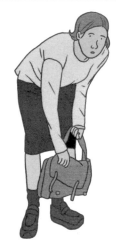

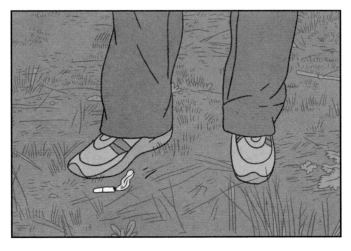

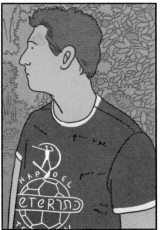

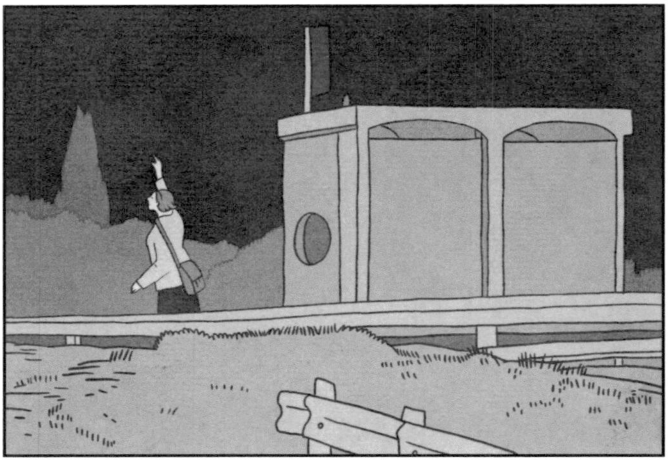

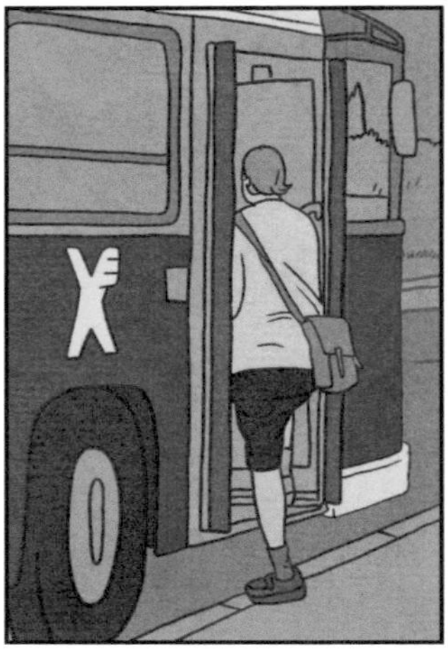

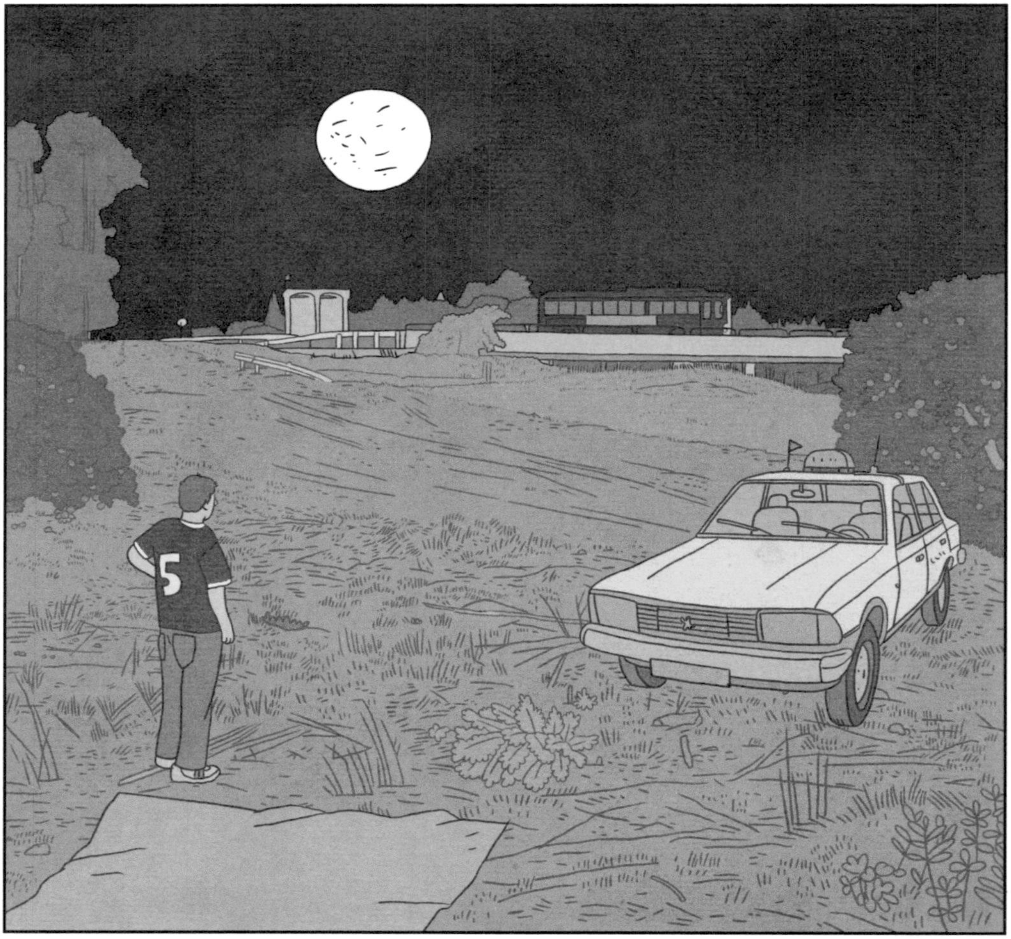

chapter four
resurrection

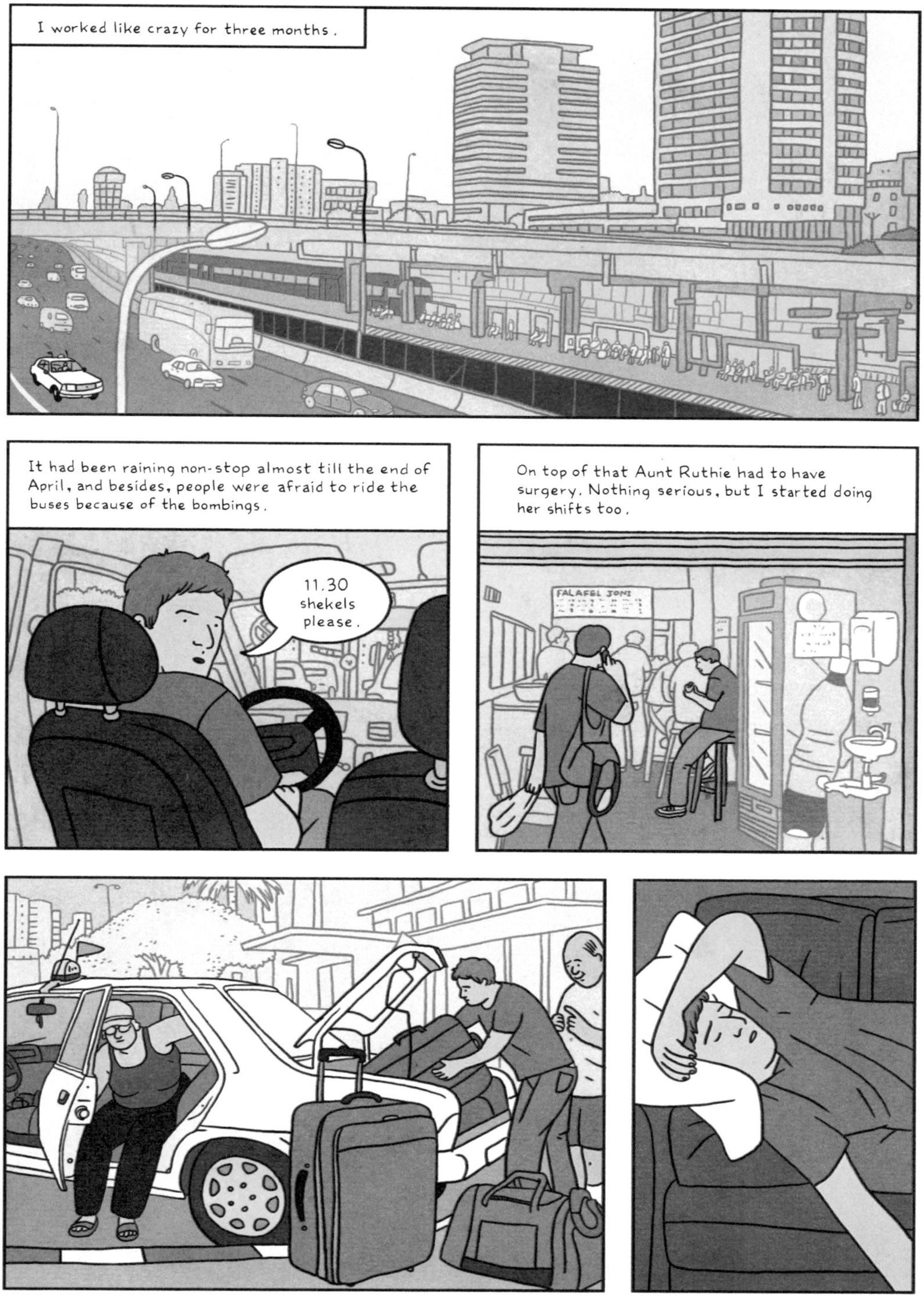
I worked like crazy for three months.
It had been raining non-stop almost till the end of April, and besides, people were afraid to ride the buses because of the bombings.
11.30 shekels please.
On top of that Aunt Ruthie had to have surgery. Nothing serious, but I started doing her shifts too.
FALAFEL JONI

One day, the mysterious
case of the unidentified
corpse came to a close.

Shuki Taasa, a heavy gambler, had gone camping by the sea
of Galilee, without telling anyone.

His kids were sure he'd gone underground, hiding from
loansharks.

It took them a couple of months
to figure out that something
must have happened to him.

I watched on TV while they dug up his body from the grave
that Numi had cleaned so diligently all those months ago.

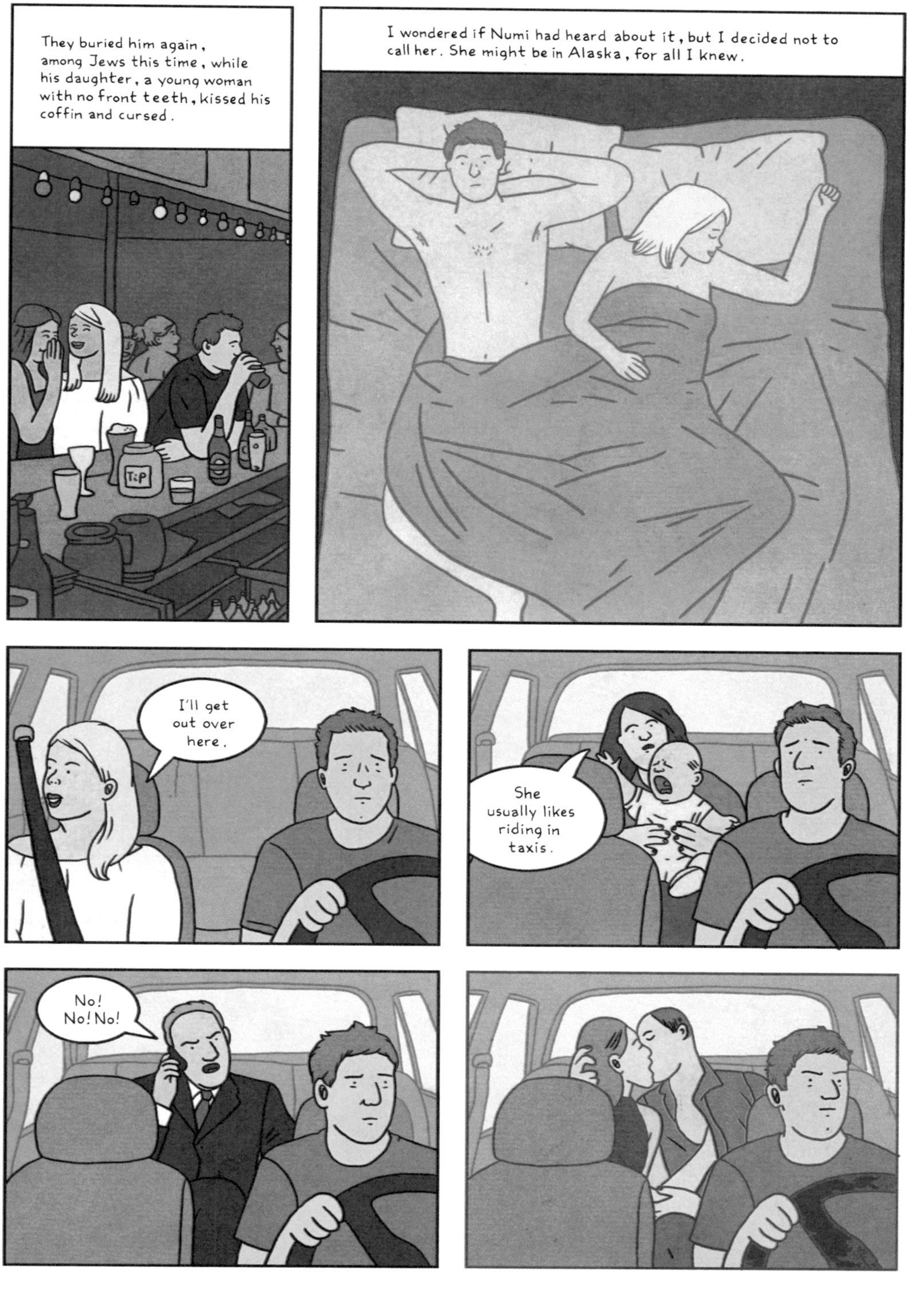
They buried him again, among Jews this time, while his daughter, a young woman with no front teeth, kissed his coffin and cursed.
TIP
I wondered if Numi had heard about it, but I decided not to call her. She might be in Alaska, for all I knew.
I'll get out over here.
She usually likes riding in taxis.
No! No! No!

I developed a theory, as yet unfounded, that my father had been having an affair with Aunt Ruthie.

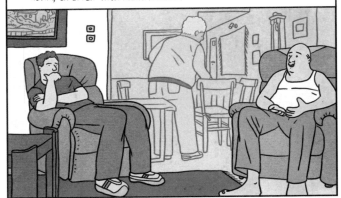

Despite her eternal animosity towards him - or maybe because of it ... it explains too many things.

I don't have any proof, but that time, long ago, when he kicked me out of his house, he had been so uptight. And Aunt Ruthie had been there, after all.

The way I see it now, if i'd showed up just fifteen minutes earlier I might have caught them in the act.

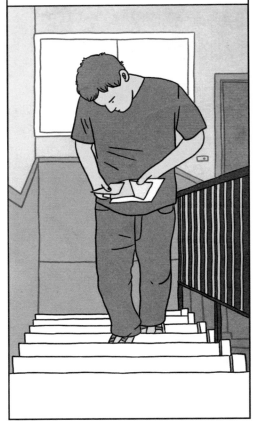

To:
Kobi Franco
30 Feirberg st.
Tel-Aviv 63827

Shapira & Gliksman Associates
Lilenblum 16 Tel-Aviv Tel. 03-6850159   6850934

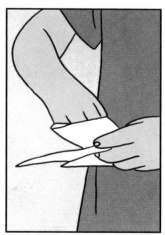

בנק לאומי
bank leumi
FRANCO GABRIEL
PAY Kobi Franco
176,000xx
One hundred Seventy six thousand shekels
N.I.S
5/6/2002
DATE
G. Franco
SIGNATURE
What the fuck!

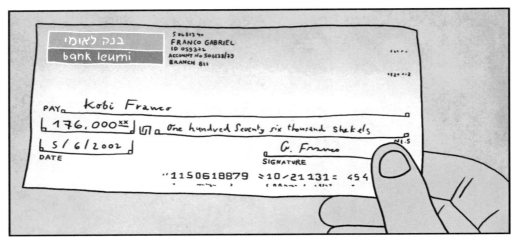

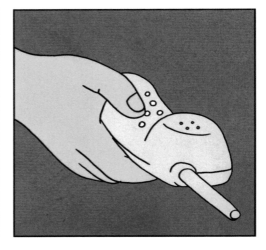

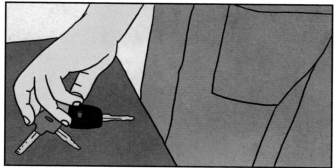

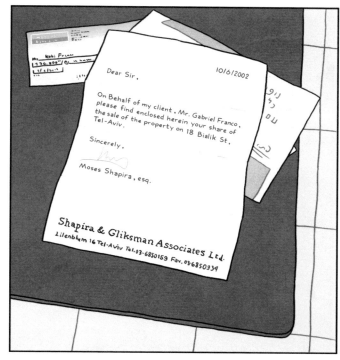

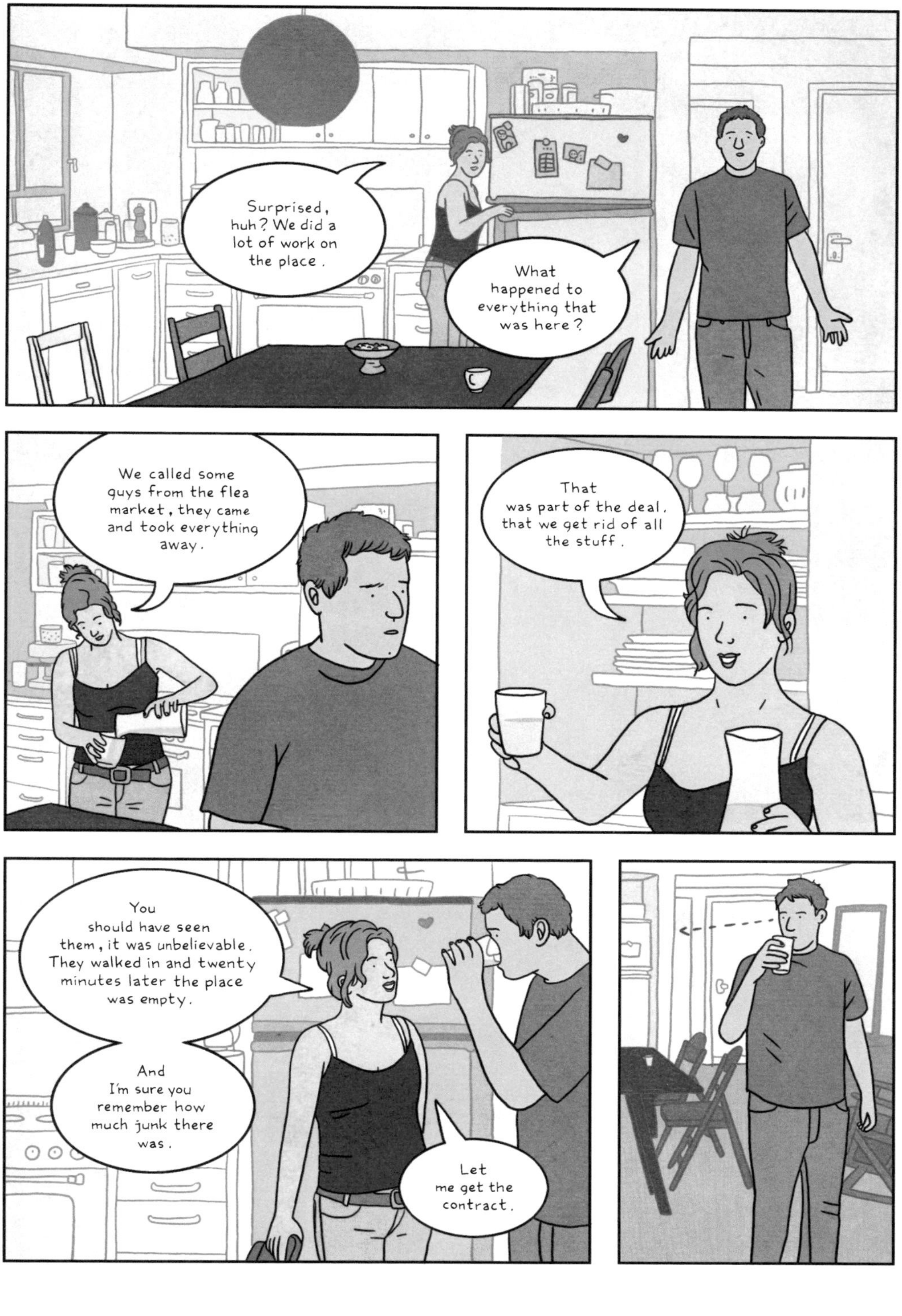
Surprised, huh? We did a lot of work on the place.
What happened to everything that was here?
We called some guys from the flea market, they came and took everything away.
That was part of the deal, that we get rid of all the stuff.
You should have seen them, it was unbelievable. They walked in and twenty minutes later the place was empty.
And I'm sure you remember how much junk there was.
Let me get the contract.

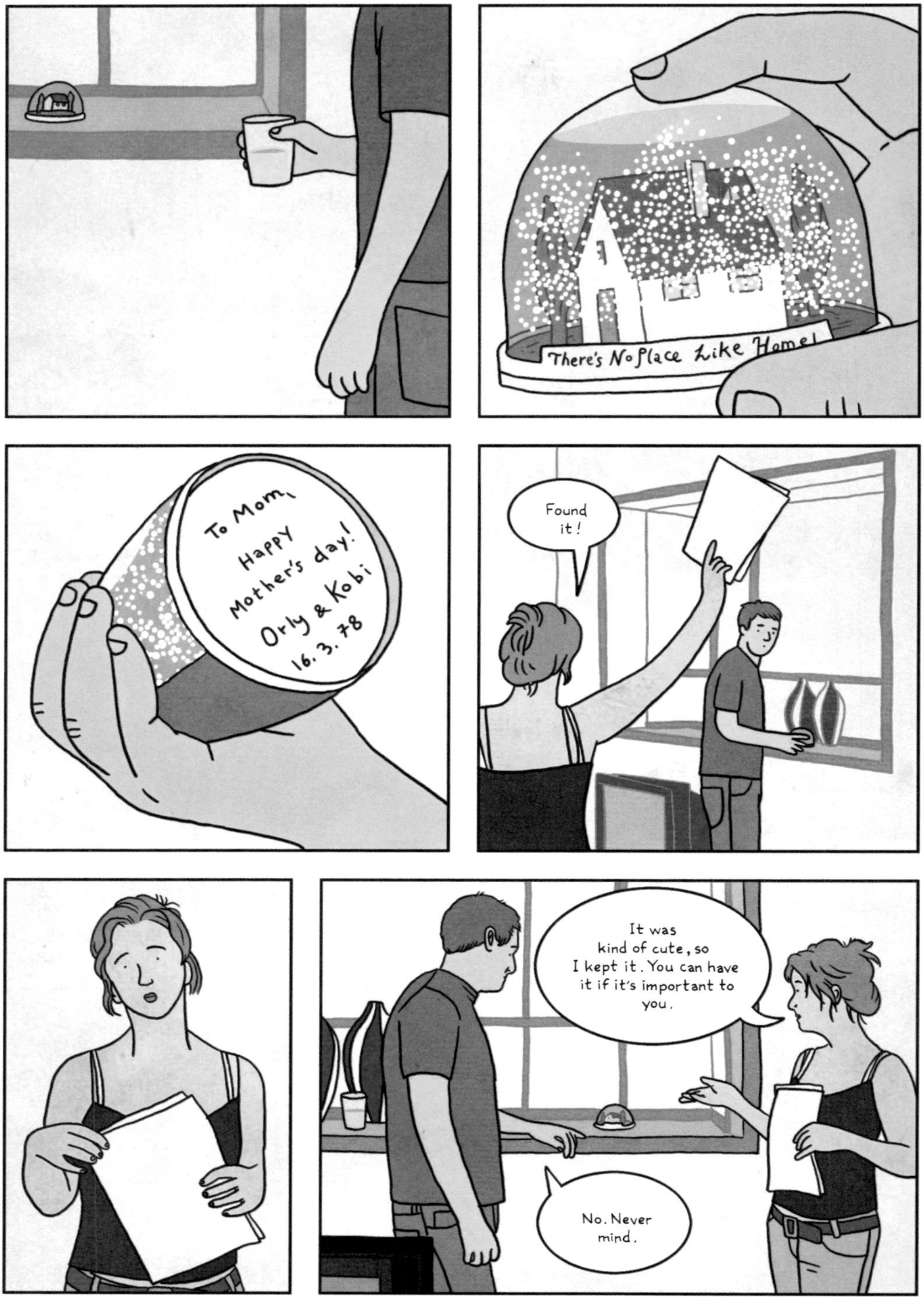
There's No Place Like Home!
To Mom,
Happy Mother's day!
Orly & Kobi
16.3.78
Found it!
It was kind of cute, so I kept it. You can have it if it's important to you.
No. Never mind.

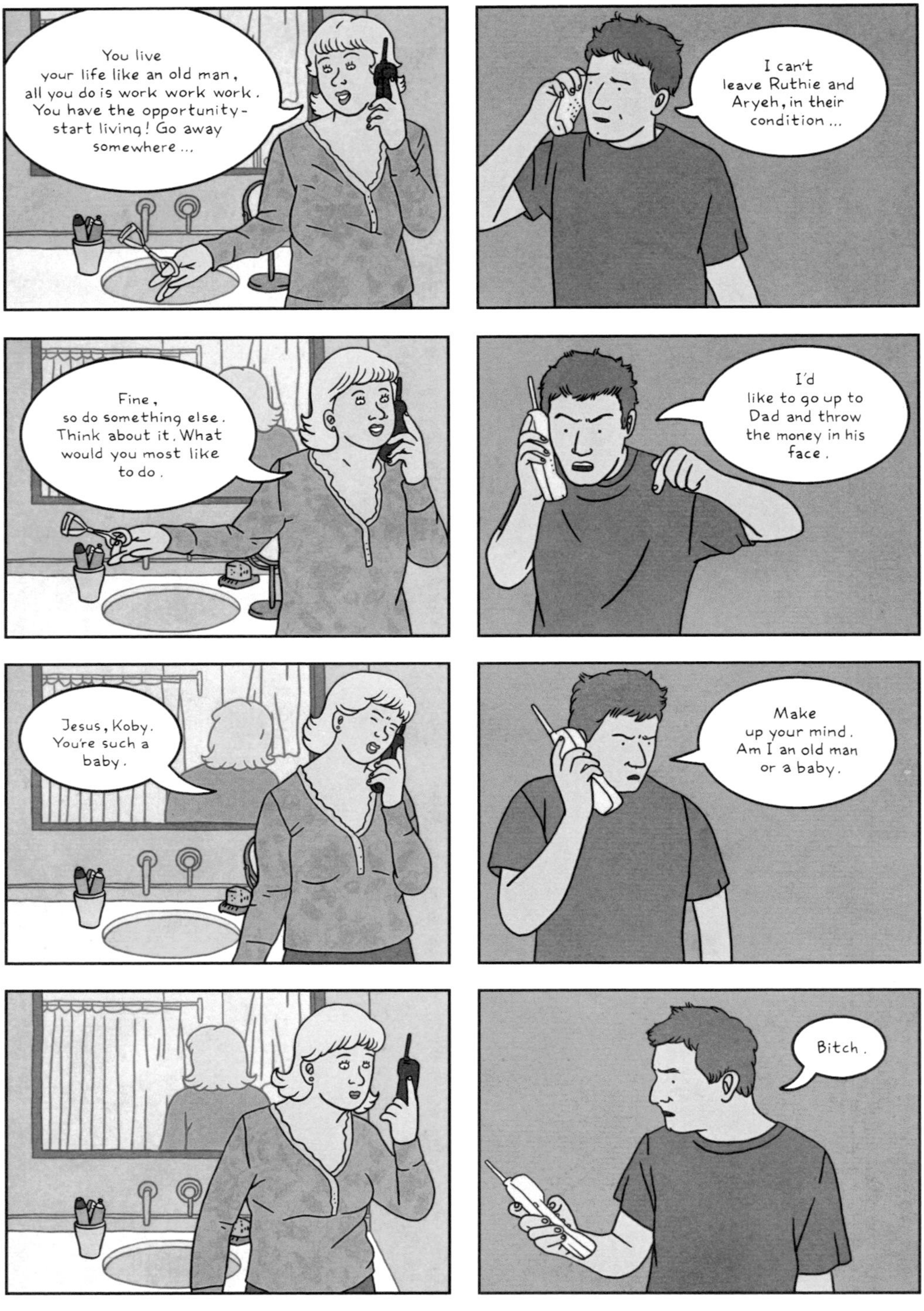
You live your life like an old man, all you do is work work work. You have the opportunity- start living! Go away somewhere...
I can't leave Ruthie and Aryeh, in their condition...
Fine, so do something else. Think about it. What would you most like to do.
I'd like to go up to Dad and throw the money in his face.
Jesus, Koby. You're such a baby.
Make up your mind. Am I an old man or a baby.
Bitch.

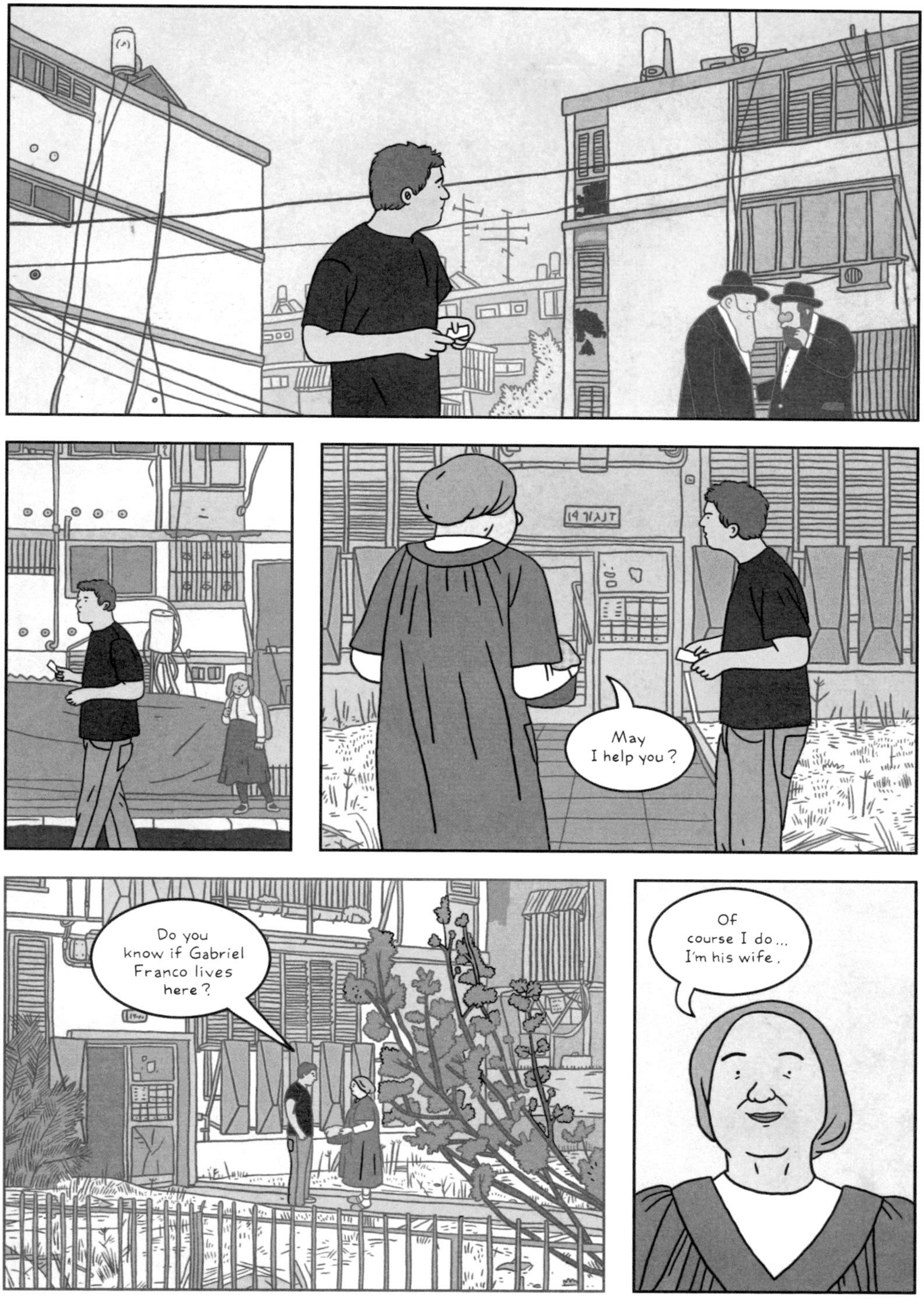
May I help you?
Do you know if Gabriel Franco lives here?
Of course I do... I'm his wife.

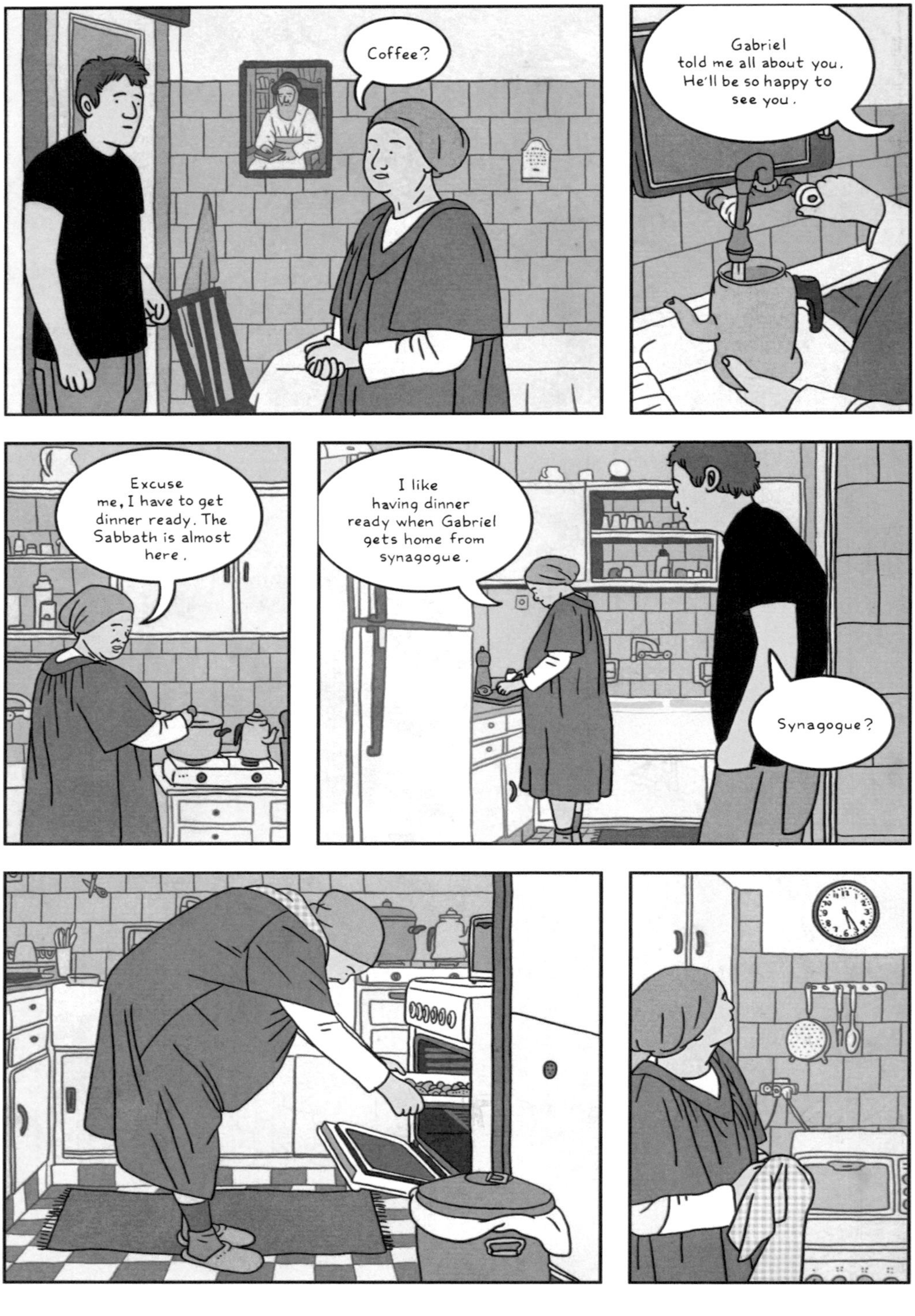

Coffee?
Gabriel told me all about you. He'll be so happy to see you.
Excuse me, I have to get dinner ready. The Sabbath is almost here.
I like having dinner ready when Gabriel gets home from synagogue.
Synagogue?

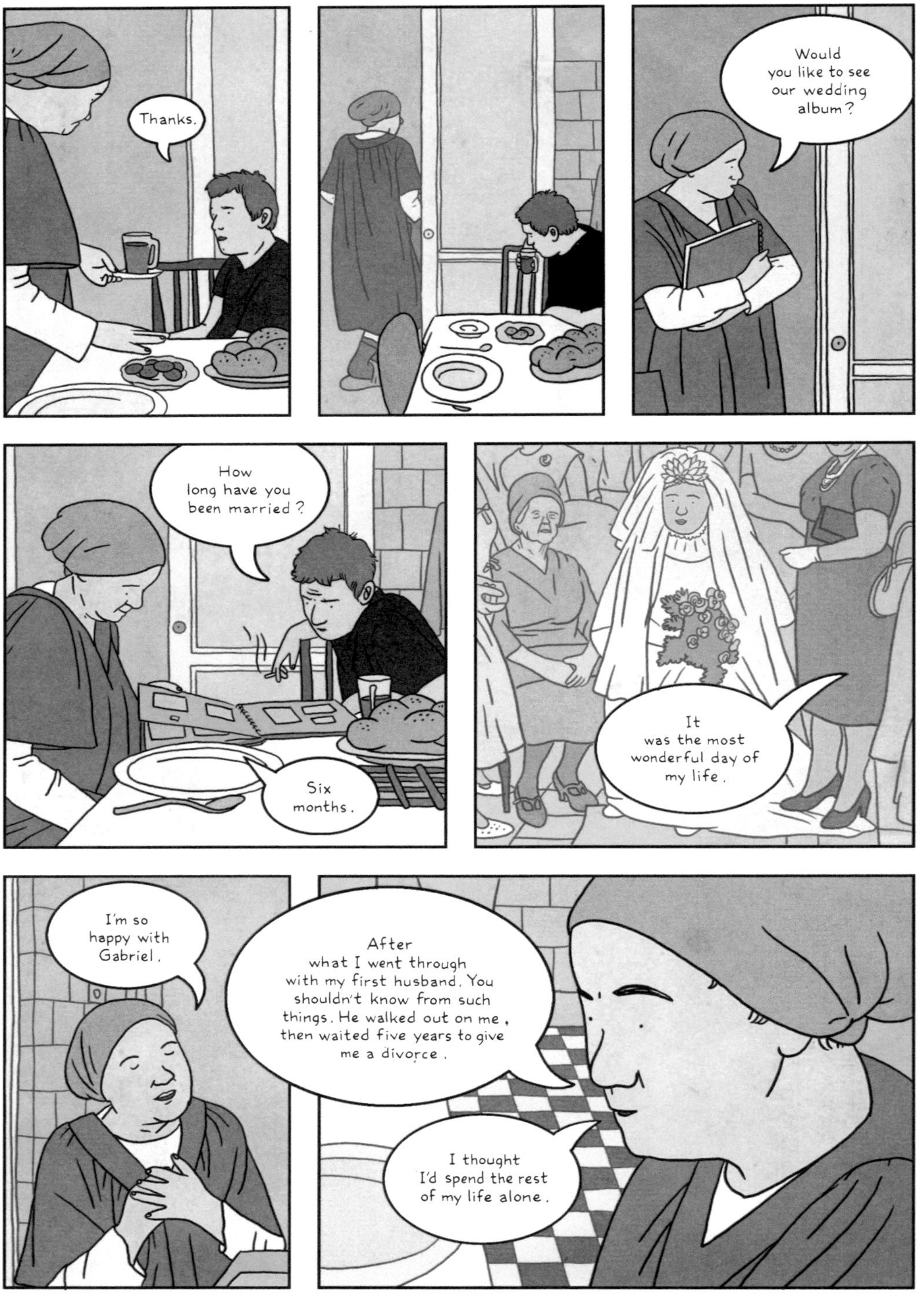
Thanks.
Would you like to see our wedding album?
How long have you been married?
Six months.
It was the most wonderful day of my life.
I'm so happy with Gabriel.
After what I went through with my first husband. You shouldn't know from such things. He walked out on me, then waited five years to give me a divorce.
I thought I'd spend the rest of my life alone.

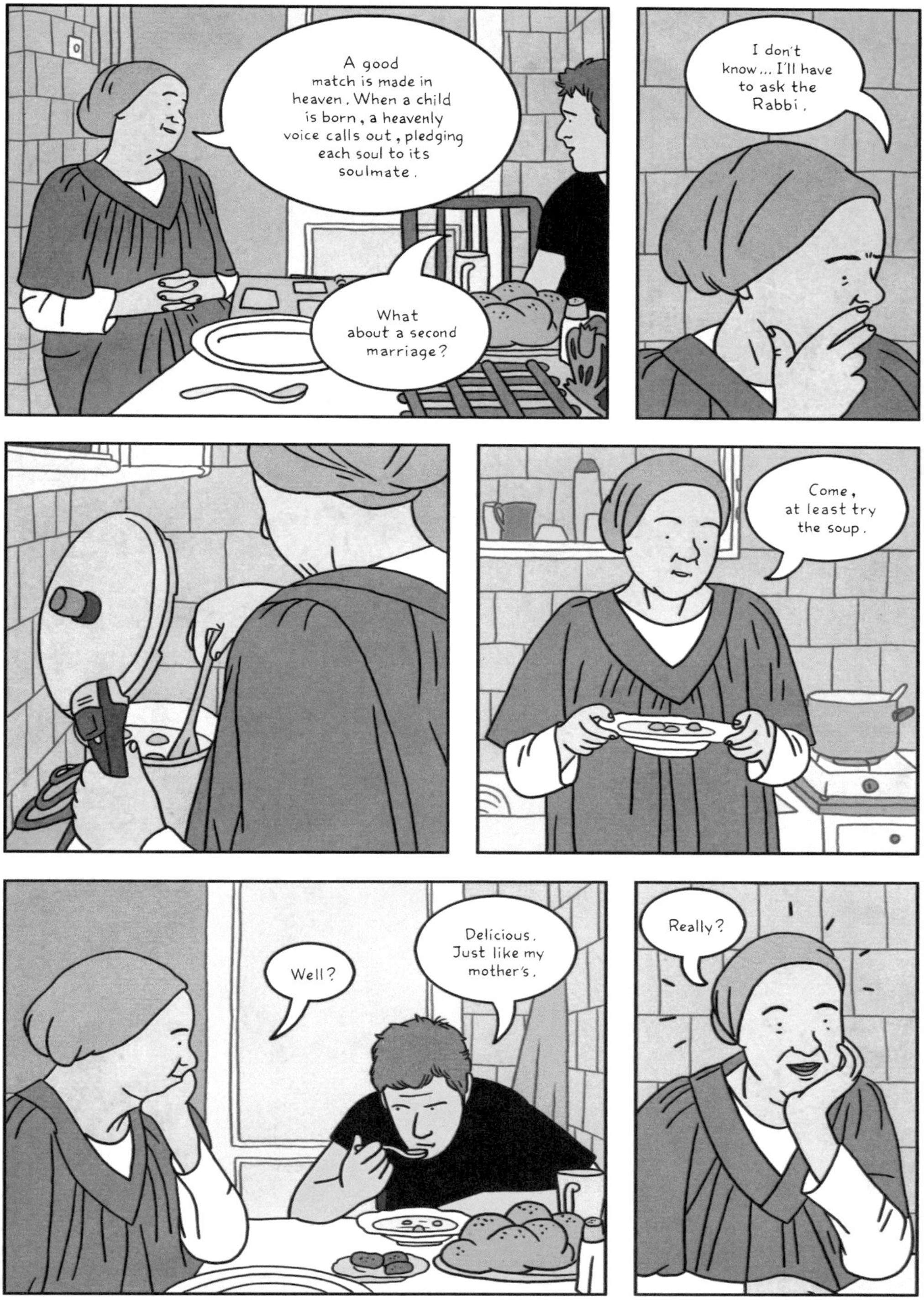
A good match is made in heaven. When a child is born, a heavenly voice calls out, pledging each soul to its soulmate.
What about a second marriage?
I don't know... I'll have to ask the Rabbi.
Come, at least try the soup.
Well?
Delicious. Just like my mother's.
Really?

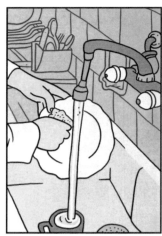

What's the matter with him? How long does he expect me to wait?

The chicken is ruined! Bone dry!

CLANK

One hour later.

I shouldn't have thrown it away. I could have made chicken salad.

I really should go.

Why? Gabriel will be here any minute.

I've waited enough.

It's a shame you missed each other. Do you want to leave him a message?

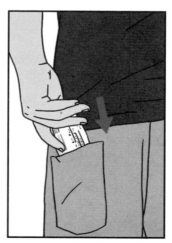

No. Just tell him I was here.

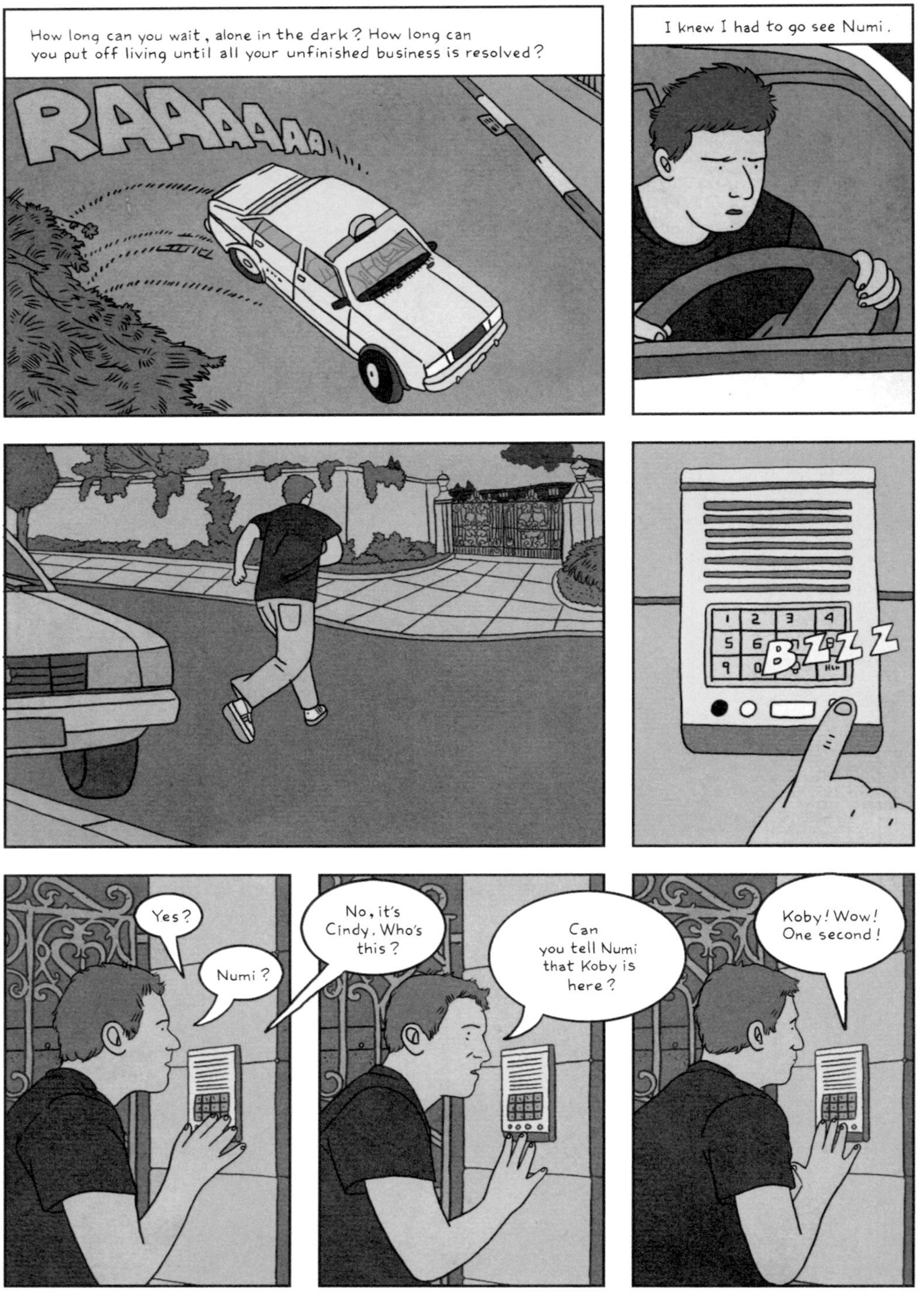
How long can you wait, alone in the dark? How long can you put off living until all your unfinished business is resolved?
RAAAAAA
I knew I had to go see Numi.
BZZZ
Yes?
Numi?
No, it's Cindy. Who's this?
Can you tell Numi that Koby is here?
Koby! Wow! One second!

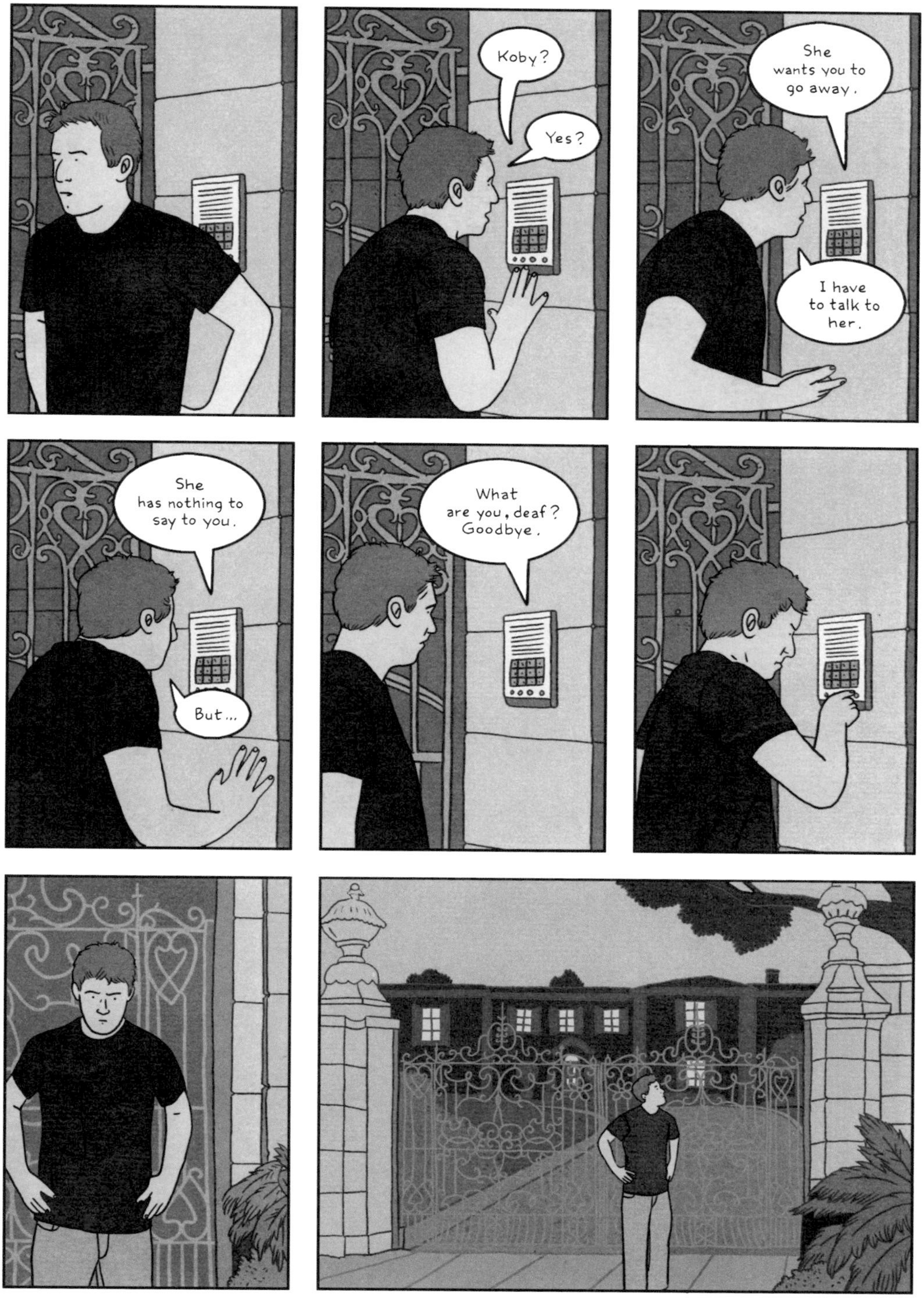
Koby?
Yes?
She wants you to go away.
I have to talk to her.
She has nothing to say to you.
But...
What are you, deaf? Goodbye.

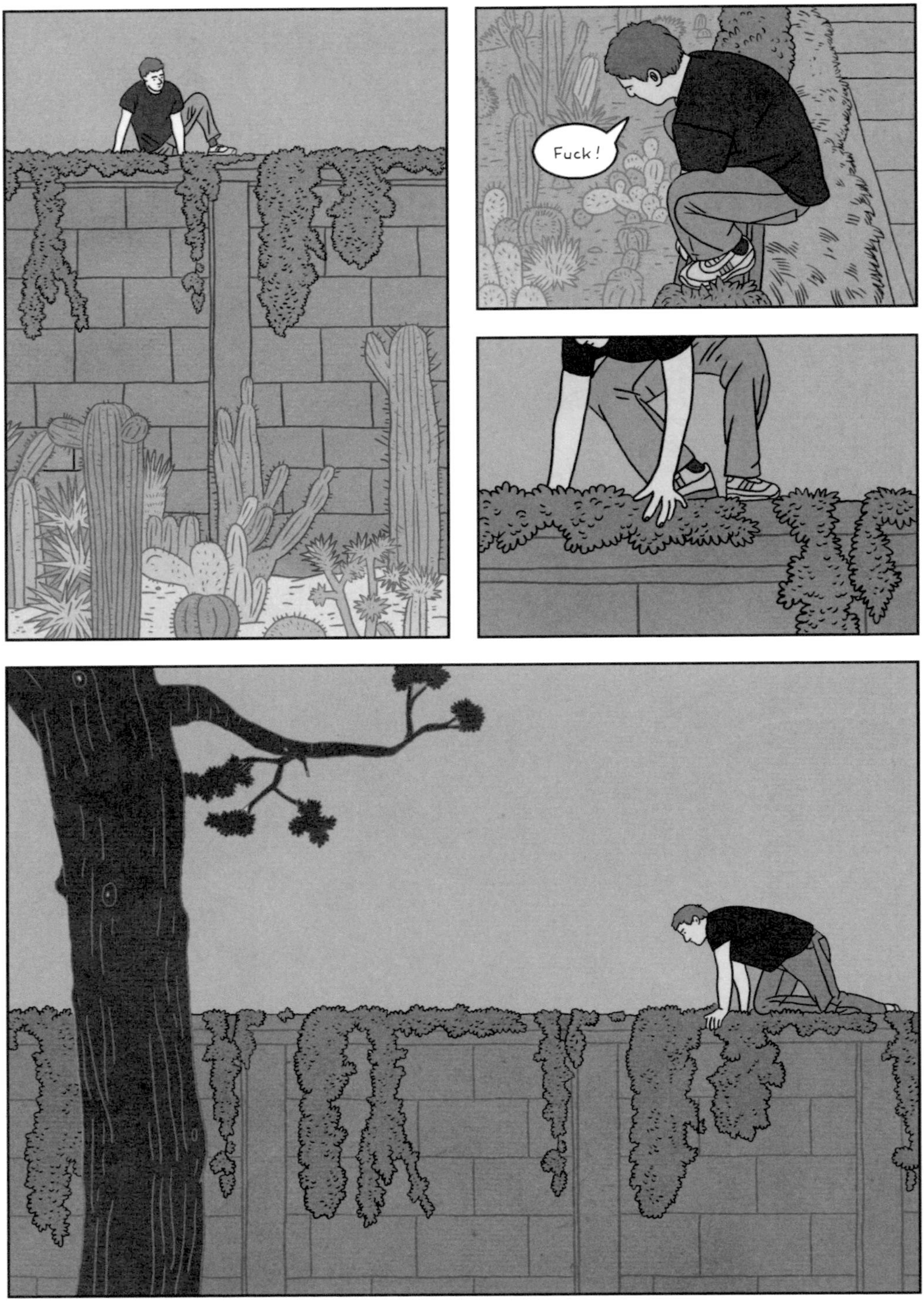
Fuck!

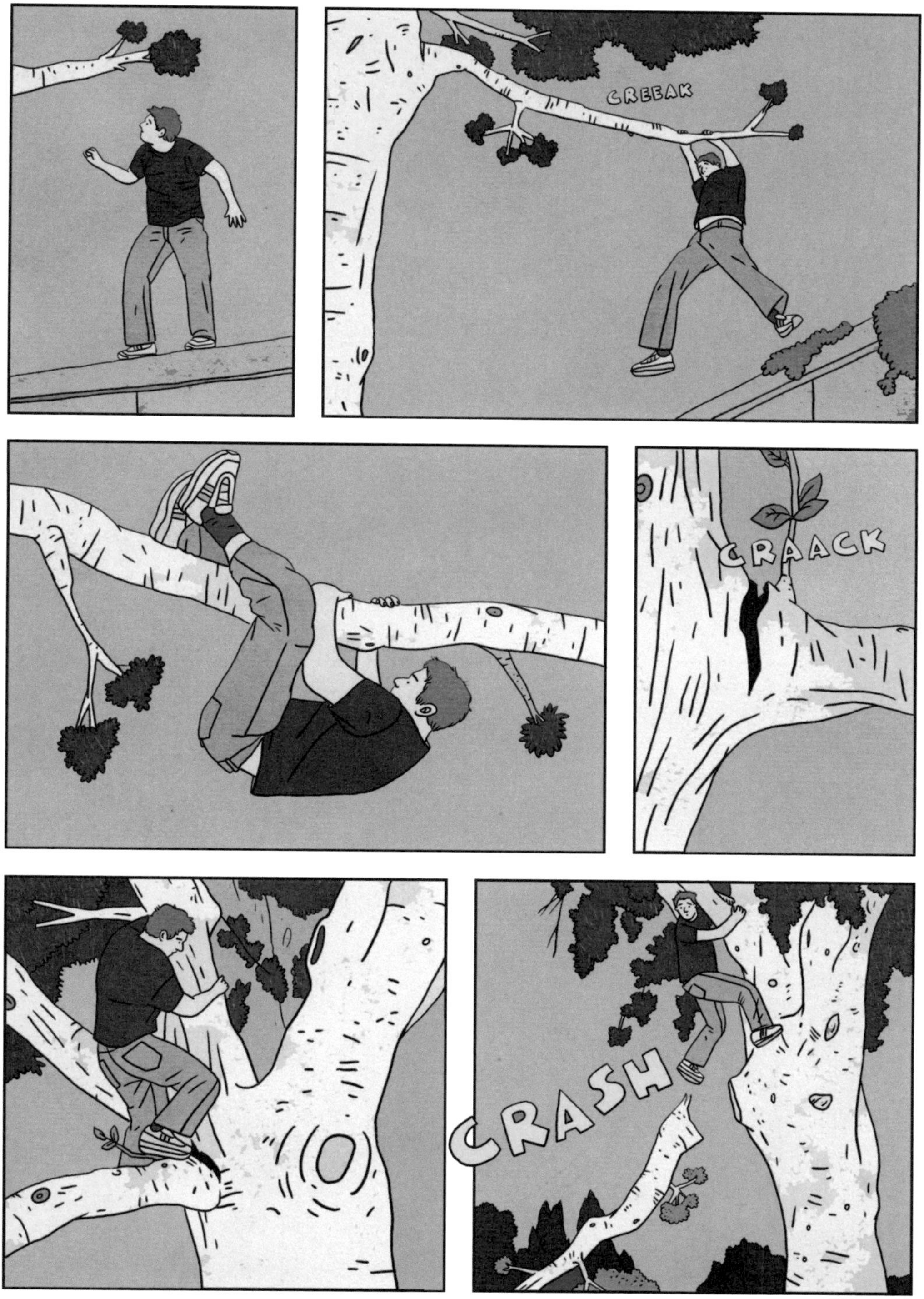
CREEAK
CRAACK
CRASH

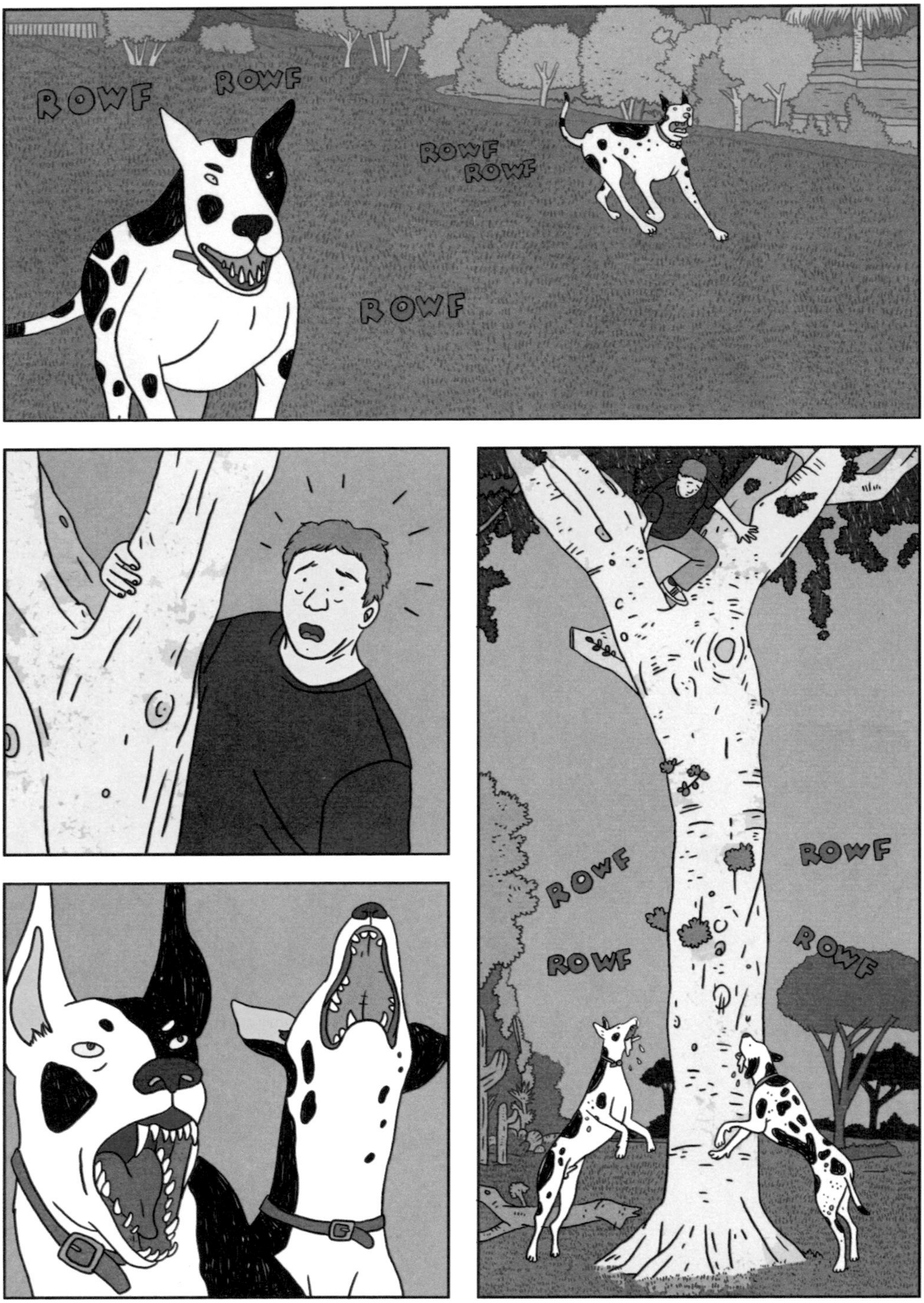
ROWF
ROWF
ROWF
ROWF
ROWF
ROWF
ROWF
ROWF
ROWF

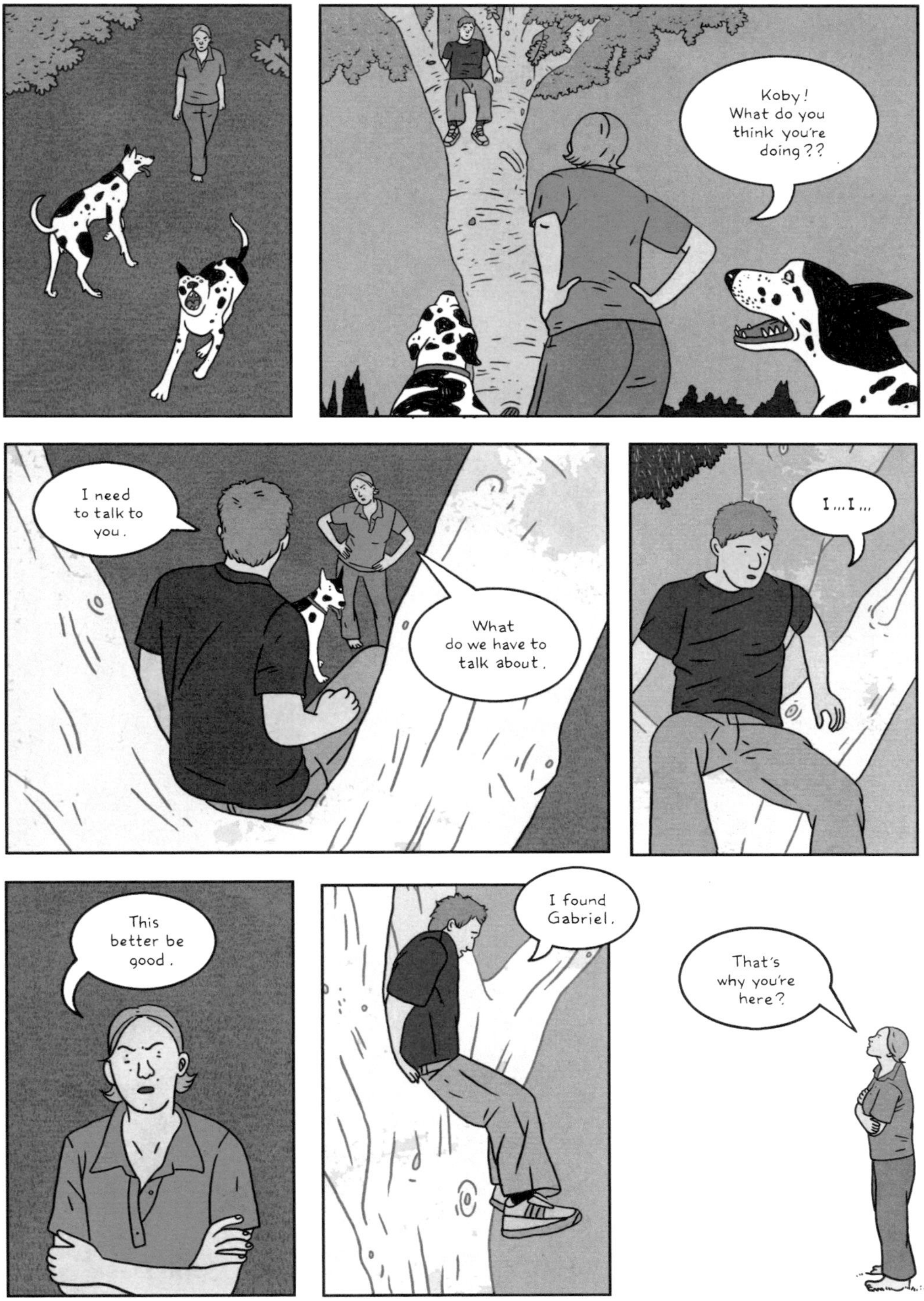
Koby! What do you think you're doing??
I need to talk to you.
What do we have to talk about.
I...I...
This better be good.
I found Gabriel.
That's why you're here?

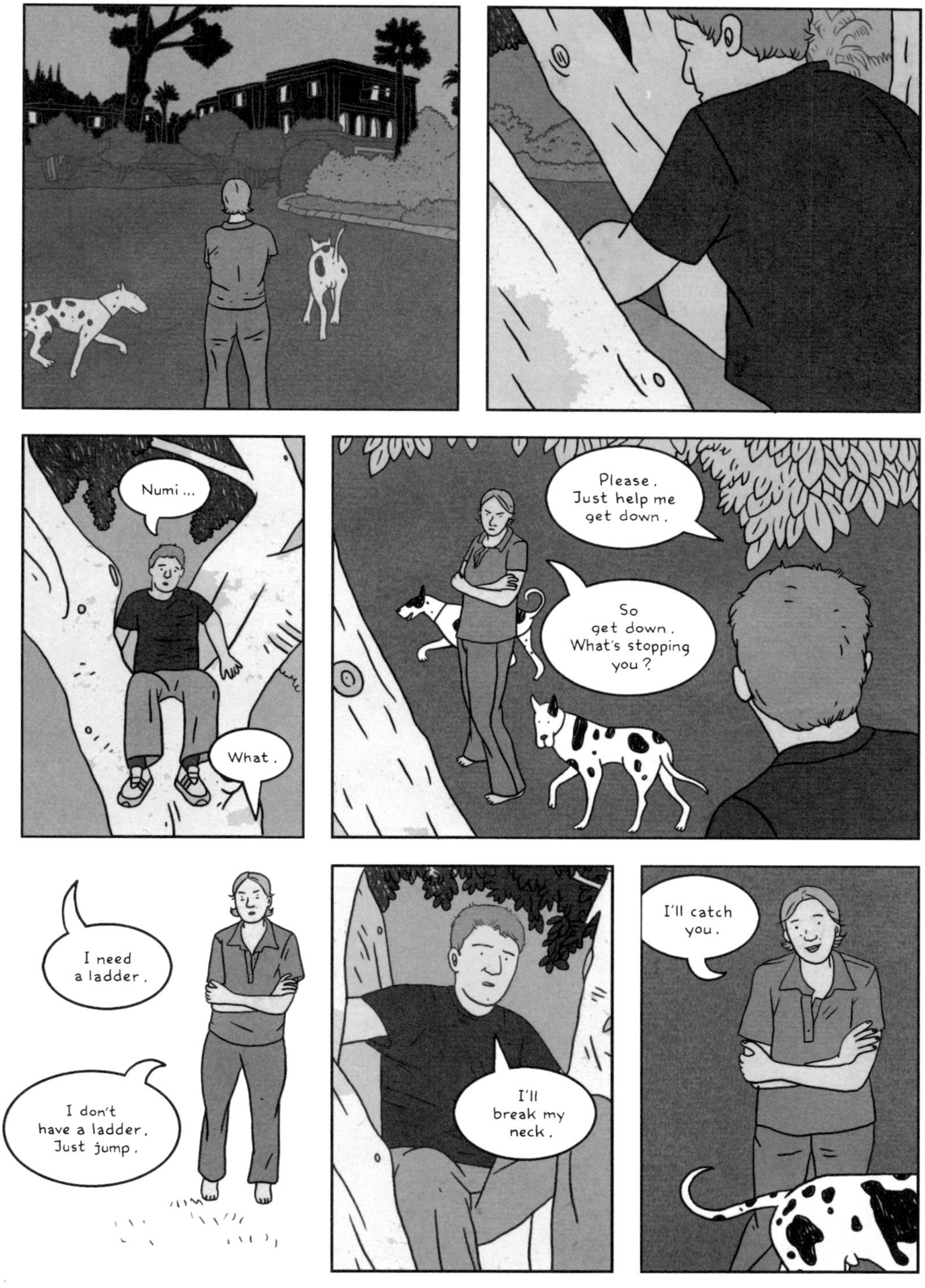
Numi ...
What.
Please. Just help me get down.
So get down. What's stopping you?
I need a ladder.
I don't have a ladder. Just jump.
I'll break my neck.
I'll catch you.

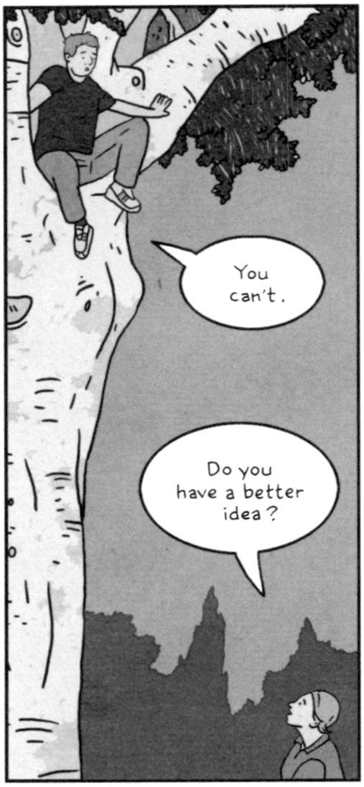
You can't.
Do you have a better idea?

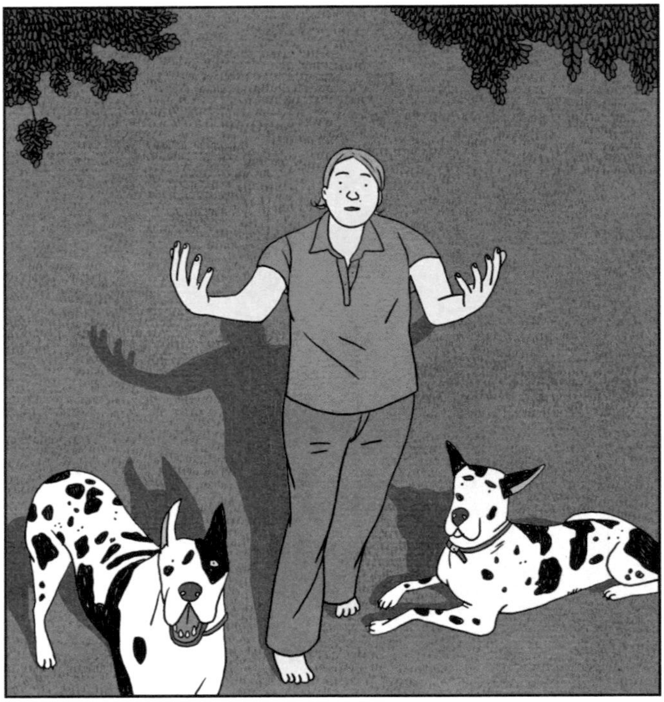

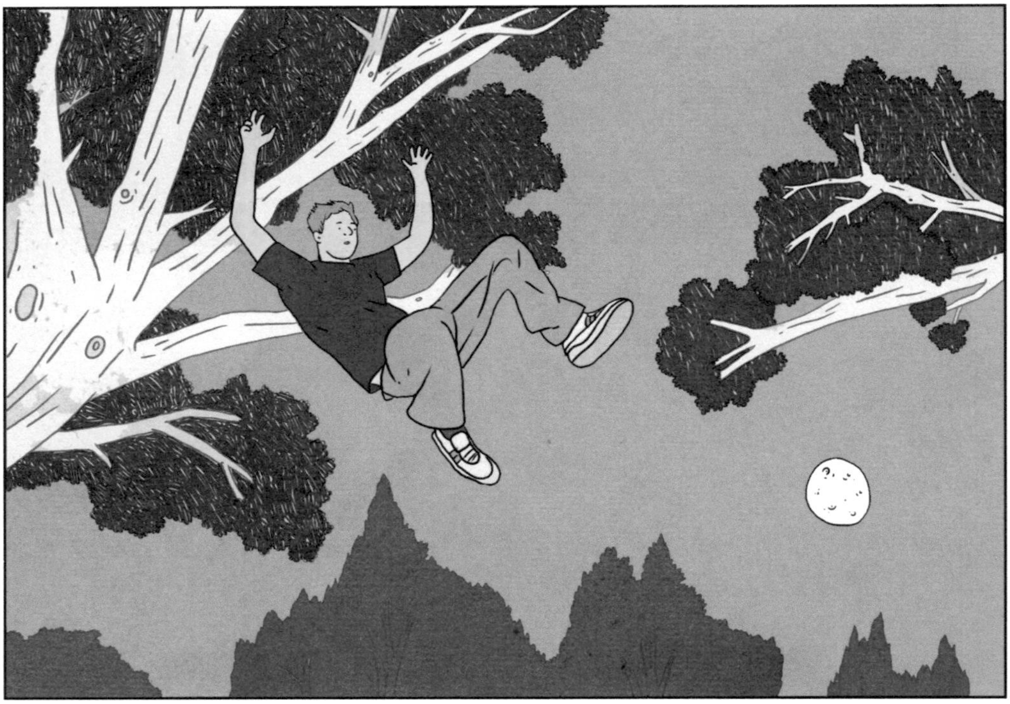

Photo by Ephrat Beloosesky

Rutu Modan was born in Tel-Aviv in 1966. She graduated *cum laude* from the Bezalel Academy of Art and Design in Jerusalem. After graduating, she began regularly writing and illustrating comic strips and stories for Israel's leading daily newspapers, as well as co-editing the Israeli edition of *MAD* magazine. She is a co-founder of Actus Tragicus, an alternative comic artists collective and independent publishing house. She collaborated with Israeli author Etgar Keret on her first graphic novel, *Nobody Said it Was Going to Be Fun*, an Israeli bestseller. Modan has worked as an illustrator for magazines and books in Israel and abroad, including *The New York Times*, *New Yorker* and *Le Monde*, and others. She is the recipient of four Best Illustrated Children's Book Awards from the Israel Museum in Jerusalem, the Young Artist of the Year by the Israel Ministry of Culture, the International Board on Books for Young People Honor List for Children's Book Illustration and is a chosen artist of the Israel Cultural Excellence Foundation since 2005. She has been nominated for the Angoulême Festival's Goccini Award, Eisner, and Ignatz Awards.

Modan currently teaches comics and illustration at the Bezalel Academy of Art and Design and lives in Tel-Aviv with her family.